This book is dedicated to the world of

LINUX

and to those who have made it what it is...

...and to the Knights that say "Ni!"

Heartfelt Thanks

to

Nancy Davis, the best editor in the world and a sweet friend.

and

Harold who helped me get everything up and running. Without him this book wouldn't exist.

and

Julian, my wonderful little guy, for putting up with Mama while she pounded away at the keyboard. Ki!

START GUIDE

WORDPERFECT 8

FOR LINUX

Phyllis Davis

Visual QuickStart Guide
WordPerfect 8 for Linux
Phyllis Davis

Peachpit Press
1249 Eighth Street
Berkeley, CA 94710
510-524-2178
800-283-9444
510-524-2221 (fax)

Find us on the World Wide Web at: http://www.peachpit.com

Peachpit Press is a division of Addison Wesley Longman

Copyright © 1999 by Phyllis Davis

Editor: Nancy Davis
Production Coordinator: Lisa Brazieal
Interior design and production: Phyllis Davis
Cover design: The Visual Group

Notice of Rights

All rights reserved. No part of this book may be reproduced or transmitted in any form by any means, electronic, mechanical, photocopying, recording, or otherwise, without the prior written permission of the publisher. For information on getting permission for reprints and excerpts, contact Gary-Paul Prince at Peachpit Press.

Notice of Liability

The information in this book is distributed on an "As Is" basis, without warranty. While every precaution has been take in the preparation of the book, neither the author nor Peachpit Press, shall have any liability to any person or entity with respect to any loss or damage caused or alleged to be caused directly or indirectly by the instructions contained in this book or by the computer software and hardware products described in it.

Trademarks

Visual QuickStart Guide is a registered trademark of Peachpit Press, a division of Addison Wesley Longman. Corel, Corel WordPerfect, QuickList, and QuickMenu are registered trademarks of Corel Corporation or Corel Corporation Limited in Canada, the United States and/or other countries. Linux is a registered trademark of Linus Torvalds, and the bulk of Linux is copyright ©1993 by Linus Torvalds. Red Hat is a registered trademark of Red Hat, Inc. Throughout this book trademarked names are used. Rather than put a trademark symbol in every occurrence of a trademarked name, we state that we are using the names only in an editorial fashion and to the benefit of the trademark owner with no intention of infringement of the trademark.

ISBN 0-201-70051-4

9 8 7 6 5 4 3 2 1

 Printed on recycled paper

Printed and bound in the United States of America

TABLE OF CONTENTS

Chapter 4   **Working with Text**   **51**

TABLE OF CONTENTS

TABLE OF CONTENTS

THE BASICS

Welcome to the world of WordPerfect 8 for Linux! I am a long time WordPerfect devotee and am *very* pleased to see it up and running on the Linux platform.

My purpose in writing this book is to show just how easy it is to create professional documents using the tools that WordPerfect 8 offers. In keeping with the *Visual QuickStart Guide* format, my aim is to present easy, step-by-step directions with illustrations to take the mystery out of even the most complicated word processing procedure.

WordPerfect 8 for Linux offers a complete, professional set of tools for creating many kinds of documents, from birthday cards, brochures, and newsletters, to reports, memos, and information-intensive documents that include charts and tables. This program has incredible power and loads of features, all incorporated into a user interface that will be familiar to those who've used other word processing programs. As sophisticated as WordPerfect 8 is, it's also easy to use. You can run with it as far as you please.

WordPerfect is feature-rich. If you take it one step at a time, you'll be creating professional documents in no time. For those of you who are acquainted with previous WordPerfect DOS and Windows versions, use this book as a guide to new features and techniques, and as a handy reference.

Let's get started!

Why Linux?

Why should you run WordPerfect on Linux? There are many good answers to this question as witnessed by the fact that Linux is the fastest growing operating system today. Perhaps you have chosen Linux because:

◆ It is the predominant operating system of Web servers.

◆ It is more stable than any version of Microsoft Windows. (I've been running it for months and haven't had one crash yet!)

◆ It is extremely affordable.

◆ You believe in the tenants of the open-source movement.

On the other hand, maybe you've heard a lot about Linux and are just starting to experiment with it.

Whatever reason you have for choosing Linux, WordPerfect 8 for Linux is an excellent tool for your professional word processing needs.

You'll be glad to know that WordPerfect 8 for Linux is as easy to use as any word processor running on Microsoft Windows. In other words, you don't have to be a technical genius to get WordPerfect up and running. And the best news yet: you can save and open files in WordPerfect 8 for Linux that are compatible with many Microsoft Windows file formats, including Microsoft Word for Windows. (Turn to page 44 for details on how to do this.)

Learning More About Linux

If you'd like to learn more about Linux, my husband's wonderful book will help speed you on your way (no, I'm not biased!). His book: *Red Hat Linux 6: Visual QuickPro Guide* by Harold Davis (Peachpit Press). This book comes with a full working copy of Linux on the CD-ROM.

Some Web sites you can visit for more information about Linux and the Linux community:

Very useful Linux links: `http://www.bearhome.com/linux/links.html`

Red Hat home site: `http://www.redhat.com/`

Linux Links, a portal for Linux information: `http://www.linuxlinks.com/`

Companion Web Sites

Peachpit Press has created companion Web sites for its Linux titles. These companion Web sites include text excerpts from the books, links to other resources, discussion threads, and chat areas.

The companion site for *WordPerfect 8 for Linux: Visual QuickStart Guide* can be found at:
`http://www.peachpit.com/vqs/linuxwp8/`

The companion site for *Red Hat Linux 6: Visual Quick Pro Guide* can be found at:
`http://www.peachpit.com/vqp/linux`

The Way WordPerfect Works

WordPerfect 8 is a full-featured word processing program that you can use to create many kinds of text-based documents—letters, reports, memos, envelopes, and Web pages.

WordPerfect 8 documents are created in the *document window*. The *program window* appears when WordPerfect is launched. Anything changed using the program window effects all documents created in WordPerfect.

Documents are *saved* in the WordPerfect 8 .wpd file format. They can be *imported* from or *exported* to other file formats.

The *insertion point* is used to position text, graphics, tables, and charts on the page. The insertion point also shows you where you are in a document. The *shadow cursor* lets you position text anywhere in a document, even if nothing has been typed there before.

Formatting in WordPerfect is handled on *character* and *paragraph* levels. Character formatting involves changing and individual characters. Paragraph formatting deals with paragraphs as a whole.

WordPerfect lets you be creative with character formatting. You can change *fonts, font sizes*, and other *font attributes*, such as bold, italic, underline, and color. You can set the spacing between lines of text.

With paragraph formatting, you can indent the first line of a paragraph, using a *tab setting*. Or you can indent the entire left side of a paragraph using an *indent*. A *double indent* moves both the left and right sides of a paragraph in towards the center of the page. You can also set the spacing between paragraphs.

Text can be placed into *columns* that vertically or horizontally divide the page. There are two main types of columns— *newspaper* and *parallel*.

Page setup involves how the page looks as a whole. You can adjust top, bottom, left, and right margins, and set header and footer size and appearance. Pages can be added and deleted. *Subdocuments* can be inserted into a *master document.*

Graphics that ship with WordPerfect and those you have stored in other clipart libraries can be inserted into documents to add distinction and interest. Images can be resized horizontally, vertically, or proportionately. Borders and fills can be added to graphics. Text can be set to *flow* around, behind, or in front of a graphic.

Charts and tables can be created to organize and display information in useful, graphical ways. Using the chart mode of WP Draw, you can create pie, bar, line, hi-lo, area, and scatter charts. Tables of virtually any dimension can be inserted into a document. Using *Speed Format*, you can quickly make a table with a custom look.

Merges help you quickly amalgamate an address list with a form letter or other document to create personalized copies. Envelopes can also be created using merge *field codes*.

With WordPerfect, you can create *macros* using the *macro recorder*. Macros are mini-programs that automatically perform keystrokes and commands.

You can change the view of a document to make editing easier. You can *zoom in* to get a close up look and work with small details or *zoom out* to see the document as a whole.

You can use precision tools such as *guidelines*, *tab settings*, *margin settings*, and *rulers* to align text, tables, charts, and images, making your documents precise.

When you finish a document, the file can be *printed*. If you've created a Web document, it can be saved in HTML format for the Internet.

The WordPerfect 8 Screen (Figure 1)

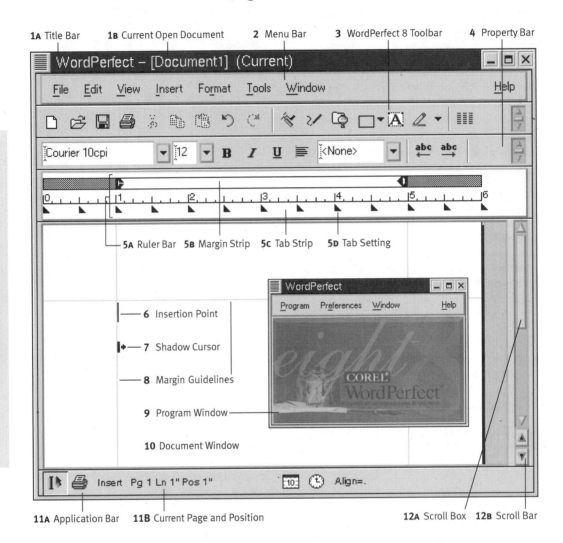

1A Title Bar   **1B** Current Open Document   **2** Menu Bar   **3** WordPerfect 8 Toolbar   **4** Property Bar

5A Ruler Bar   **5B** Margin Strip   **5C** Tab Strip   **5D** Tab Setting

6 Insertion Point

7 Shadow Cursor

8 Margin Guidelines

9 Program Window

10 Document Window

11A Application Bar   **11B** Current Page and Position   **12A** Scroll Box   **12B** Scroll Bar

Key to the WordPerfect 8 Screen

1A–B *Title Bar*
Displays the program name and current document name.

2 *Menu Bar*
Click any menu title to access commands fly-outs, and dialog boxes, as well as the various toolbars, views, and Ruler Bar.

3 *WordPerfect 8 Toolbar*
One of the sixteen toolbars, the WordPerfect 8 Toolbar buttons and drop-down lists give you quick access to standard word processing commands such as New, Open, Save, Print, Cut, Copy, Paste, Undo, and Redo. It also includes several WordPerfect 8 commands such as Create Columns and Create Table.

4   *Property Bar*
The Property Bar is a *context sensitive* toolbar. Buttons and drop-down lists change dynamically, depending upon what is selected. This gives you easy access to the most important commands associated with the selected tool or item.

5A–D   *Ruler Bar*
The Ruler Bar displays current tab and left/right margin settings, indents, and column boundaries. It can be used to set all these things. You can quickly access commands associated with the Ruler Bar by right clicking on the Ruler Bar and using the QuickMenu that appears.

6   *Insertion Point*
This blinking vertical bar shows you where you are in a document. You can use it to position text, graphics, or tables.

7   *Shadow Cursor*
One of the wonderful features of WordPerfect, the shadow cursor lets you position text, graphics, tables, or charts anywhere in a document, even in *white space*. There's no need to insert blank lines manually by pressing the Enter key on the keyboard to move to where you want to position an item.

8   *Margin Guidelines*
These non-printing horizontal and vertical gray lines display the top, bottom, left, and right margin boundaries. Guidelines are also displayed when tables and columns are used.

9   *Program Window*
This smaller window appears when WordPerfect is launched. Any changes made using the program window effect all documents.

10   *Document Window*
This is the place where most of the action happens. The document you create appears in the document window. All text, graphics, tables, charts, etc. are displayed here. Any changes you make in the document window effect only the document currently open and *active*. You can open as many as 100 document windows at one time.

11A–B   *Application Bar*

This tiny horizontal panel at the bottom of the document window displays important information about a document, including the current page and position, date, time, and currently selected text alignment. It can also be used to quickly insert the date and time into a document.

12A–B   *Scroll Bars*

The horizontal and vertical bars that appear at the bottom and right side of the document window as needed. (Since the width of the entire page is shown in Figure 1, no horizontal scroll bar is needed; therefore, it's not present.) Scroll bars are used to move through a document by either clicking the scroll arrows or dragging the scroll box.

THE WORDPERFECT 8 SCREEN

Terms Used in This Book

◆ *Click* means to quickly press and release the left mouse button.

◆ *Double-click* means to quickly press and release the left mouse button twice.

◆ *Right click* means to quickly press and release the right mouse button.

◆ *Choose* means to use the mouse pointer to highlight a menu item and click.

WordPerfect 8 Controls

Figures 2a–g show the controls you will use when working with WordPerfect 8 dialog boxes.

Figure 2a. *Text boxes and spin buttons.* You can enter text or numbers in text boxes. Spin buttons are used to increase or decrease a number. To increase a number, click the up arrow. To decrease a number, click the down arrow.

Figure 2b. Push buttons. Push buttons usually start a user specified action and/or close dialog boxes, cancel an action, or answer no to an action to keep it from starting. A selected push button has a black border around it. A push button with text that is followed by an ellipsis (...) will open another dialog box when clicked.

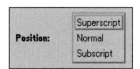

Figure 2c. *Drop-down lists.* Drop-down lists present a selection of items from which to choose. To open the list, click the list box button or the little arrow to the right of the list box. Some drop-down lists allow you to enter text.

Figure 2d. *List buttons.* List buttons appear in dialog boxes with two possible looks: the first is a tiny folder on the button, the second is a left pointing triangle. When a list button is clicked, a file manager dialog box opens to let you select a file or move to another directory.

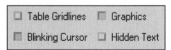

Figure 2e. *Check boxes.* Click a check box to turn an option on or off. Depending upon your WordPerfect settings, a check may or may not appear in the box when it is selected (if there is no check mark, the entire box will be a darker gray). The default Word-Perfect setting is for no check mark to appear, so that's the way it's shown throughout this book. In the example shown here, Blinking Cursor and Graphics are selected.

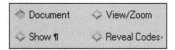

Figure 2f. *Radio buttons.* Radio buttons are usually contained in an area, and you can select only one item from two or more options. Click the diamond to select an option. The diamond that is darker gray (Document, in this example) is selected. Some folks call these option buttons.

Figure 2g. *Preview areas.* Some dialog boxes include a preview area that lets you see how changes look before you click OK and apply them to a document. As you add and delete characters or options, these items appear or disappear from the preview.

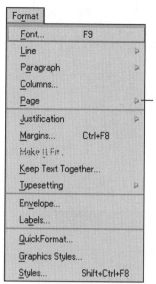

Figure 3. Click a menu title on the Menu Bar to open the menu.

This arrow indicates a fly-out

Menus

There are 8 menus available on the Menu Bar. These menus give access to commands, fly-outs (submenus that open off of main menus), and dialog boxes.

To open a menu and select an item:

1. Position the mouse pointer over a menu title and click. The menu will open (**Figure 3**). If you see a tiny arrow to the right of a menu item, it means that there is an available fly-out. To open the fly-out, click the tiny arrow (**Figure 4**).

2. Move the mouse down to highlight the item you want to select.

3. Click to select the item.

✔ Tip

■ A menu item with an ellipsis (...) after it means that this item will open a dialog box.

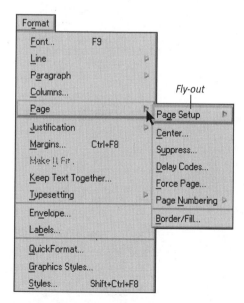

Fly-out

Figure 4. Click the tiny arrow to open the fly-out. As you can see in this figure, some fly-outs also have fly-outs. For instance, there is a tiny arrow to the right of the Page Numbering fly-out menu item.

Keyboard Shortcuts

Many menu commands have keyboard equivalents. Keyboard shortcuts (also called *hot keys*) always use the Ctrl, Shift, or Alt keys (or a combination of them) plus a letter or number key. Many times the letter is a mnemonic. For instance, the Copy command uses the letter C.

As an example, the keyboard shortcut for the Copy command is Ctrl+C.

For details on how to create custom keyboard shortcuts, turn to pages 210–212.

MENUS; KEYBOARD SHORTCUTS

Large Menus and Dialog Boxes

WordPerfect 8 menus and dialog boxes contain many commands and items to select. Consequently, some of them are quite large. Several of the figures in this *Visual QuickStart Guide* are too big to display in their entirety or become very small when sized to fit the page. In order to fit these large items, some menus and dialog boxes have been shortened using a jagged edge (**Figures 5a–b**). The menu or dialog box item being selected is shown, but lower or middle items are removed to conserve space. When a large dialog box is shown and its contents are very tiny, a circle is drawn around the area under discussion (**Figure 6**).

Figure 5a. Menus in some figures have been cropped using a jagged edge.

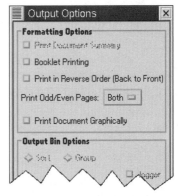

Figure 5b. Dialog boxes in some figures have been cropped using a jagged edge to conserve space.

This Book is Based on the WordPerfect 8 Personal Edition

WordPerfect 8 for Linux is available in three versions, the downloadable Free Version, the Personal Edition, and the Server Edition. (For details on the differences between these versions, turn to page 20.)

This book is based upon the Personal Edition. If you are using the Server Edition of WordPerfect, every feature I discuss here will be available in your copy of WordPerfect. If you are using the downloadable Free Version, there will be some features which will be grayed out and unavailable to you. For instance, you won't be able to create macros or charts.

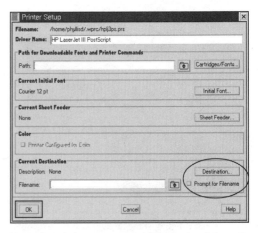

Figure 6. A circle appears around the area under discussion in a large dialog box.

Figure 7. Choose Toolbars from the View menu.

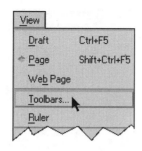

Toolbars

There are sixteen toolbars available in WordPerfect 8. They give access to commands and dialog boxes with just the click of a button. Two toolbars are available, by default, when you launch WordPerfect for the first time. They are the WordPerfect 8 Toolbar and the Property Bar.

To access the toolbars:

1. Choose Toolbars from the View menu (**Figure 7**). The Toolbars dialog box will open (**Figure 8**).

2. In the Available toolbars list box, select the check boxes next to the toolbars you want to display.

3. Click OK. The Toolbars dialog box will close and the toolbars you selected will appear.

or

Right click on a toolbar at the top of the document window and choose the toolbar you want to display from the QuickMenu that appears (**Figure 9**).

Figure 8. Select the toolbars you want to view from the Available toolbars list box, then click OK.

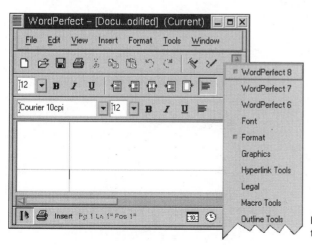

Figure 9. Right click on a toolbar and choose the toolbar you want to view from the QuickMenu.

For Users of Previous WordPerfect Versions

For those of you out there who are users of previous WordPerfect versions and are moving to WordPerfect 8 for Linux, welcome!

You might like to know that you don't have to leave your favorite keyboard strokes and shortcuts, and toolbars behind.

With WordPerfect 8 for Linux, you can set your keyboard to work as it does in WordPerfect 6 for DOS, or WordPerfect 5.1, 6, 7, or 8 for Windows. Instead of the WordPerfect 8 Toolbar, you can set the WordPerfect 6 or 7 Toolbar.

To change keyboard settings to previous WordPerfect versions:

1. Choose Preferences in the program window (**Figure 10**). The Preferences dialog box will open (**Figure 11**).

2. Click Keyboard. The Keyboard Preferences dialog box will appear (**Figure 12**).

3. Select the keyboard you want to use from the Keyboards list box.

4. Click Select. The Keyboard Preferences dialog box will close.

5. Click Close to close the Preferences dialog box and return to the document window.

Figure 10. Choose Preferences in the program window.

Figure 11. Click Keyboard in the Preferences dialog box.

Figure 12. Highlight the keyboard you want to use, then click Select.

Figure 13. Right click on a toolbar, then choose WordPerfect 6 or WordPerfect 7 from the QuickMenu.

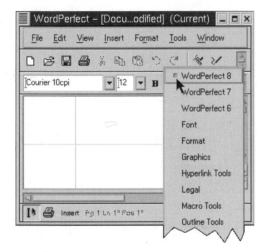

Figure 14. Right click on the WordPerfect 8 toolbar, then choose WordPerfect 8 from the QuickMenu that appears to hide that toolbar.

To display the WordPerfect for Windows 6 or 7 Toolbar:

1. Right click on the WordPerfect 8 Toolbar. A QuickMenu will appear (**Figure 13**).

2. Choose either WordPerfect 7 or WordPerfect 6 from the QuickMenu. The toolbar you selected will appear at the top of the document window.

✔ Tip

■ When a toolbar is displayed, a tiny square appears next to the item on the QuickMenu.

To hide the WordPerfect 8 Toolbar:

1. Right click on the WordPerfect 8 Toolbar. A QuickMenu will appear (**Figure 14**).

2. Choose WordPerfect 8 from the QuickMenu. The WordPerfect 8 Toolbar will disappear from the top of the document window.

FOR PREVIOUS WORDPERFECT VERSION USERS

Viewing a Document

The View menu gives you two commands for changing the *view quality*. View quality is the way a document is displayed in the document window.

The two view qualities, *draft view* and *page view* both display a document in the WYSIWYG (What You See Is What You Get) environment, imitating how it will look when printed. This imitation includes using the fonts in the document window that the printer will use to print. Font attributes, including bold, italics, and underlines are displayed in the document window as they will appear on the printed page.

However, there are some differences between the two views. Here's a brief description of each view:

◆ **Draft view** (**Figure 15**) is handy when working with a large or complex document. It redraws faster on the screen and uses less screen space because items such as headers, footers, and footnotes are not displayed. Also, page breaks are displayed using a double line.

◆ **Page view** (**Figure 16**) shows everything in a document, including the headers, footers, footnotes, and watermarks. Each time a new page appears, the entire page is graphically displayed, meaning that any unused part of the page is displayed.

To change view quality:

1. Open the View menu by clicking the menu title (**Figure 17**).

2. Select either Draft or Page from the View menu.

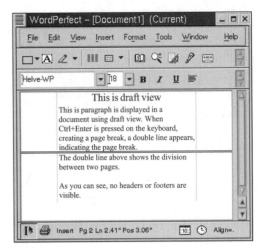

Figure 15. While draft view displays in a WYSIWYG environment, it only shows basic text, formatting, and page breaks. Even if headers or footers are present, they are not displayed.

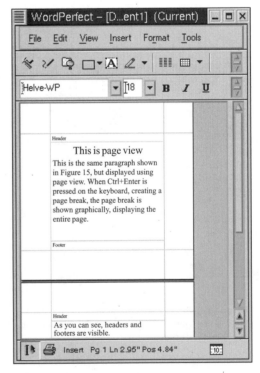

Figure 16. Page view displays in a WYSIWYG environment, showing all text, formatting, and page breaks. Headers and footers are also displayed.

Figure 17. Choose either Draft or Page from the View menu or press Ctrl+F5 or Shift+Ctrl+F5, respectively.

Zooming In and Out to See a Document

The Zoom command is used to magnify or reduce the view of a document. You can zoom in to see detail or zoom out to view an entire document. Zooming in or out has no effect on the document or the size of the text, only your view of it.

To zoom to a different magnification:

Click the Zoom button on the WordPerfect 8 Toolbar, then choose the magnification you want from the drop-down list (**Figure 18**).

or

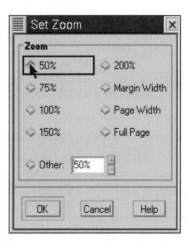

1. Choose Zoom from the View menu (**Figure 19**). The Set Zoom dialog box will open (**Figure 20**).

2. Select a radio button next to the magnification you would like to use, then click OK. The document will zoom in or out in the document window.

Figure 18. Click the Zoom button on the WordPerfect 8 Toolbar, then choose the magnification you would like to use.

Figure 19. Choose Zoom from the View menu.

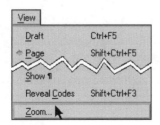

Figure 20. Select a magnification from the Zoom area, then click OK.

The Property Bar

The Property Bar (**Figure 21**), located by default near the top of the document window below the WordPerfect 8 Toolbar, is a context-sensitive command bar. It displays different buttons and options depending on which tool or item (such as a graphic or table) is selected. For instance, when a graphic is selected, the Property Bar contains only graphic-related commands.

Figure 21. The Property Bar is context-sensitive. In this example, the insertion point was blinking in the document, waiting for text to be typed, thus text related commands and options are displayed.

It's a Pop-up Menu! No, Wait! It's a QuickMenu!

When you right click on the Gnome or KDE Desktop, a *pop-up menu* appears that you can use to choose a command or open a dialog box (**Figure 22**). (Some folks just call these *pop-ups*.) Gnome and KDE both use the term "pop-up menu" for this item.

WordPerfect also uses pop-up menus, but calls them *QuickMenus*. They are referred to as QuickMenus in both the WordPerfect online Help file and the *WordPerfect User's Guide* that ships with the Personal Edition. To try to avoid any confusion, here's how these useful menus are named in this book:

◆ When working with the Gnome and KDE Desktops in Chapters 2 and 3, I use the term pop-up menu.

◆ When working in WordPerfect, I use the term QuickMenu.

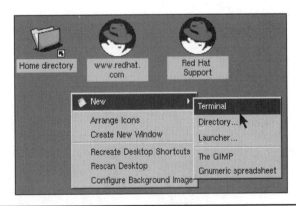

Figure 22. This pop-up menu with open fly-out is accessed by right clicking on the Gnome Desktop. Pop-up menus are called QuickMenus in WordPerfect 8.

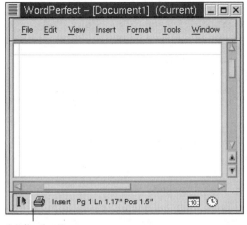

Application Bar

Figure 23. The Application Bar displays important information as you work on a document. For instance, the selected printer will be displayed in a balloon window when the mouse is positioned over the printer icon.

The Application Bar

The Application Bar (**Figure 23**) is your guide to what's happening in the document window. It gives information about the position of the insertion point and on which page you're working.

You can customize the Application Bar to display other information including the date and time, font in use, keyboard selection, and zoom magnification. Any of these items added to the Application Bar also perform another purpose: you can click them to change the setting. For instance, if you click the Zoom button on the Application Bar, the Set Zoom dialog box will open (**Figure 20**), letting you select another zoom setting.

You can customize the Application Bar by right clicking on the Application Bar, then choosing Settings from the QuickMenu (**Figure 24**). The Application Bar Preferences dialog box will open (**Figure 25**), ready to help you customize the Application Bar. For a complete discussion about customizing the Application Bar, turn to pages 153–154.

Figure 24. Right click on the Application Bar and choose Settings from the QuickMenu.

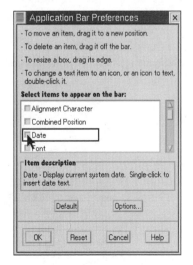

Figure 25. You can set what is available on the Application Bar using the Application Bar Preferences dialog box.

Getting Help

WordPerfect 8 for Linux comes with a comprehensive online help system that has been developed with users' requests in mind. There are five parts in the help system:

◆ **The User's Guide**—this is the paper manual that ships with the Personal Edition of WordPerfect 8. You can read it at your leisure, even away from the computer.

◆ **Online Help**—this opens a window where you can look for your topic using a table of contents or search engine (**Figure 26**).

◆ **PerfectExpert**—the PerfectExpert is a tutor that gives you step-by-step instructions on how to complete specific tasks (**Figure 27**).

◆ **QuickTips**—these are the balloons that appear when the mouse passes over a button or drop-down list on a toolbar (**Figure 28**).

◆ **Technical Support**—folks who purchase the Personal Edition of WordPerfect 8 for Linux are entitled to 30 days free support from the date of purchase. For technical assistance in the U.S., call 1-613-728-6852, and have your license number handy.

Figure 26. With Online Help, you can use the Contents to look for a topic or perform a search.

Figure 27. The PerfectExpert takes you step-by-step through tasks you need to perform to create a document.

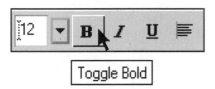

Figure 28. When you pass the mouse over a button or menu item, a QuickTip appears, telling you what the item does.

Figure 29. Click the Help menu title at the right end of the Menu Bar, then choose the type of help you would like to use.

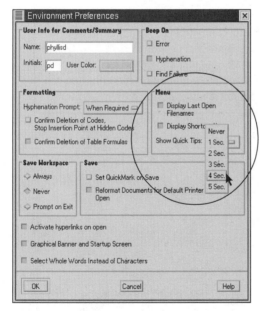

Figure 30. In the Menu area, use the Show Quick Tips drop-down list to set how long a QuickTip is displayed.

To open online Help or the PerfectExpert:

1. Click the Help menu title on the Menu Bar (**Figure 29**).

2. Select the type of help you want to use:

   ◆ Choose Contents to look through the help file's table of contents.

   ◆ Choose Search for Help on to look up a specific topic.

   ◆ Choose PerfectExpert to open the PerfectExpert window.

✔ Tip

■ If you are working with Macros, and need help, choose Macros from the Help menu. This will open a macro-specific help file.

To see QuickTips:

Slowly move the mouse pointer over any button. A balloon help window will appear, telling you what the button does.

To display/hide QuickTips:

1. In the program window, choose Preferences (**Figure 10**). The Preferences dialog box will open (**Figure 11**).

2. Click Environment. The Environment Preferences dialog box will open (**Figure 30**).

3. In the Menu area, use the Show Quick Tips drop-down list to select how long a QuickTip will display.

4. Click OK to close the Environment Preferences dialog box.

5. Click OK again to close the Preferences dialog box and return to the document window.

HOW TO OPEN HELP; DISPLAY/HIDE QUICKTIPS

Moving Around Dialog Boxes

It's easy to move around dialog boxes using the keyboard or the mouse. With the mouse, it's obvious: click what you would like to select or to move to a different area of the dialog box. If you don't want to take your hands from the keyboard, there are various keystrokes you can use to move around:

◆ Tab moves you to the next option

◆ Shift+Tab moves you to the previous option

◆ Arrow keys are used to move within a list box or group of options

◆ Esc works just like the Cancel button, closing the dialog box with no changes

◆ Enter works just like the OK button, starting a selected action

Hardware Considerations

While Linux will run on virtually any type of Intel compatible computer, running a 486 processor with a minimum of 4 MB of RAM is suggested. For WordPerfect 8 for Linux, Corel Corporation recommends a minimum of 9 MB memory and 87 MB hard disk space for a full installation. Please bear in mind that these are minimum suggestions and you will no doubt enjoy working with WordPerfect more if you are using current hardware.

Summary

In this chapter you learned about:

◆ Why you might use Linux

◆ Linux on the Web

◆ Peachpit companion Web sites

◆ How WordPerfect works

◆ The WordPerfect screen

◆ WordPerfect controls

◆ The Application Bar

◆ QuickMenus vs. pop-up menus

You also learned how to:

◆ Use a menu

◆ Use keyboard shortcuts

◆ Access toolbars

◆ Change keyboard and toolbar settings to previous WordPerfect versions

◆ Change view quality

◆ Zoom in and out

◆ Get help

INSTALLING WORDPERFECT 8

The term *Linux* means two things. First, it means the kernel or heart of the Linux operating system. Second, it means a *distribution* of software programs that is built around the Linux kernel.

The latest Linux distributions all incorporate version 2 of the Linux kernel. In this sense, at the heart, the distributions are the same. However, the programs that make up the distributions can vary considerably. For instance, the Red Hat distribution is different from the Caldera distribution, although both are based upon the same Linux kernel.

One way in which distributions vary is the look and feel of the Desktop Environments they include. A Linux Desktop Environment is loaded on top of Linux just as Microsoft Windows is loaded on top of DOS. In other words, the look and feel of your Linux windows depends upon the desktop environment you use.

You may be interested to know that some Linux distributions—such as Red Hat 6—ship with more than one desktop environment. It is up to you to decide which one you want to work with.

The most common Desktop Environments in use today are Gnome and KDE. Red Hat—the best-selling distribution of Linux—installs the Gnome Desktop as its default. Caldera—the next best-selling distribution—defaults to KDE. From the viewpoint of a WordPerfect for Linux user, it doesn't matter which one you use, because WordPerfect works the same in either desktop environment.

When writing the *WordPerfect 8 for Linux: Visual QuickStart Guide*, I used the Red Hat Linux 6 distribution with the Gnome Desktop. This is what you will see when a figure in this book shows the desktop.

If you want to learn more about Red Hat Linux 6 and the Gnome desktop, take a look at the *Red Hat Linux 6: Visual QuickPro Guide* (Peachpit Press).

What is the Linux X11 Windows Server?

Technically, WordPerfect 8 for Linux will run on any Linux system that is capable of displaying *X11 Windows*. X11 Windows is the mechanism that works behind the scenes in Unix systems, such as Linux, to display windowing environments such as Gnome. It is an enhanced version of what used to be called X Windows. So the real bottom line of whether your system can run Word-Perfect 8 for Linux is whether it has an X11 Windows server.

The Difference Between the WordPerfect Versions

WordPerfect 8 for Linux is available in three versions: the downloadable version which is available at no charge, the Personal Edition, which this book is based on, and the Server Edition.

The downloadable version is a fully functional word processor that will let you import and export Microsoft Office 97 document file formats. It includes an online help system, over 90 built-in spreadsheet functions, and lets you export Web-ready documents in HTML format.

The Personal Edition includes all of the features in the downloadable version plus the ability to draw pictures and create charts, create document suites using the ExpressDocs feature, and install any of the 130 fonts that ship with the program. In addition, the CD-ROM contains over 5000 clipart images, 200 photographs, and 180 textures that can be used to create dynamic reports and documents.

The Server Edition includes all the features in the Personal Edition plus support for the Oracle Database engine, advanced application customization programs, and the ability to access WordPerfect 8 for those folks using non-GUI terminal distributions of Linux.

WordPerfect and Linux Licensing

Unlike the Linux operating system, WordPerfect is a commercial product; it is neither *freeware* nor *open source software*. You are legally obliged to comply with Corel Corporation's terms of license. For the free, downloadable version, this means that each user must register with Corel within 90 days, otherwise the free version will expire and not work anymore. Also, the free version is intended for personal, not business use.

The Personal Edition comes with a single-user license. For information about licensing the Server Edition, contact Corel Corporation.

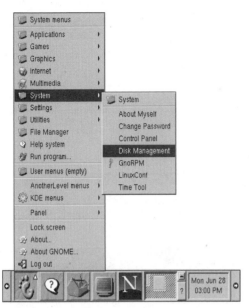

Figure 1. Choose Disk Management from the System fly-out on the Gnome main menu.

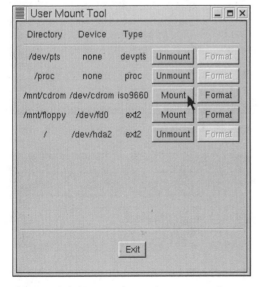

Figure 2. Click the Mount button that corresponds to the CD-ROM.

Installing the Personal Edition

This section describes how to install the WordPerfect 8 Personal Edition which ships on a CD-ROM. If you want to find out how to download and install the free version, turn to page 29.

To install the WordPerfect 8 Personal Edition on your computer you will need to mount the CD-ROM drive, then go to the command line using a Terminal Window. To do both of these you will have to log on as *root* or *su to root*. If you don't have access to root, see your system administrator.

To mount the CD-ROM drive:

1. Insert the WordPerfect CD-ROM into your computer's CD-ROM drive.

2. Choose Disk Management from the System fly-out on the Gnome main menu (**Figure 1**). The User Mount Tool dialog box will open (**Figure 2**).

3. Click the Mount button found to the right of your computer's CD-ROM location. In Figure 2 this location is **/mnt/cdrom**. The CD-ROM drive will mount and the button you just clicked will read "Unmount."

4. Click Exit to close the User Mount Tool dialog box.

MOUNT THE CD-ROM

To install WordPerfect:

1. Create a directory where you want to install WordPerfect (**Figure 3**). Often this directory is created under the /usr directory.

2. Click the Terminal emulation program button on the Gnome Panel (**Figure 4**). A Terminal window will open (**Figure 5**).

3. Change to the directory where the CD-ROM is mounted (**Figure 6**). This is the same pathname shown in the User Mount Tool dialog box (**Figure 2**). In Figure 5 cd /mnt/cdrom has been typed to change directories.

4. Press Enter on the keyboard.

5. Type pwd then press Enter on the keyboard. This will verify that you are in the correct location (**Figure 7**).

6. Type ls then press Enter on the keyboard. This will list the contents of the directory where you are located.

INSTALL WORDPERFECT 8

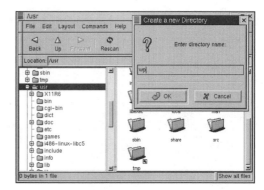

Figure 3. Create a new directory where you want to install WordPerfect.

Figure 4. Click the Terminal button to open a Terminal window.

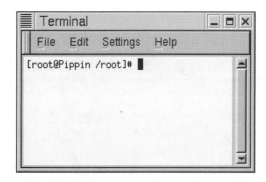

Figure 5. The Terminal window.

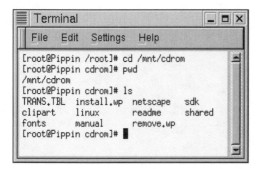

Figure 7. Type pwd to make sure you're in the right place, then type ls to view the contents of the WordPerfect CD-ROM.

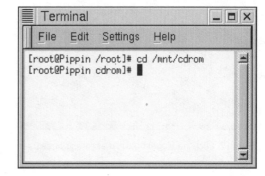

Figure 6. Change to the directory where the CD-ROM is mounted.

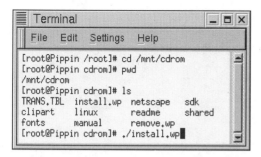

Figure 8. Type ./install.wp to start the installation.

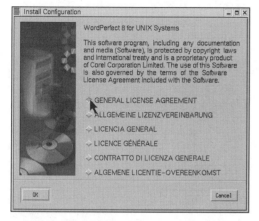

Figure 9. Select the language you want to use for the installation.

7. Type ./install.wp then press Enter on the keyboard (**Figure 8**). The WordPerfect installation program will start and the first panel of the Install Configuration dialog box will open (**Figure 9**). This panel is used to set the language you want to use.

8. Click the button next to the language you would like to use for the installation process. In Figure 9 English has been selected.

9. Click OK. The next panel will open, showing the license agreement (**Figure 10**).

10. Click Agree to continue with the installation. The panel will open (**Figure 11**). This panel is used to tell the installation program where to install WordPerfect.

11. Enter the full pathname of the directory you created in step 1. In **Figure 11**, the directory pathname is /usr/wp.

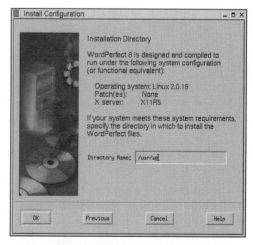

Figure 10. Click Accept to continue with the installation.

Figure 11. Type the full pathname of the directory where you want to install WordPerfect 8.

12. Click OK. The next panel will open (**Figure 12**). This panel is used to select the type of installation you would like—Full, Medium, or Minimum.

13. Select the installation type you would like, then click OK. The next panel will open (**Figure 13**). If you have another version of WordPerfect installed on your computer, you can set this installation to mimic that previous installation. This means that any printer or terminal drivers that you are already using will appear as defaults for this new WordPerfect 8 installation.

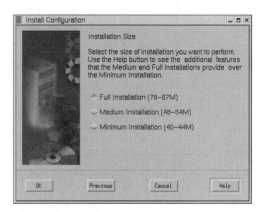

Figure 12. Select the type of installation you would like, then click OK.

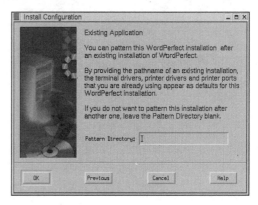

Figure 13. If you wish to mimic another WordPerfect installation, enter the full pathname where the existing WordPerfect software is installed in the Pattern Directory text box. Otherwise, leave the text box blank.

What are the different installation types?

◆ **Minimum Installation** includes all the programs and data files needed to run WordPerfect; though, it does not include the features listed in the medium or full installation. It requires up to 44 MB free hard disk space.

◆ **Medium Installation** includes everything installed in the Minimum Installation plus Grammatik and a thesaurus. It requires up to 54 MB free hard disk space.

◆ **Full Installation** includes everything installed in the Medium Installation plus online help, sample macros and online macro help, WordPerfect Draw and sample graphics files, sample documents, and sound capabilities. It requires up to 87 MB free hard disk space.

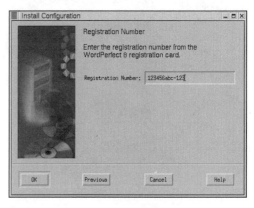

Figure 14. Type in your registration number, then click OK to continue.

Figure 15. Click the button next to Update the magic file, then click OK.

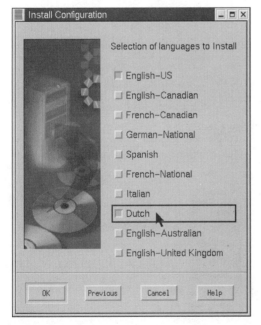

Figure 16. Click the check box(es) next to the languages you would like to install, then click OK.

14. If you wish to mimic another WordPerfect installation, enter the full pathname where the existing WordPerfect software is installed in the Pattern Directory text box. Otherwise, leave the text box blank.

15. Click OK. The next panel will appear (**Figure 14**). This panel is used to enter the registration number that came with your copy of WordPerfect.

16. Type the registration number in the text box.

17. Click OK. The next panel will display (**Figure 15**). This dialog box is used to edit the *magic file*. Unlike Windows where the operating system "knows" the type of file by the file suffix—for instance, .wpd for a WordPerfect document—Linux has no built in way to distinguish file types. In Linux, the magic file is used to store information about file types to let the operating system distinguish file types.

18. If you wish to update the magic file, and you most likely will wish to do so, select the radio button next to Update the magic file to select it. The Linux magic file will automatically be updated when WordPerfect is installed. WordPerfect will work with Linux and the magic file to distinguish the types of files you create.

19. Click OK. The next panel will open (**Figure 16**). This panel lets you select the languages you would like to install.

20. Click the check box(es) next to the languages you want to install (you can select more than one).

21. Click OK. The next panel will display (**Figure 17**). This panel is used to select the printer drivers for the printer you are using.

22. To select printer drivers:

A. Scroll down the list of printer drivers until you find one you want to install, then click to highlight it. To select more than one driver, hold down the Ctrl key while clicking.

B. Click Select to select the printers. An asterisk will appear next to each selected driver in the list.

or

Scroll down the list of printer drivers until you find one you want to install, then double-click to select it. An asterisk will appear next to the selected printer driver.

23. To view the list of printer drivers you have selected, click List. The Selected Entries dialog box will open (**Figure 18**).

24. When you have finished viewing the list, click OK to close the Selected Entries dialog box and return to the Install Configuration window.

25. To remove a printer driver you have chosen, scroll through the list to find that printer driver, then double-click on it.

26. To remove all selected printer drivers, click None in the Install Configuration window.

27. When you have finished selecting printer drivers, click OK. The next panel will appear (**Figure 19**). This panel is used to assign the printer drivers to the printer installed on your Linux computer.

Figure 17. Highlight the printer drivers you want to install, then click Select.

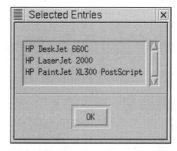

Figure 18. The Selected Entries dialog box displays the list of the selected printer drivers.

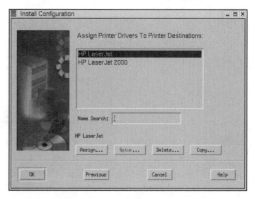

Figure 19. Click the Assign button to assign the selected printer drivers to a specific printer.

Figure 20. Use the Destinations dialog box to assign a printer driver to a printer.

Figure 21. Click to highlight the printer, then click OK.

28. Highlight the printer drivers you want to assign to a printer.

29. Click Assign to locate the printer. The Destinations dialog box will open (**Figure 20**).

30. Highlight the printer device by clicking on it (**Figure 21**).

31. Click OK to close the Destinations dialog box and return to the Install Configuration window.

32. When you are finished assigning printer drivers to specific printers, click OK. The next panel will open (**Figure 22**). This panel is used to select optional features. These features are:

- ◆ CDE Desktop Icon—this item will place a WP icon on your desktop.

- ◆ Word Perfect Online Manual

- ◆ Netscape Browser 3.04

33. Click the check boxes next to the optional features you want to install, then click OK. The next panel will open (**Figure 23**). This panel lets you review the installation options you have selected.

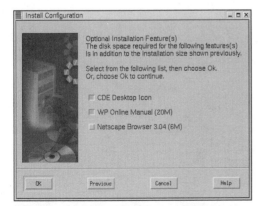

Figure 22. Click the check boxes next to the optional features you want to install, then click OK.

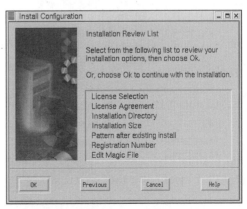

Figure 23. You can review the installation options you've selected by highlighting one, then clicking OK.

34. If you want to change an item, select the item from the list, then click OK. The installation program will return you to the appropriate panel, where you can make changes.

or

If you are happy with what you see in the list, don't select anything in the list box, and click OK to continue the installation. The Installing Files dialog box will open (**Figure 24**) and WordPerfect will be installed on your computer. When the installation is complete, a README Review dialog box will open (**Figure 25**).

35. Highlight any item you want to read about, then click View. When you are finished reading the various items, click Done to finish the installation. ***Congratulations!*** WordPerfect is installed!

Unmounting the CD-ROM

To finish up, you need to unmount the CD-ROM.

To unmount the CD-ROM:

1. Choose Disk Management from the System fly-out on the Gnome main menu (**Figure 1**). The User Mount Tool dialog box will open (**Figure 26**).

2. Click the Unmount button found to the right of your computer's CD-ROM location. In Figure 2 this location is /mnt/cdrom. The CD-ROM drive will unmount and the button you just clicked will read "Mount."

3. Click Exit to close the dialog box.

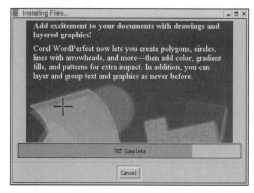

Figure 24. The Installing Files dialog box shows you the installation's progress.

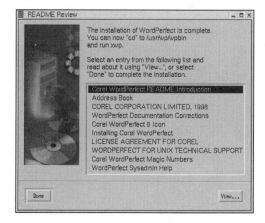

Figure 25. Click Done to finish the installation.

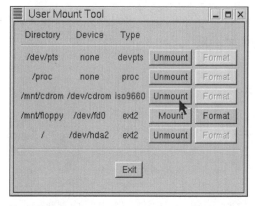

Figure 26. Click Unmount to unmount the CD-ROM.

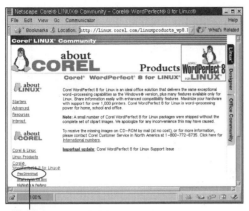

Click here

Figure 27. Open Corel's Linux products Web site in your browser, then click Free Download.

Click here

Figure 28. Click the CNET Downloads button.

Click here

Figure 29. Click the Download Now button.

Downloading and Installing the Free Version of WordPerfect

The free version of WordPerfect can be downloaded from Corel Corporation's Web site. While this program is offered at no charge, it is about 24 megabytes. It can be downloaded in one zipped file or seven zipped file segments. If you are using a dial-up connection to access the internet, downloading this version will take hours. If you purchased and are running the Red Hat Linux 6 distribution, this "free" WordPerfect version is available on the second CD-ROM in the three disk set.

To download Corel WordPerfect 8:

1. In your Internet browser, open `http://linux.corel.com/linuxproducts_wp8.htm` Corel's Linux products Web site will open (**Figure 27**).

2. Click on the Free Download link at the left of the Web page below WordPerfect 8 for Linux. The Corel Free Download Web page will open (**Figure 28**).

3. Click the CNET Downloads button to proceed to Download.com. The CNET download page will open in a new browser window (**Figure 29**).

(continued)

DOWNLOAD WORDPERFECT 8

4. Click Download Now. A new window with the Corel WordPerfect for Linux User Agreement will open (**Figure 30**).

5. Click the Yes, I Accept button at the lower left-hand corner. The User Agreement window will close and the CNET download window will open showing full and segmented downloads (**Figure 31**).

6. Click to download the entire file in one download, or click in series to download each of seven segments, one after the other.

✔ Tip

■ The full WordPerfect installation requires about 70 Mb of free hard drive space.

To install the free version of WordPerfect:

1. Create a directory where you want to install WordPerfect (**Figure 32**). Often this directory is created under the /usr directory.

2. Copy the file (or files) that you downloaded to your new directory.

3. Click the Terminal button on the Gnome Panel (**Figure 33**). A Terminal window will open (**Figure 34**).

4. Change to the directory where you just copied the downloaded files. If you downloaded one file, it will be named guilg.gz. If you downloaded the seven segments, they will be named gui00.gz...gui06.gz.

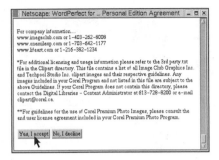

Figure 30. Click Yes, I accept to continue to the download window.

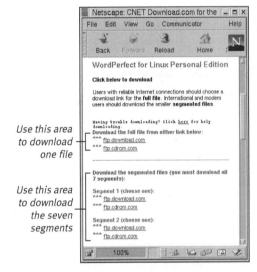

Figure 31. Use the different areas to download either the single file or the seven segments.

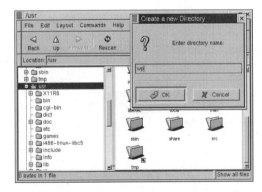

Figure 32. Create a directory where you want to unzip the downloaded files.

Figure 33. Click the Terminal button to open a Terminal window.

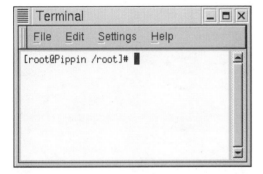

Figure 34. The Terminal window.

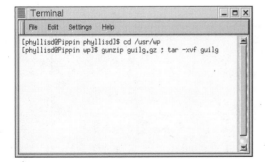

Figure 35. Type gunzip guilg.gz ; tar -xvf guilg to unzip the single file download or type gunzip gui00.gz ; tar -xvf gui00 to unzip the first segment of the seven segment download.

5. To unzip the file(s):

Type gunzip guilg.gz ; tar -xvf guilg if you downloaded the one file, then press Enter on the keyboard (**Figure 35**).

or

A. Type gunzip gui00.gz ; tar -xvf gui00 then press Enter on the keyboard to unzip the first segment if you downloaded the seven segments.

B. Type gunzip gui01.gz ; tar -xvf gui01 then press Enter on the keyboard to unzip the second segment.

C. Continue typing in sequential commands until you have unzipped all seven segments.

6. When you have finished unzipping the file(s), type ./Runme to start the installation program. Follow steps 8–32, starting on page 23 to install the free version of WordPerfect.

✔ Tips

■ You don't need to have a license number to install the free version of WordPerfect, but every time you use the free version of WordPerfect, you will be asked for one. To obtain a license number for the free version, follow the steps on the page 32.

■ If you don't obtain a license number and register it with your free copy of WordPerfect, the free version of the WordPerfect program will stop working after 90 days.

INSTALL THE FREE VERSION OF WORDPERFECT 8

To obtain a license number for the free version:

1. In your Internet browser, open http://venus.corel.com/nasapps/wp8linuxreg/register.html. Corel's Linux registration Web site will open (**Figure 36**).

2. Fill out the registration form.

3. Click Submit. Your license number will appear on the next page.

4. Write down the license number or print the Web page.

5. Enter the license number when prompted during the installation or enter the number in the initial box when you launch WordPerfect.

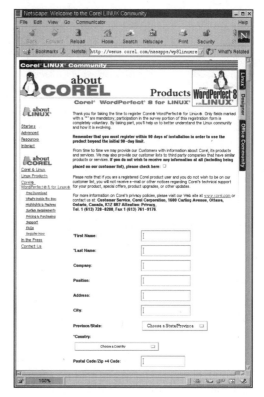

Figure 36. Open Corel's Linux registration Web site at http://venus.corel.com/nasapps/wp8linuxreg/register.html. Scroll down the Web page to find the registration form. Enter all the necessary information, then click Submit.

OBTAIN A LICENSE NUMBER

Summary

In this chapter you learned about:

◆ The Linux Desktop Environments

◆ The Linux X11 Windows server

◆ The difference between the WordPerfect versions

◆ WordPerfect and Linux licensing

◆ Installing the Personal Edition

◆ Downloading the free version

◆ Installing the free version

◆ Obtaining a license number for use with the free version

STARTUP

When WordPerfect is launched, a small rectangular window, called the *program window,* appears on the screen (**Figure 1**). Any changes you make using the program window, effect all documents created in WordPerfect.

The *document window* is the area on the screen where documents are created (**Figure 1**). Any changes you make using the document window effect only the current document you are working on. The part of the document window where you actually work with the text of the document is called the *workspace.*

You can have as many as 100 document windows open at one time (depending upon how much memory your computer has). When more than one document window is displayed, the window whose title bar is highlighted is *active.* If you type or change anything in the document window, it's the active document that changes. The first time you launch WordPerfect, a new document window appears, ready for typing.

Document window ⸺

Program window ⸺

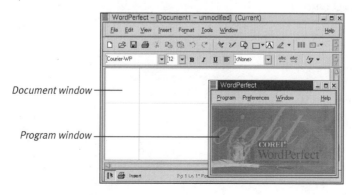

Figure 1. The WordPerfect program and document windows.

Menu Items and Desktop Shortcuts

Launching WordPerfect is quick and easy once you add an item to the Gnome or K Main Menu or add a shortcut on the Desktop.

To put a menu item on the Gnome Main Menu:

1. Choose Menu editor from the Settings fly-out on the Gnome Main Menu (**Figure 2**). The GNOME menu editor dialog box will open with User Menus selected in the tree view window (**Figure 3**).

2. On the Menu Bar, click New Item to add a new menu item under User Menus.

3. On the Basic tab page, type WordPerfect in the Name text box (**Figure 4**).

4. Type the full pathname of the location where WordPerfect is installed plus the command to launch WordPerfect in the Command text box. In Figure 4, /usr/wp/wpbin/./xwp has been typed.

5. Click the Icon button to choose an appropriate icon.

6. Click Save.

7. Close the GNOME menu editor dialog box by clicking the Close button. The WordPerfect menu item will appear on the Gnome Main Menu (**Figure 5**).

✔ Tip

■ If you are logged on as root, you can add the WordPerfect menu item to the Systems menu on the Gnome Main Menu. (You could add it under Applications.) Once an icon is added to the System menu, it is available to all users; whereas, an item added to the User menu is only available for that user.

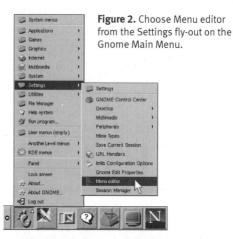

Figure 2. Choose Menu editor from the Settings fly-out on the Gnome Main Menu.

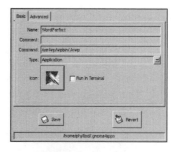

Figure 3. The GNOME menu editor dialog box opens with User Menu selected in the tree view window.

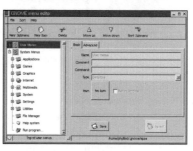

Figure 4. Use the Basic tab page to enter the program name, command line information, and select an icon.

Figure 5. The WordPerfect menu item appears as a user menu on the Gnome Main Menu.

Figure 6. Choose Menu Editor from the Utilities fly-out on the K Main Menu.

To put a menu item on the K Main Menu:

1. Choose Menu Editor from the Utilities fly-out on the K Main Menu (**Figure 6**). The Menu Editor window will appear (**Figure 7**).

2. Right click on the Empty button and select New from the pop-up menu (**Figure 8**). The kmenuedit dialog box will open (**Figure 9**).

3. Type WordPerfect in the Name text box.

4. Click the icon button to the right of the dialog box and select an icon from the Select Icon dialog box.

5. On the Execute tab page, type the full pathname of the location where WordPerfect is installed plus the command to launch WordPerfect in the Execute text box. In **Figure 9**, `/usr/wp/wpbin/./xwp` has been typed.

6. Click OK to close the kmenuedit dialog box and return to the Menu Editor window.

7. Choose Save from the File menu.

8. Press Ctrl+Q on the keyboard to close the Menu Editor. The WordPerfect menu item will appear under the Personal fly-out on the K Main Menu (**Figure 10**).

Figure 7. The K Desktop Menu Editor.

Figure 8. Choose New from the pop-up menu.

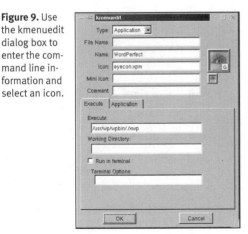

Figure 9. Use the kmenuedit dialog box to enter the command line information and select an icon.

Figure 10. The WordPerfect menu item appears on the K Main Menu.

To put a shortcut on the Gnome Desktop:

1. Right click on the Gnome Desktop. A pop-up menu will appear (**Figure 11**).

2. Choose Launcher from the New fly-out. The Desktop entry properties dialog box will appear (**Figure 12**).

3. On the Basic tab page, type WordPerfect in the Name text box.

4. In the Command text box, type in the full path where the WordPerfect program is installed (**Figure 13**). In **Figure 13**, /usr/wp/wpbin/xwp has been entered. (Notice that this is not a typical Linux command line. Usually, there would be a period (.) before the /xwp as shown in Figure 4.)

5. Select Application from the Type drop-down list.

6. Click the Icon button to select an appropriate icon from the Choose an icon dialog box.

7. Click OK. The shortcut will appear on the Desktop (**Figure 14**).

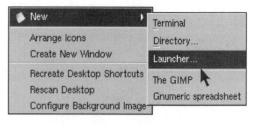

Figure 11. Choose Launcher from the New fly-out on the pop-up menu.

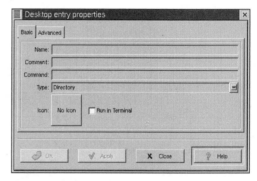

Figure 12. The Basic tab page of the Desktop entry properties dialog box is used to enter the information you need to create a shortcut.

Figure 14. The WordPerfect shortcut appears on the Gnome Desktop.

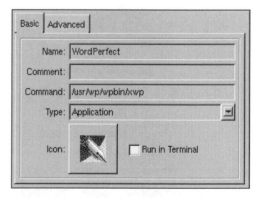

Figure 13. On the Basic tab page, enter the name of the program and the command line, then choose an icon.

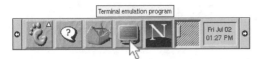

Figure 15. Click the Terminal emulation program button on the Gnome panel.

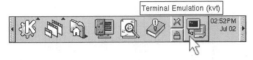

Figure 16. Click the Terminal Emulation button on the K panel.

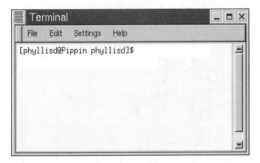

Figure 17. Use the Terminal window to move to the directory where WordPerfect is installed, then enter the command to launch the program.

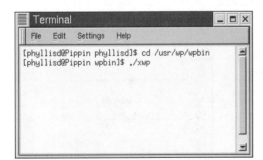

Figure 18. Change to the wpbin directory, then type ./xwp and press Enter on the keyboard to launch WordPerfect.

To launch WordPerfect using a menu item or shortcut:

If you are using the Gnome Desktop, choose WordPerfect from the User fly-out on the Gnome Main Menu (**Figure 5**) or double-click the WordPerfect icon on the Gnome Desktop (**Figure 14**).

or

If you are using the K Desktop, choose WordPerfect from the Personal fly-out on the K Main Menu (**Figure 10**).

To launch WordPerfect from the command line:

1. Click the Terminal emulation program button on the Gnome panel (**Figure 15**) or click the Terminal Emulation button on the K panel (**Figure 16**). A Terminal window will open (**Figure 17**).

2. At the prompt, change directories to where WordPerfect was installed.

3. Change to the wpbin directory.

4. Type ./xwp (**Figure 18**), then press Enter on the keyboard to launch WordPerfect.

USE A SHORTCUT OR COMMAND LINE TO LAUNCH

Starting a New Document

When you start a new document, you can either open the new document and close the current document at the same time, or start a new document window while keeping the current one open.

Figure 19. Choose New from the File menu.

To start a new document and close the current document:

1. Choose New from the File menu (**Figure 19**). A new document will open. If you have made changes to the current document, a Save dialog box will appear asking if you want to save the changes (**Figure 20**).

2. You can:

   ◆ Click Yes to save the current document before closing it;

   ◆ Click No to close the current document without saving it; or

   ◆ Click Cancel to cancel the new document command, and return to the active document.

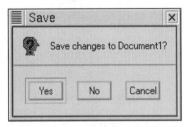

Figure 20. The Save dialog box asks whether you want to save changes that you've made to a document.

To start a new document and keep the current one open:

Using the program window, choose New Window from the Program menu (**Figure 21**) or press Ctrl+N on the keyboard. A new window will open on top of the active window.

Figure 21. Choose New Window from the Program menu.

Document Windows Roll Up

If you are working on several documents at once and want to get one out of the way, double-click on the Title Bar. The document window will roll up. Double-click on the Title Bar again to unroll the document window.

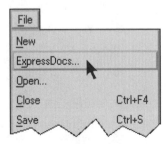

Figure 22. Choose ExpressDocs from the File menu.

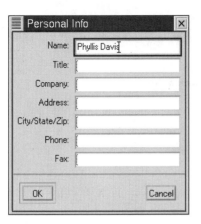

Figure 23. Enter your information in the Personal Info dialog box.

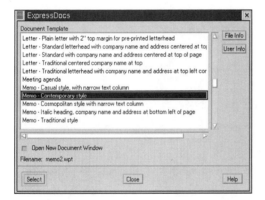

Figure 24. The ExpressDocs dialog box is used to select a template and change file and user information.

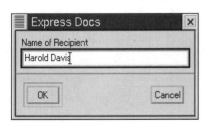

Figure 25. Depending on the template you choose, a series of dialog boxes open, asking for pertinent information.

Using ExpressDocs

Every document you create is based upon a *template*. The template sets the formatting and layout of the document. You can use a template as many times as you wish to create documents that look the same and have similar content. This can be particularly useful if you constantly use a particular kind of document, such as a letterhead, or need to generate reports. You can create your own templates or use the ones that ship with WordPerfect, called *ExpressDocs*.

There are more that 70 ExpressDocs included with WordPerfect that let you quickly create professional documents. Many of them are part of document suites that include such items as a letter, memo, and brochure that use the same layout and design for a consistent look. There are several suites, including Contemporary, Cosmopolitan, Elegant, and Traditional.

To start a new document using ExpressDocs:

1. Choose ExpressDocs from the File menu (**Figure 22**). The first time you use ExpressDocs a Personal Info dialog box will appear (**Figure 23**) along with the ExpressDocs dialog box (**Figure 24**). The information that you enter in this dialog box can be used in future documents created with ExpressDocs.

2. Enter your personal information, if you wish, into the appropriate text boxes in the Personal Info dialog box.

3. When you are finished entering your information, click OK to close the dialog box and return to the ExpressDocs dialog box.

4. Scroll down the Document Template list box until you find the type of document you want to create.

(continued)

5. Click on the item to highlight it, then click Select. In **Figure 24**, Memo – Contemporary style has been selected. Depending upon the type of ExpressDoc you selected, various dialog boxes will appear, prompting you for information (**Figure 25**). In the contemporary memo style example, a dialog box requesting the Name of Recipient has appeared.

6. Enter the information requested by the various dialog boxes, if you wish. If you don't want to enter information now, you can enter it later when working on the documents.

7. Each time you finish with a dialog box, click OK to close that dialog box and move on to the next one.

8. When the ExpressDocs template has finished requesting information from you, the document will appear, ready for you to start typing in the document window (**Figure 26**).

✔ Tips

■ If you want the ExpressDocs template to create a document in a new document window, make sure the check box next to Open New Document Window is selected in the ExpressDocs dialog box (**Figure 27**). Otherwise, the ExpressDoc template will create the document in the active document window.

■ You can change any of the text that an ExpressDocs template adds to a document.

■ If you want to change the personal information that you entered in the Personal Info dialog box, click User Info at the right of the ExpressDocs dialog box (**Figure 24**).

Figure 26. A document appears in the document window, ready for typing.

Figure 27. To make the ExpressDocs document open in a new document window, click the check box next to Open New Document Window.

Figure 28. Choose Save As from the File menu.

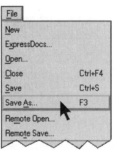

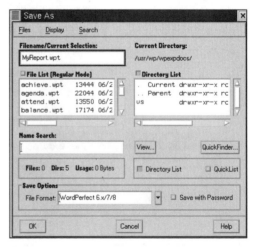

Figure 29. In the Save As dialalog box, use the Directory List box to move to the /wp/wpexpdocs/ directory.

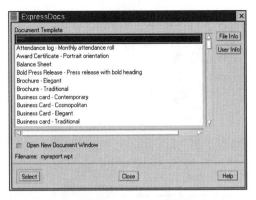

Figure 30. Your custom template will appear at the top of the Document Template list box as 4 asterisks.

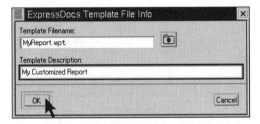

Figure 31. In the ExpressDocs Template File Info dialog box, enter a description of your template in the Template Discription text box, then click OK.

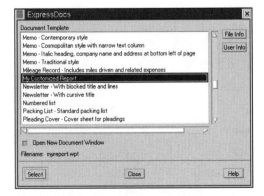

Figure 32. The new template description you entered replaces the 4 asterisks and your custom template appears alphabetically in the Document Template list box.

To create your own ExpressDocs:

1. Create the document that you want to use as a template.

2. Choose Save As from the file menu (**Figure 28**) or press F3 on the keyboard. The Save As dialog box will open (**Figure 29**).

3. Use the Directory List box to move to the directory where WordPerfect is installed.

4. Change to the **wpexpdocs** directory.

5. In the Filename/Current Selection text box, type in the name of your template with a **.wpt** extension.

6. Click OK to close the dialog box.

7. Choose ExpressDocs from the File menu (**Figure 22**). The ExpressDocs dialog box will open with you template displayed as 4 asterisks at the top of the Document Template list box (**Figure 30**).

8. Click File Info in the ExpressDocs dialog box. The ExpressDocs Template File Info dialog box will open (**Figure 31**).

9. Type a description of your template in the Template Description text box.

10. Click OK. Your template will appear in the Document Template list box, ready for use (**Figure 32**).

✔ Tip

■ If you don't have the right permissions, you cannot save a document in the **wpexpdocs** directory. You will need to log on as root or see your system administrator for assistance.

To open an existing document:

1. With the program window active, choose Open Window from the Program menu (**Figure 33**). The Open dialog box will appear (**Figure 34**).

2. Select the file you want to open using the directory and file lists.

3. Click OK. The document will open in a new document window.

or

1. Choose Open from the File menu in the document window (**Figure 35**). The Open dialog box will appear (**Figure 34**).

2. Select the file you want to open using directory and file lists.

3. Click Open. A Save dialog box will appear, asking whether you want to save the current document (**Figure 20**).

4. You can:

   ◆ Click Yes to save the document;

   ◆ Click No to close the document without saving changes; or

   ◆ Click Cancel to cancel the open document command and return to the active document.

5. If you clicked Yes or No, the Save dialog box will close and the file you selected will open in the document window.

✔ Tip

■ To quickly open one of the last documents you worked on, select it from the bottom of the Program menu in the program window.

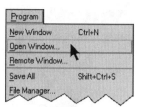

Figure 33. Choose Open Window from the Program menu.

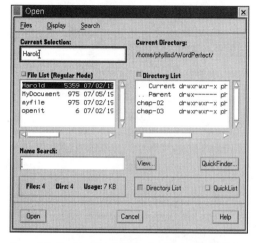

Figure 34. Use the Directory List box in the Open dialog box to move to the directory where the document is stored.

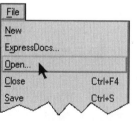

Figure 35. Choose Open from the File menu.

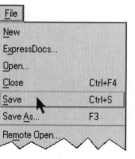

Figure 36. Choose Save from the File menu.

Figure 37. Choose Save As from the File menu.

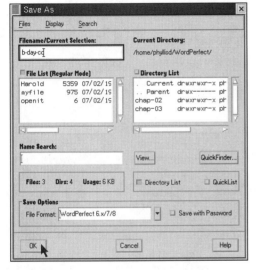

Figure 38. Move to the directory where you want to save the document, type its name in the Filename/ Current Selection text box, and then click OK.

Figure 39. Enter the password in the text box, then click OK.

To save your work:

With the document window active, choose Save from the File menu (**Figure 36**) or press Ctrl+S on the keyboard.

To save a copy of a file:

1. In the document window, choose Save As from the File menu (**Figure 37**) or press F3 on the keyboard. The Save As dialog box will open (**Figure 38**).

2. Use the Directory List to move to the directory where you want to save the file.

3. Type a name for the file in the Filename/ Current Selection text box.

4. If you want to save the file in a file format other than WordPerfect 8, use the File Format drop-down list in the Save Options area to select another file type.

5. Click OK to close the dialog box and save the document.

✔ Tips

■ To quickly move to your home directory, type a tilde (~) in the Filename/Current Selection text box, then press Enter on the keyboard.

■ You can save a document with a password, if you click the box next to Save with Password in the Save Options area (**Figure 38**). If you select this option, a Password Protection dialog box will open (**Figure 39**). To set a password, enter the password you would like to use in the Type Password for Document text box, then click OK.

SAVE YOUR WORK; SAVE A COPY OF A FILE

To import a document:

1. In the document window, choose Open from the File menu (**Figure 40**). The Open dialog box will appear (**Figure 41**).

2. Use the Directory List box to move to the directory where the document is stored.

3. Use the File List box to select the file.

4. Click Open. A Convert File dialog box may open (**Figure 42**).

5. If the Convert File dialog box appears, use the Convert File Format From list box to select the type of file.

6. Click OK. The file will open in the active document window.

✔ Tips

■ After importing a document, you should save it. Choose Save from the File menu to save the file with the same name or choose Save As from the file menu to save the file with a different name.

■ The Convert File dialog box will not appear when a WordPerfect 5.x or 6.0 format document (from any platform, DOS, OS/2, UNIX, or Windows) is imported because WordPerfect 8 automatically converts the file for you.

■ To see a list of the file formats that WordPerfect 8 supports, turn to page 58 in the *WordPerfect 8 User's Guide* that ships with the Personal Edition.

Figure 40. Choose Open from the File menu.

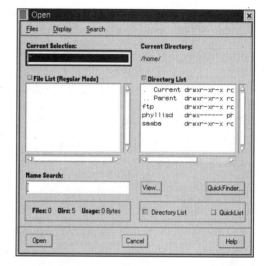

Figure 41. Use the Directory List box in the Open dialog box to move to the directory where the file is stored, highlight it in the File List box, and then click Open.

Figure 42. Use the Convert File Format From list box to select the type of file you are importing, then click OK.

IMPORT A DOCUMENT

Figure 43. Choose Save As from the File menu.

To export a document:

1. Create the document you want to export.

2. Choose Save As from the File menu (**Figure 43**). The Save As dialog box will open (**Figure 44**).

3. Use the Directory List to move to the directory where you want to save the file.

4. Type a name for the file in the Filename/Current Selection text box.

5. Use the File Format drop-down list in the Save Options area to select the file type that you would like to save the file as (**Figure 45**).

6. Click OK to close the dialog box and save the document in the new file format.

✔ Tip

- If you save a file that is password protected to another file format, the password is removed.

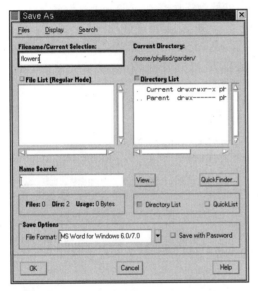

Figure 44. Move to the directory where you want to export the document and enter a name for the file in the Filename/Current Selection text box.

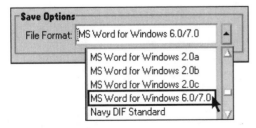

Figure 45. Scroll down the File Format drop-down list to find the file format you want to use to export the document.

Some File Extensions You May See

File extensions are the three letters that come after the period in a file name. These file extensions, which work with the Linux magic file, tell the computer what kind of file it is and how to interpret it.

WordPerfect uses several file extensions:

◆ .wpd—this is the native WordPerfect file extension that will automatically be attached to your documents when you save them.

◆ .ltr—you can save a document with this file extension to indicate a letter.

◆ .wpt—an ExpressDocs template.

Working with the QuickList

The WordPerfect QuickList is used to specify a list of directories and files that you most often. You can use the QuickList to quickly access those files and directories.

To create a QuickList:

1. Choose Open from the File menu (**Figure 35**). The Open dialog box will appear (**Figure 46**).

2. If the QuickList box is not displayed, click the check box next to QuickList near the bottom right of the dialog box (**Figure 47**). The QuickList box will open above the Directory List box (**Figure 48**).

3. Right click on the QuickList box. A QuickMenu will appear (**Figure 49**).

4. Choose Edit QuickList from the bottom of the QuickMenu. The Edit QuickList dialog box will open (**Figure 50**).

5. Click Add. The Add QuickList Item dialog box will open (**Figure 51**).

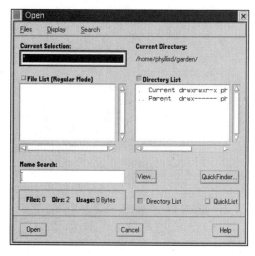

Figure 46. The Open dialog box without the QuickList displayed (it would appear above the Directory List box).

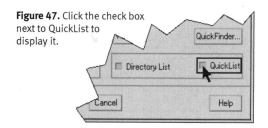

Figure 47. Click the check box next to QuickList to display it.

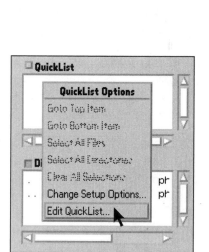

Figure 49. Choose Edit QuickList from the QuickMenu that appears.

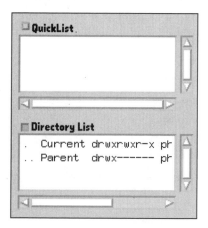

Figure 48. The QuickList appears above the Directory List box.

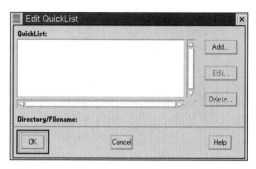

Figure 50. The Edit QuickList dialog box is used to add, edit, and delete QuickList entries.

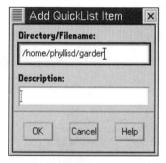

Figure 51. To add a file to the QuickList, type the path and filename; to add a directory, enter its path and the directory name.

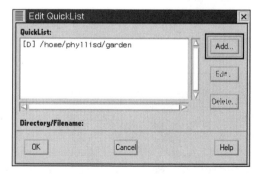

Figure 52. The file or directory appears in the QuickList box. If a directory has been added, [D] appears before the entry (as shown in this figure). If a file has been added, [F] appears before the entry.

6. If you want to add a directory to the QuickList, type the directory name and its path in the Directory/Filename text box.

or

If you want to add a document, type its full path and filename in the Directory/Filename text box.

7. You can type a description of the document or directory in the Description text box, if you wish.

8. Click OK to return to the Edit QuickList dialog box. The document or directory will be added to the QuickList box (**Figure 52**).

9. Click OK again. The file or directory will appear in the QuickList in the Open dialog box (**Figure 53**).

✔ Tip

■ To delete a QuickList item, right click on the QuickList box, then select Edit QuickList from the QuickMenu. Highlight the item you want to delete in the QuickList box in the Edit QuickList dialog box (**Figure 50**), then click Delete. Click Yes in the Delete dialog box that appears.

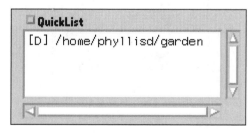

Figure 53. When you click OK and return to the Open dialog box, the entry appears in the QuickList.

CREATE A QUICKLIST

To use the QuickList:

1. Choose Open from the File menu (**Figure 54**). The Open dialog box will appear (**Figure 55**).

2. In the QuickList box, highlight the file you want to open or double-click on the directory you want to move quickly to, then select a file from the File List box.

3. Click Open to open the file.

✔ Tip

- The QuickList is also available in the SaveAs dialog box. You can use the QuickList to rapidly move to a directory where you would want to save a file, or to select a document file that you frequently overwrite.

To close a document:

Choose Close from the File menu in the document window (**Figure 56**) or press Ctrl+F4 on the keyboard, or click the Close button at the upper right-hand corner of the document window (**Figure 57**).

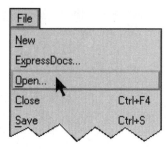

Figure 54. Choose Open from the File menu.

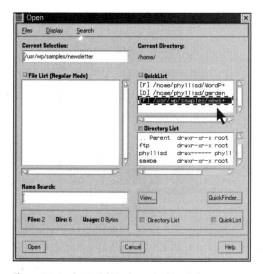

Figure 55. In the QuickList box, double-click on a directory to move to that location or highlight the file you want to open, then click Open.

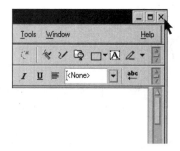

Figure 57. Click the Close button at the upper right-hand corner of the document window.

Figure 56. Choose Close from the File menu.

Figure 58. Choose Preferences in the program window.

Figure 59. Click the Environment button.

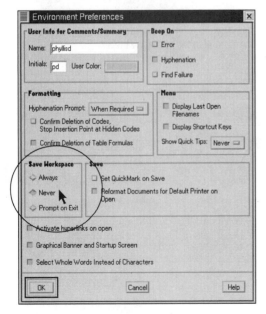

Figure 60. In the Environment Preferences dialog box, click the radio button next to the item you want to select in the Save Workspace area.

Saving your Workspace

You can set the workspace options to always open a new document, ask you whether you want to save the workspace, or automatically save the workspace without asking you.

To save your workspace:

1. With a document open, choose Preferences in the program window (**Figure 58**). The Preferences dialog box will open (**Figure 59**).

2. Click the Environment button. The Environment Preferences dialog box will open (**Figure 60**).

3. In the Save Workspace area, select the radio button for the item you would like to choose:

   ◆ **Always** automatically saves your workspace without asking;

   ◆ **Never** always opens a new document window (the default); or

   ◆ **Prompt on Exit** asks whether you want to save the workspace.

4. Click OK to close the Environment Preferences dialog box.

5. Click Close to close the Preferences dialog box.

✔ Tip

■ Saving your workspace is very handy if you want to work on the same documents the next time you launch WordPerfect.

Exiting WordPerfect

Shutting down WordPerfect is very easy. There are three ways to do it.

To exit WordPerfect 8 for Linux:

With the document window active, press Ctrl+Shift+F4 on the keyboard.

or

Choose Exit from the Program menu in the program window (**Figure 61**)

or

Click the Close button in the upper right-hand corner of the program window (**Figure 62**).

Figure 61. Choose Exit from the Program menu in the program window.

Figure 62. Click the Close button in the upper right-hand corner of the program window.

Summary

In this chapter you learned how to:

- Put a menu item on the Gnome and K Main Menus
- Launch WordPerfect
- Start a new document
- Start a new document using ExpressDocs
- Create your own ExpressDocs
- Open a document

- Save your work
- Save a copy of a file
- Import and export a file
- Use the QuickList
- Close a document
- Save your workspace
- Exit WordPerfect

Working with Text

4

The power of Word processing programs has forever changed the way people work. Back in the days of the dinosaur, folks used typewriters to create documents. (Yes, I'm a dinosaur, I learned to type on an IBM Selectric!) Unfortunately, when a mistake was made, whiteout or an eraser were necessary tools. Copies of a document had to be photocopied or created using carbon paper. Newsletters with artwork had to be cut and pasted with scissors and glue.

Computers and word processing programs have changed all that. Today, you can create, format, and edit your documents while you work, and save them for the future. Printing multiple copies is a breeze. Adding pictures and tables is easy—with a few clicks of the mouse, the sky's the limit!

This chapter helps you take the first steps toward creating professional documents using WordPerfect. In this chapter, you'll enter, delete, select, and move text, use the *shadow cursor* to move the *insertion point*, undo and redo your actions, and copy, cut, and paste (without scissors or glue, of course!)

Entering Text

Let's get going! Entering text in a WordPerfect document is as easy as typing on your keyboard.

To enter text:

1. Launch WordPerfect and start a new document (**Figure 1**). (Turn to Chapter 3, *Startup*, for details on how to do this.) A vertical bar, the *insertion point*, will be blinking on the page in the document window.

2. Type your text. As you type, corresponding characters will appear on the screen (**Figure 2**).

✔ Tip

- If you see red or blue diagonal lines below any words, this means that there might be a spelling or grammar error. To find out more about Spell-As-You-Go and Grammar-As-You-Go, turn to Chapter 9, *Checking Your Work*.

To start a new paragraph:

When you have finished typing a paragraph, press the Enter key on the keyboard. The insertion point will move down to the next line where you can start typing the next paragraph (**Figure 3**).

✔ Tip

- Starting a new paragraph inserts an invisible hard return code into your document. You can view this code by turning on formatting symbols as described on page 70.

To start a new page:

Position the insertion point where you want the new page to start, then press Ctrl+Enter on the keyboard.

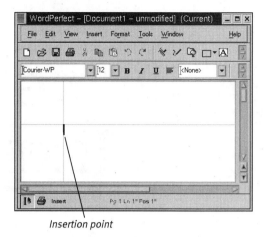

Insertion point

Figure 1. A new document opens, ready for typing.

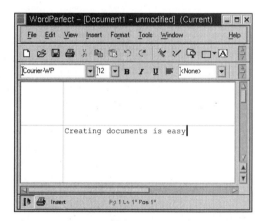

Figure 2. As you type, the characters appear on the page.

Figure 3. When you press Enter, a new paragraph starts.

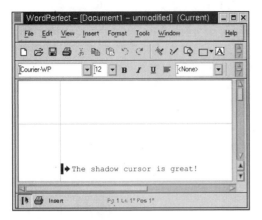

Figure 4. The shadow cursor lets you position text anywhere in a document.

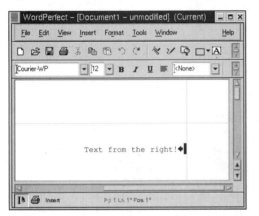

Figure 5. The shadow cursor points in the direction the text will flow.

The Shadow Cursor

You may have already noticed a small blue line and arrow that appear when you move the mouse pointer over text or white space on the page in the document window. This is the *shadow cursor*. The shadow cursor shows you where the insertion point will appear when you click the mouse. You don't need to press the Enter key on the keyboard to insert blank lines between text or pictures. All you need to do is click where you want the text to go, and then start typing.

If you move the shadow cursor around the page in the document window, you will notice that it changes the way it looks depending upon where it is on the page. If you move it to the left margin, the cursor's arrow points to the right, indicating the direction the text will move when you type (**Figure 4**). If you move the cursor to the right margin, the little arrow points to the left, showing which way the text will move (**Figure 5**). And, if you move the cursor to the very center of the page, it will display tiny arrows on both sides of the line, indicating the text will be centered when you type.

You can view or hide the shadow cursor at any time, and also set its color, appearance, and what items it *snaps to*.

A Few Things You Should Know

If you're new to word processing programs, there are a few things you should know:

◆ As you type a document, you don't need to press the Enter key at the end of every line. WordPerfect will automatically take care of moving you down to the next line when you run out of space. This is called *word wrapping*. You'll only need to press Enter when you want to start a new paragraph.

◆ If you make a mistake, you can fix it by deleting the error. You can add or delete text anywhere in the document at any time.

◆ If you want to indent text, use the Tab key, don't press the space bar. You can set tabs using the ruler. This is discussed in Chapter 5, *Formatting Your Text*.

◆ The unused area of a document is referred to as *white space*.

To view or hide the shadow cursor:

Choose Shadow Cursor from the View menu (**Figure 6**).

or

1. Right click on the document window. A QuickMenu will appear (**Figure 7**).

2. Choose Shadow Cursor from the QuickMenu.

To change the way the shadow cursor looks:

1. In the program window, choose Preferences (**Figure 8**). The Preferences dialog box will appear (**Figure 9**).

2. Click Display. The Display Preferences dialog box will open (**Figure 10**).

3. To change the shadow cursor's color:

   A. Click the Color button in the Shadow Cursor area (**Figure 11**). A color palette will appear.

   B. Click the new color you want to use. The palette will close and the new color will display in the Color button.

4. To change the shadow cursor's shape:

   A. Click the Shape button in the Shadow Cursor area (**Figure 12**). A shape selector will appear.

   B. Click the new shape that you want to use. The selector will close and the new shape will display in the Shape button.

5. To set an item that the shadow cursor will snap to, select an radio button from the Snap to list in the Shadow Cursor area (**Figure 13**). These options are:

VIEW THE SHADOW CURSOR; CHANGE ITS LOOK

Figure 6. Choose Shadow Cursor from the View menu.

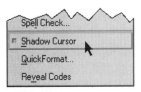

Figure 7. Choose Shadow Cursor from the QuickMenu.

Figure 8. Choose Preferences in the program window.

Figure 9. Click Display in the Preferences dialog box.

Figure 10. Use the Shadow Cursor area to set options.

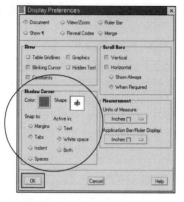

Figure 11. Choose a new color from the color palette.

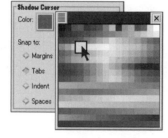

Figure 12. Choose a different shape using the shape selector.

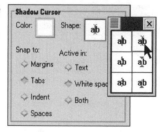

Figure 13. Click the radio button next to the item you want the cursor to snap to.

Figure 14. Click the radio button next to the area where you want the cursor active.

◆ **Margins**—the shadow cursor will snap to the left or right margins or to the center of the page between the margins. If you click in white space, on the page, the insertion point will snap to one of these positions.

◆ **Tabs**—the shadow cursor will snap to the current tab settings. If you click in white space, the insertion point will snap to the closest tab. When you enter your text, it will continue from that position until the end of the line then wrap to the beginning of the next line.

◆ **Indent**—the shadow cursor will snap to the current tab settings. If you click in white space, the insertion point will snap to the closest tab. When you enter text, it will continue from that position until the end of the line, then wrap to the indented position.

◆ **Spaces**—the shadow cursor will snap to the closest space. If you click in white space, that's where the insertion point will appear.

6. To set where you want the shadow cursor active, select an radio button next to one of the items in the Active in list (**Figure 14**). You can set the cursor to appear only in text or white space, or set it to appear in both areas.

7. When you are finished selecting options, click OK to close the Display Preferences dialog box.

8. Click OK to close the Preferences dialog box and return to the document window.

Moving the Insertion Point

You can also move the insertion point through text using the arrow keys on the keyboard. (You can't move the insertion point around in white space with the keyboard, only with the shadow cursor.)

To move the insertion point using the keyboard:

Use the appropriate arrow key to move in the direction you want to go. For instance, if you press the up arrow key, ⬆, the insertion point will move up one line; if you press the right arrow key, ➡, the insertion point will move one character to the right. There are many keystrokes and combinations. Some of them are listed in the sidebar on the next page.

Inserting and Deleting Text

With WordPerfect you can add or delete text from your document at any time.

To insert text:

1. Use the shadow cursor or keyboard strokes to move the insertion point to the place where you want to add text (**Figure 15**).

2. Type the text that you want to add (**Figure 16**).

✔ Tip

- When you add characters to existing text, any text to the right of the insertion point automatically moves to the right to make room for the new characters and word wrapping automatically readjusts the lines of text.

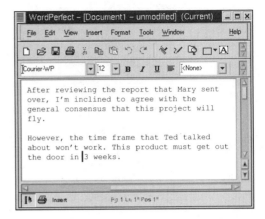

Figure 15. Position the insertion point using keyboard strokes or the shadow cursor where you want to add text to your document.

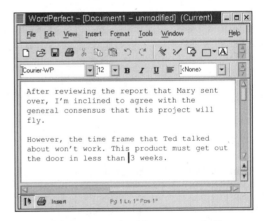

Figure 16. As you type, the old text automatically moves to the right to make room for the new text.

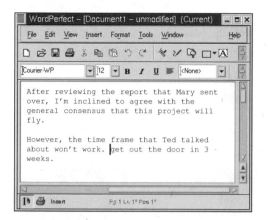

Figure 17. Position the insertion point where you want to delete text. If you press the Backspace key, the text to the right of the insertion point is deleted. If you press the Delete key, the text on the left of the insertion point is deleted.

To delete text:

1. Use the shadow cursor or keyboard strokes to move the insertion point to the place where you want to delete text (**Figure 17**).

2. Press the Backspace key on the keyboard to delete characters to the right of the insertion point.

    or

    Press the Delete key on the keyboard to delete characters to the left of the insertion point.

✔ Tip

■ When text is deleted, any text to the right of the insertion point automatically moves to the left to close the space left by the deleted characters. Word wrapping automatically readjusts the lines of text.

DELETE TEXT; USEFUL KEYSTROKES

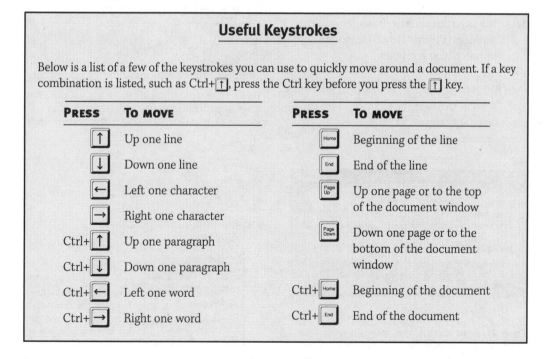

Useful Keystrokes

Below is a list of a few of the keystrokes you can use to quickly move around a document. If a key combination is listed, such as Ctrl+[↑], press the Ctrl key before you press the [↑] key.

PRESS	TO MOVE	PRESS	TO MOVE
[↑]	Up one line	[Home]	Beginning of the line
[↓]	Down one line	[End]	End of the line
[←]	Left one character	[Page Up]	Up one page or to the top of the document window
[→]	Right one character	[Page Down]	Down one page or to the bottom of the document window
Ctrl+[↑]	Up one paragraph		
Ctrl+[↓]	Down one paragraph		
Ctrl+[←]	Left one word	Ctrl+[Home]	Beginning of the document
Ctrl+[→]	Right one word	Ctrl+[End]	End of the document

Inserting Symbols

In addition to the regular characters found on your keyboard, you can also insert special symbols into your documents. These symbols include characters from other languages, math, science, and typography.

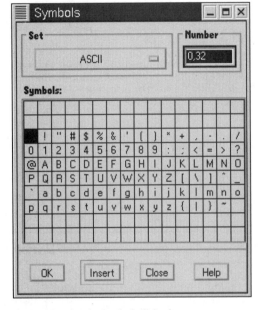

Figure 18. Choose Symbol from the Insert menu.

To insert symbols:

1. Position the insertion point in the document where you would like the symbol to appear.

2. Choose Symbol from the Insert menu (**Figure 18**) or press Ctrl+W on the keyboard. The Symbols dialog box will appear (**Figure 19**).

3. Use the Set drop-down list to select the type of characters you want to select (**Figure 20**).

4. In the Symbols grid, click the character you want to use.

5. Click Insert to add the character into the document (**Figure 21**) and leave the Symbols dialog box open.

   or

   Click OK to insert the character into the document (**Figure 21**) and close the Symbols dialog box.

Figure 19. Using the Symbols dialog box, you can insert special characters from many types of sets, including Typographic Symbols, Hebrew, and Japanese.

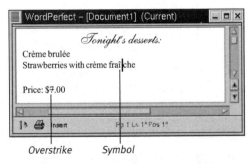

Overstrike   *Symbol*

Figure 21. When you click Insert or OK, the symbol you selected appears next to the insertion point in the text.

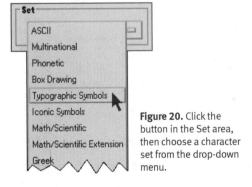

Figure 20. Click the button in the Set area, then choose a character set from the drop-down menu.

Insert Symbols

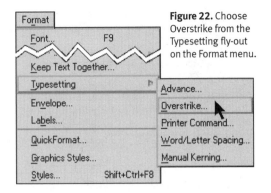

Figure 22. Choose Overstrike from the Typesetting fly-out on the Format menu.

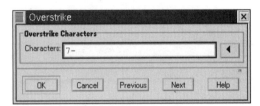

Figure 23. In the Overstrike Characters area, enter the characters you want printed as an overstrike in the text box.

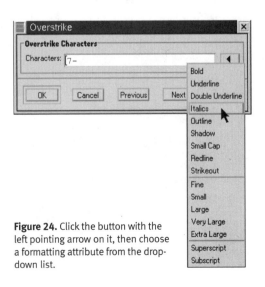

Figure 24. Click the button with the left pointing arrow on it, then choose a formatting attribute from the drop-down list.

Creating Custom Symbols using Overstrike

Using the keyboard, you can create characters not included in the symbols sets accessed on the previous page. If you want to create custom characters, you should know that some printers don't have the capabilities to print them.

To create custom symbols:

1. Position the insertion point in the document where you would like the custom symbol to appear.

2. Choose Overstrike from the Typesetting fly-out on the Format menu (**Figure 22**). The Overstrike dialog box will open (**Figure 23**).

3. In the Characters text box, type the characters you would like printed as an overstrike. Do not add spaces between the characters. Also, character order doesn't matter.

4. To add a formatting attribute to the custom symbol:

   A. Click the button with the left pointing arrow on it, to the right of the Characters text box (**Figure 24**).

   B. Choose a formatting attribute from the drop-down list.

5. Click OK. The characters you entered in the text box will appear printed as an overstrike in your document (**Figure 21**).

✔ Tip

■ To insert a symbol into the Characters text box in the Overstrike dialog box, press Ctrl+W on the keyboard while the Overstrike dialog box is open. The Symbols dialog box will appear and you can select and insert the symbol you want.

CREATE CUSTOM SYMBOLS

Selecting Text

You can select characters, words, paragraphs, even entire documents to move, copy, cut, delete, or format them. There are three ways to select text: by dragging the mouse, clicking the mouse, or positioning the insertion point, then using the Select fly-out on the Edit menu (**Figure 25**). You will know the text has been selected when it is highlighted.

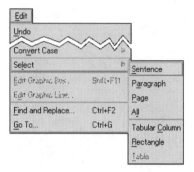

Figure 25. You can use the Select fly-out on the Edit menu to select various parts of a document.

To select a character:

Position the insertion point to the left of the character, hold down the Shift key on the keyboard, then press the right arrow key, →.

or

Position the shadow cursor to the left of the character, press the left mouse button, and drag to select the character.

To select a word:

Position the mouse over the word, and then double-click.

or

1. Position the shadow cursor to the left of the text you want to select.

2. Press the left mouse button and drag until the text is selected (**Figure 26**).

3. Release the mouse button.

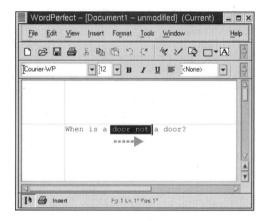

Figure 26. Drag the mouse until the text is selected.

To select a sentence:

Position the insertion point within the sentence, then choose Sentence from the Select fly-out on the Edit menu (**Figure 27**).

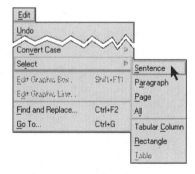

Figure 27. Choose Sentence from the Select fly-out on the Edit menu.

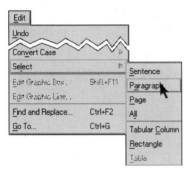

Figure 28. Choose Paragraph from the Select fly-out on the Edit menu.

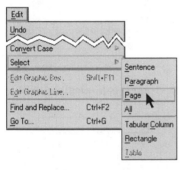

Figure 29. Choose Page from the Select fly-out on the Edit menu.

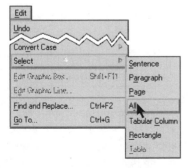

Figure 30. Choose All from the Select fly-out on the Edit menu.

To select a paragraph:

Position the mouse over the paragraph you want to select, and then triple-click.

or

Position the insertion point within the paragraph, then choose Paragraph from the Select fly-out on the Edit menu (**Figure 28**).

To select the contents of a page:

1. Position the insertion point on the page you want to select.

2. Choose Page from the Select menu on the Edit fly-out (**Figure 29**).

To select the contents of a document:

Choose All from the Select fly-out on the Edit menu (**Figure 30**).

Use the QuickMenu to Select

You can also use the QuickMenu to select portions of your text. To do so, position the insertion point within a sentence, paragraph or page. Next, move the mouse pointer over to the left margin, and then right click. The QuickMenu will appear (see below). Choose the desired selection from the QuickMenu.

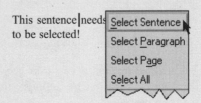

Working with Selected Text

Once you've selected the text that you want to change, you can copy it, cut it out of the document, move it, paste it in the document as many times as you wish, replace it, or delete it.

To copy text:

1. Select the text you want to copy.

2. Choose Copy from the Edit menu (**Figure 31**).

    or

    Press Ctrl+C on the keyboard.

    or

    Click the Copy button on the WordPerfect 8 Toolbar.

    or

    Right click and choose Copy from the QuickMenu that appears (**Figure 32**).

    The selected text is copied to the X Clipboard, ready for pasting.

To cut text:

1. Select the text you want to cut.

2. Choose Cut from the Edit menu (**Figure 33**).

    or

    Press Ctrl+X on the keyboard.

    or

    Click the Cut button on the WordPerfect 8 Toolbar.

    or

    Right click and choose Cut from the QuickMenu that appears (**Figure 34**).

    The selected text disappears from the document and is saved on the clipboard, ready for pasting.

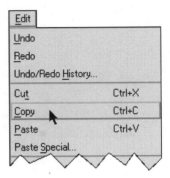

Figure 31. Choose Copy from the Edit menu or press Ctrl+C on the keyboard.

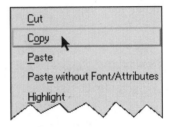

Figure 32. Choose Copy from the QuickMenu.

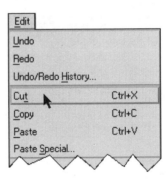

Figure 33. Choose Cut from the Edit menu or press Ctrl+X on the keyboard.

The X Clipboard

The X Clipboard is used by all X Windows programs. (See page 20 for more about X Windows programs.) The X Clipboard is an area of memory where cut or copied text or graphics are held for later use.

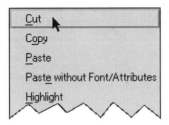

Figure 34. Choose Cut from the QuickMenu.

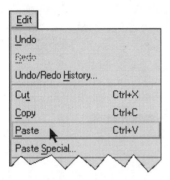

Figure 35. Choose Paste from the Edit menu or press Ctrl+V on the keyboard.

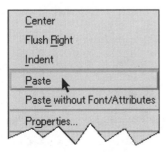

Figure 36. Choose Paste from the QuickMenu.

To paste text:

1. Copy or cut the text you want to paste.

2. Move the insertion point to the position where you want to paste the text.

3. Choose Paste from the Edit menu (**Figure 35**).

   or

   Press Ctrl+V on the keyboard.

   or

   Click the Paste button on the WordPerfect 8 Toolbar.

   or

   Right click and choose Paste from the QuickMenu that appears (**Figure 36**).

   The text appears to the right of the insertion point.

✔ Tips

■ You can paste the copied text as many times as you wish anywhere in your document.

■ The X Clipboard can only hold one thing at a time. So, if you copy or cut something new, the old contents of the clipboard are replaced.

■ The clipboard is a very handy tool. Since you can open up to 100 documents in WordPerfect at one time, you can use the clipboard to copy and paste from one document to another.

To move text using drag-and-drop:

1. Select the text you want to cut and paste.

2. Position the mouse pointer over the selected text.

3. Press the left mouse button and drag until the insertion point appears where you want to paste the text (**Figure 37**). A tiny rectangle appears attached to the mouse pointer.

4. Release the mouse button. The text "hops" from its old position to the new position (**Figure 38**).

✔ Tip

■ Moving text is the same as cutting and pasting text.

To copy and paste text using drag-and-drop:

1. Select the text you want to copy and paste.

2. Position the mouse pointer over the selected text.

3. Hold down the Ctrl key on the keyboard, press the left mouse button, and then drag until the insertion point appears where you want to paste the text (**Figure 39**).

4. Release the mouse button, then the Ctrl key. The text is copied and pasted into the new position (**Figure 40**).

To replace text:

Select the text you want to replace, then start typing. The selected text is deleted and the new text appears in its place.

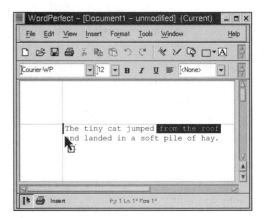

Figure 37. Drag the insertion point to the position where you want to move the text.

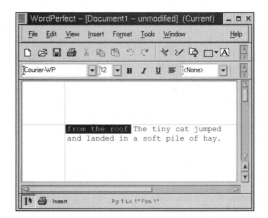

Figure 38. When you release the mouse button, the text appears selected in its new position.

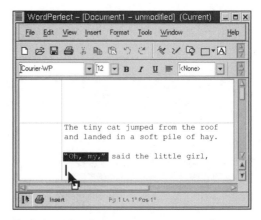

Figure 39. Select the text you want to copy and paste.

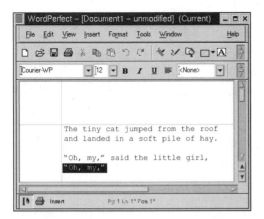

Figure 40. When the mouse button is released, the copied text appears selected, pasted in the new position.

Saving Your You-know-what

Undo is a favorite command of many users. If you delete something by accident, don't panic! You can undo it!

But, if you decide you really did want to delete that text after restoring it with undo, you can use redo to reverse the undo.

WordPerfect 8 for Linux comes with an amazing feature, you can undo or redo more that one action at a time up to 300 actions using the Undo/Redo History dialog box!

To undo an action:

Choose Undo from the Edit menu (**Figure 41**), or click the Undo button on the WordPerfect 8 Toolbar.

To redo an action:

Choose Redo from the Edit menu (**Figure 42**), or click the Redo button on the WordPerfect 8 Toolbar.

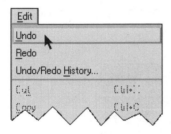

Figure 41. Choose Undo from the Edit menu to reverse an action.

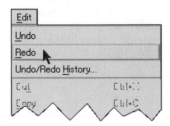

Figure 42. Choose Redo from the Edit menu to reverse an Undo command.

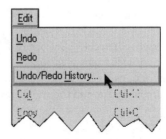

Figure 43. Choose Undo/Redo History to undo and/or redo more than one action at a time.

To undo or redo more than one action at a time:

1. Choose Undo/Redo History from the Edit menu (**Figure 43**). The Undo/Redo History dialog box will open (**Figure 44**). This dialog box displays up to 300 Undo and Redo actions you have performed on the document.

2. To undo several actions at once:

   A. Use the Undo list box to select the actions you want to undo by holding down the Ctrl key, then clicking on the various undo actions (**Figure 45**).

   B. Click the Undo button. The actions you selected will undo.

   or

   A. Use the Redo list box to select the actions you want to redo by holding down the Ctrl key, then clicking on the various redo actions (**Figure 46**).

   B. Click the Redo button. The actions you selected will redo.

3. When you are finished selecting undo and redo actions, click Close to close the dialog box and return to your document.

✔ Tip

■ You can save undo and redo actions with a document. To do so, click the Options button in the Undo/Redo History dialog box. The Undo/Redo Options dialog box will open (**Figure 47**). Use the Number of Undo/Redo Items text box to set how many actions will be saved with the document, make sure the check box next to Save Undo/Redo Items With Document is selected, and then click OK.

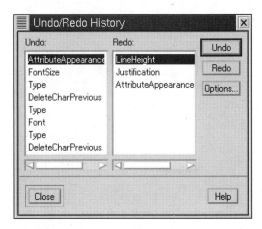

Figure 44. The Undo/Redo History dialog box lets you undo or redo up to 300 actions.

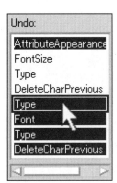

Figure 45. Hold down the Ctrl key while you click to select multiple undo actions.

Figure 46. Hold down the Ctrl key while you click to select multiple redo actions.

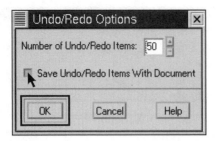

Figure 47. The Undo/Redo Options dialog box lets you save up to 300 undo and redo actions with a document.

Figure 48. Choose Find and Replace from the Edit menu.

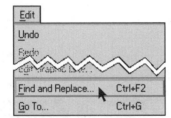

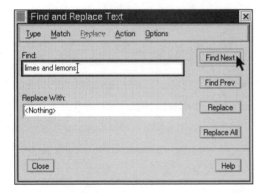

Figure 49. Type the word or phrase you want to find in the text box, then click Find Next.

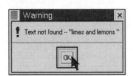

Figure 50. If the word or phrase is not found a Warning dialog box opens. "Warning" sounds a bit drastic, but it's nothing to worry about. Just click OK to close the dialog box.

Using Find and Replace

WordPerfect makes it easy to find and/or replace any kind of word or phrase in a document.

To find a word or phrase:

1. Position the insertion point where you would like the search to begin.

2. Choose Find and Replace from the Edit menu (**Figure 48**) or press Ctrl+F2 on the keyboard. The Find and Replace Text dialog box will appear (**Figure 49**).

3. Type the word or phrase you want to locate in the Find text box.

4. Click Find Next. WordPerfect will search the document for the next occurrence of the word or phrase.

5. Click Find Next again to find the next occurrence of the word or phrase.

6. Continue clicking Find Next until you have finished your search.

7. Click Close to close the dialog box.

✔ Tips

■   If you select text before you open the Find and Replace Text dialog box, the selected text will appear in the Find text box when the dialog box opens.

■   You can work on the document while the Find and Replace Text dialog box is open. This can be handy if you want to move through a document, checking various items.

■   If you try to find text that is not present in the document, a Warning dialog box will open, telling you the text is not found (**Figure 50**). Click OK to close this dialog box.

To replace a word or phrase:

1. Position the insertion point where you would like the search to begin.

2. Choose Find and Replace from the Edit menu (**Figure 48**) or press Ctrl+F2 on the keyboard. The Find and Replace Text dialog box will appear (**Figure 51**).

3. Type the word or phrase you want to locate in the Find text box.

4. Type the replacement text in the Replace With text box.

5. Click Replace. WordPerfect will search through the document for the next occurrence of the word or phrase and replace it with the new text.

6. Click Replace again to move to the next occurrence and replace the text.

7. Continue clicking Replace until you have finished searching the document. When WordPerfect has finished searching a Replace dialog box will appear, telling you how many occurrences have been replaced (**Figure 52**).

8. Click OK to close the Replace dialog box.

9. Click Close to close the Find and Replace Text dialog box and return to the document window.

✔ Tips

- If you want to delete the text you are searching for and not replace it with new text, type <Nothing> in the Replace With text box.

- If you want to replace all occurrences of a word or phrase in a document, click Replace All in the Find and Replace Text dialog box.

- If you try to find text that is not present in the document, a Warning dialog box will open, telling you the text is not found (**Figure 53**). Click OK to close this dialog box.

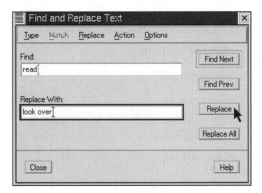

Figure 51. Type the text you want to find and replace in the text boxes, then click Replace to change the next occurrence or Replace All to change all occurrences.

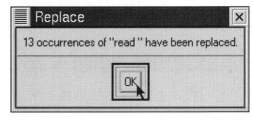

Figure 52. When the entire document has been searched, a Replace dialog box opens to tell you how many times the word or phrase was replaced.

Figure 53. If the word or phrase is not found a Warning dialog box opens. "Warning" sounds a bit drastic, but it's nothing to worry about. Just click OK to close the dialog box.

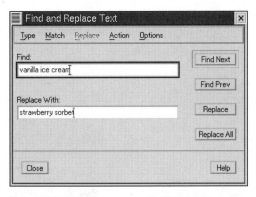

Figure 54. Type the text you want to find and/or replace in the text boxes, then use the Match and Options menus to set how the search is performed.

Figure 55. The Match menu sets the search to find whole words, specific capitalization, or specific font attributes.

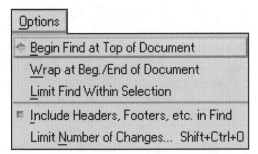

Figure 56. The Options menu sets where and what is searched. The search can begin at the top of a document, wrap to the beginning of a document if the search starts in the middle, or search within selected text. You can also set it to search only the body of the document and limit how many times a word or phrase is replaced.

Setting Find and Replace Options

You can how WordPerfect performs a search using the Match and Options menus in the Find and Replace Text dialog box.

To set find and replace options:

1. Choose Find and Replace from the Edit menu (**Figure 48**) or press Ctrl+F2 on the keyboard. The Find and Replace Text dialog box will appear (**Figure 54**).

2. Enter the text you want to find and/or replace in the appropriate text boxes.

3. To set WordPerfect to search for specific matches, choose the Match menu item. The Match menu will open (**Figure 55**). You can set WordPerfect to match:

   ◆ **Whole Word** finds whole words only.

   ◆ **Case Sensitive** exactly matches the word or phrase.

   ◆ **Font** finds the word or phrase in a specific formatting, including the font type, size, or attribute, such as bold, italics, or underline.

4. To set WordPerfect to search for specific options, choose the Options menu item. The Options menu will open (**Figure 56**). You can set the search to:

   ◆ **Begin Find at Top of Document**

   ◆ **Wrap at Beg./End of Document**— the search moves from the insertion point to the end of the document, then continues from the beginning of the document.

   ◆ **Limit Find Within Selection**— the search will only look through selected text.

(continued)

◆ **Include Headers, Footers, etc. in Find**—the search will check *all* text in a document, including text in headers, etc. If this option is not selected, the search will only occur within the body of the document.

◆ **Limit Number of Changes**—the search will limit the number of replacements when Replace All is clicked in the Find and Replace Text dialog box.

5. When you are finished selecting options, perform the search using the Find and Replace Text dialog box.

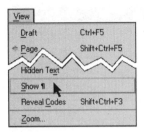

Figure 57. Choose Show ¶ from the View menu.

The Hidden World of Formatting Symbols and Codes

Everything you type—including, for instance, the spaces, tabs, and paragraph breaks—is entered into a WordPerfect document. Normally, you can't see the symbols and codes that represent these keystrokes because they're hidden, but you can display them, making it easy for you to see everything in your document.

Formatting symbols are displayed in the body of a document, right along with the text. Formatting codes are displayed at the bottom of the document window. A movable *divider line* splits the window into two.

To display formatting symbols:

Choose Show ¶ from the View menu (**Figure 57**). The hidden symbols will appear in your document (**Figure 58**).

✔ Tip

■ To hide the symbols, just choose Show ¶ from the View menu again.

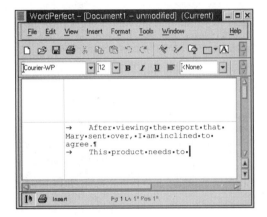

Figure 58. The hidden symbols show you every keystroke in your document.

Document is selected

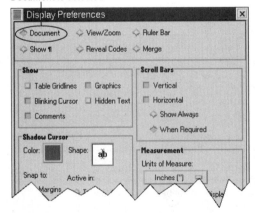

Figure 59. The Display Preferences dialog box opens with the Document radio button selected at the top of the dialog box.

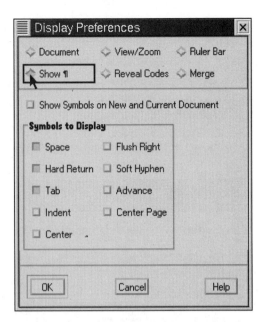

Figure 60. When the Show ¶ radio button is selected, the lower part of the Display Preferences dialog box changes to show symbols options.

To specify which symbols display:

1. In the program window, choose Preferences (**Figure 8**). The Preferences dialog box will open (**Figure 9**).

2. Click Display. The Display Preferences dialog box will appear (**Figure 59**), showing document options (notice that the Document radio button at the top of the dialog box is selected).

3. Click the radio button next to Show ¶ near the top of the dialog box. The dialog box will change to display symbols options (**Figure 60**).

4. In the Symbols to Display area, select the options you want to display by clicking the box next to the feature. In **Figure 60** Space, Hard Return, and Tab have been selected.

5. Click OK to close the dialog box and return to the Preferences dialog box.

6. Click Close to close the Preferences dialog box and return to the document window. Your document will display the symbols you selected (**Figure 61**).

✔ Tip

■ If you don't see the symbols displayed in your document, you need to turn them on. Choose Show ¶ from the View menu (**Figure 57**).

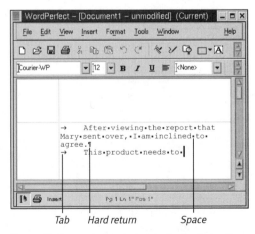

Tab   Hard return   Space

Figure 61. The symbols selected to display (using the Display Preferences dialog box) appear in the document.

To view formatting codes:

Choose Reveal Codes from the View menu (**Figure 62**), or click the right mouse button and choose Reveal Codes from the Quick-Menu that appears (**Figure 63**), or press Shift+Ctrl+F3 on the keyboard. A divider line will appear, splitting the window into two.

To hide formatting codes:

Choose Reveal Codes from the View menu (**Figure 62**).

or

1. Right click on the lower part of the document window where the formatting codes are displayed. A QuickMenu will open (**Figure 64**).

2. Choose Hide Reveal Codes from the Quick-Menu. The divider line will disappear.

✔ Tip

■ The difference between the hidden symbols and codes is that the symbols indicate what you typed and appear up in the text of the document, whereas the codes show everything you typed plus special features, such as text and page formatting down at the bottom of the document window.

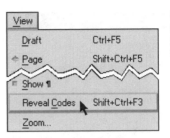

Figure 62. Choose Reveal Codes from the View menu.

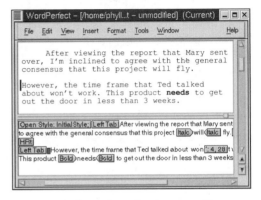

Figure 63. The formatting codes show everything you've typed, plus any special commands.

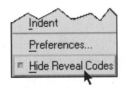

Figure 64. Choose Hide Reveal Codes from the QuickMenu.

Summary

In this chapter you learned how to:

- Enter text
- Start a new paragraph
- Use the shadow cursor
- Move the insertion point
- Cut, copy, and paste text

- Insert, replace and delete text
- Undo and redo actions
- Find and replace text
- Show and hide formatting symbols and codes

FORMATTING YOUR TEXT

5

In the last chapter you discovered how to enter and manipulate text. The next step on the road to WordPerfect proficiency is learning how to format text. WordPerfect lets you control exactly how characters look, by letting you change the size and shape of text, as well as setting how paragraphs look as a whole, by letting you set *justification*, line spacing, and indentation.

This chapter is split into two parts. The first deals with *character formatting* and the second with *paragraph formatting*.

Character formatting changes the way characters look. These changes can include the *font* or typeface the text is set in, and items that emphasize text such as **bold**, *italics*, and <u>underlines</u>.

Paragraph formatting sets how an entire paragraph looks. Some things you can do to change the way a paragraph appears are setting justification and adding indents.

Remember the golden rule of layout and design, though, when changing the way things look: *less is more*. There are so many options that you will discover in this chapter and Chapter 7, *Fun with Text*, that you may be tempted to excess. Try to <u>limit</u> the *amount* of FORMATTING you use, **TOO** much may be rather DISTRACTING and **make a document hard to read**.

Character Formatting

Font formatting comes in all shapes and sizes (literally!). You can change fonts, add emphasis, make text bigger or smaller, and change text position, moving it up for superscript or down for subscript.

When formatting text, you can select the text you want to format or format as you type by turning a format command on, typing the text, then turning the format command off.

To make text bold:

1. Select the text you want to format.

2. Click the Bold button on the Property Bar or press Ctrl+B on the keyboard.

or

A. Choose Font from the Format menu (**Figure 1**) or press F9 on the keyboard. The Font dialog box will open (**Figure 2**).

B. In the Appearance area, click the check box next to Bold (**Figure 3**).

C. Click OK to close the dialog box.

The text will be bold (**Figure 4**).

or

1. As you type, click the Bold button on the Property Bar or press Ctrl+B on the keyboard.

2. Type the bold text.

3. Turn off the bold formatting by clicking the Bold button on the Property Bar or pressing Ctrl+B on the keyboard again.

The text will be bold (**Figure 4**).

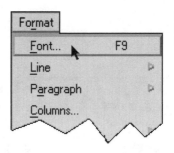

Figure 1. Choose Font from the Format menu.

Figure 2. The Font dialog box is used to change fonts, font sizes, and appearance.

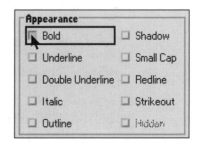

Figure 3. Click the check box next to Bold, then click OK.

Figure 4. The text you selected or type is bold.

Figure 5. Click the check box next to Italic, then click OK.

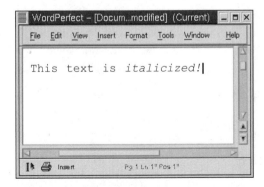

Figure 6. The text you selected or type is italicized.

To add italics:

1. Select the text you want to format.

2. Click the Italic button on the Property Bar or press Ctrl+I on the keyboard.

   or

   A. Choose Font from the Format menu (**Figure 1**) or press F9 on the keyboard. The Font dialog box will open (**Figure 2**).

   B. In the Appearance area, click the check box next to Italic (**Figure 5**).

   C. Click OK to close the dialog box.

   The text will be italicized (**Figure 6**).

or

1. As you type, click the Italic button on the Property Bar or press Ctrl+I on the keyboard.

2. Type the italic text.

3. Turn off the italic formatting by clicking the Italic button on the Property Bar or pressing Ctrl+I on the keyboard again.

   The text will be italicized (**Figure 6**).

✔ Tip

■ To remove italic or bold formatting, select the text that is italicized or bold, then click the Italic or Bold button on the Property Bar.

ADD ITALICS

ADD UNDERLINES

To underline text:

1. Select the text you want to format.

2. Click the Underline button on the Property Bar or press Ctrl+U on the keyboard.

   or

   A. Choose Font from the Format menu (**Figure 1**) or press F9 on the keyboard. The Font dialog box will open (**Figure 2**).

   B. In the Appearance area, click the check box next to Underline (**Figure 7**).

   C. Click OK to close the dialog box.

   The text will be underlined (**Figure 8**).

or

1. As you type, click the Underline button on the Property Bar or press Ctrl+U on the keyboard.

2. Type the underlined text.

3. Turn off the underline formatting by clicking the Underline button on the Property Bar or pressing Ctrl+U on the keyboard again.

   The text will be underlined (**Figure 8**).

✔ Tip

■ To remove underlining, select the text that is underlined, then click the Underline button on the Property Bar.

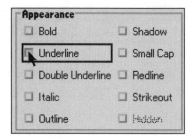

Figure 7. Click the check box next to Underline, then click OK.

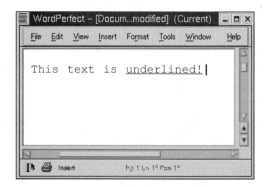

Figure 8. The text you selected or type is underlined.

A Quick Way to Add the Date

With WordPerfect it's easy to add the date even if you can't remember what day it is! This feature can be handy when writing memos, faxes, and letters.

To insert the date:

1. Position the insertion point where you want the date to appear.

2. Press Ctrl+D on the keyboard.

Tip

■ If you want the date to appear right justified on a line by itself, press Shift+Ctrl+F7 on the keyboard.

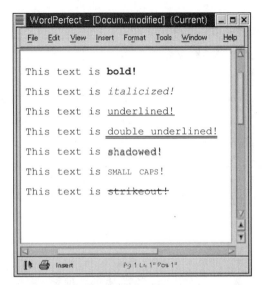

This text is **bold!**

This text is *italicized!*

This text is underlined!

This text is double underlined!

This text is shadowed!

This text is SMALL CAPS!

This text is strikeout!

Figure 9. There are many ways to emphasize text. This figure shows just a few of the options available in WordPerfect 8.

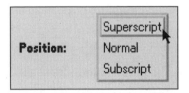

Figure 10. Choose Superscript or Subscript from the Position drop-down list.

Figure 11. The text you selected or type appears as superscript or subscript.

To add other types of text formatting:

1. Select the text you want to format.

2. Choose Font from the Format menu (**Figure 1**) or press F9 on the keyboard. The Font dialog box will appear (**Figure 2**).

3. In the Appearance area, select the type of formatting you want to use (**Figure 7**). **Figure 9** displays some of the formatting choices you can select.

4. Click OK to close the dialog box. The text you selected will redraw with the formatting you selected.

To make text superscript or subscript:

1. Select the text you want to change.

2. Choose Font form the Format menu (**Figure 1**) or press F9 on the keyboard. The Font dialog box will appear (**Figure 2**).

3. Use the Position drop-down list to select Superscript or Subscript (**Figure 10**).

4. Click OK to close the dialog box. The text you selected will redraw as superscript or subscript (**Figure 11**).

ADD OTHER FORMATTING; SUPER- AND SUBSCRIPTS

Center and Flush Right

WordPerfect also lets you quickly center a single line of text, or align it to the right margin with a command called *flush right*.

To center a line of text:

1. Position the insertion point where you want to center the line of text.

2. Choose Center from the Line fly-out on the Format menu (**Figure 12**) or press Shift+F7 on the keyboard.

3. Type the centered line of text, then press Enter on the keyboard (**Figure 13**).

To move text flush right:

1. Position the insertion point where you want to add the flush right text.

2. Choose Flush Right from the Line fly-out on the Format menu or press Shift+Ctrl+F7 on the keyboard.

3. Type the line of flush right text, then press Enter on the keyboard (**Figure 13**).

To move text flush right with dot leaders:

1. Position the insertion point where you want to add the flush right text.

2. Choose Flush Right with Dot Leaders from the Line fly-out on the Format menu (**Figure 14**). A horizontal line of dots (the dot leader) will appear in the document window next to the insertion point.

3. Type the line of flush right text next to the dot leader, then press Enter on the keyboard (**Figure 13**).

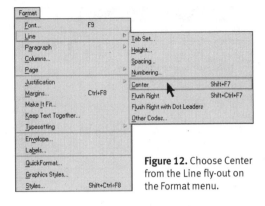

Figure 12. Choose Center from the Line fly-out on the Format menu.

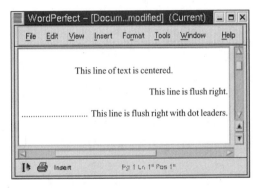

Figure 13. The three lines of text shown here are centered, flush right and flush right with dot leaders.

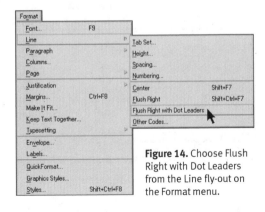

Figure 14. Choose Flush Right with Dot Leaders from the Line fly-out on the Format menu.

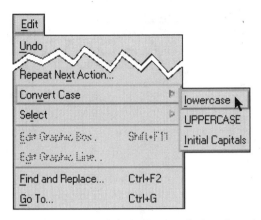

Figure 15. To change the capitalization of selected text, choose one of the options—lowercase, UPPERCASE, or Initial Capitals—on the Convert Case fly-out on the Edit menu.

Capitalization and Your Text

hAVE yOU eVER pRESSED THE cAPS lOCK kEY BY mISTAKE? I have! WordPerfect makes it very easy to correct such a situation. There's no need to retype the text.

To change text capitalization:

1. Select the text you want to change.

2. Choose Convert Case from the Edit menu to open the fly-out (**Figure 15**).

3. Choose the capitalization you would like from the fly-out, lowercase, uppercase, or initial capitals, where the first letter of each word is capitalized. The selected text will change to the capitalization you selected.

A WordPerfect Font Primer

Fonts come in several types and work in different ways in WordPerfect:

◆ *Printer fonts* are built-in to your printer. Every printer has the capability to print at least one font.

◆ *Type 1 fonts*, also called *soft fonts*, are sold like software on disks or are downloadable from the Web. Over 130 Type 1 fonts ship on the WordPerfect 8 Personal Edition CD-ROM.

◆ *Font cartridges* let you add printer fonts by inserting a font cartridge directly into a printer.

◆ *Print wheels* are used with daisy wheel printers. You can purchase print wheels to add to your font collection, changing them as you need to change fonts while printing. Type 1 fonts do not work with daisy wheel printers.

Fonts can be either *scalable* or *non-scalable*. Scalable fonts can be printed in almost any point size. Type 1 fonts are scalable. Non-scalable fonts use only a fixed set of point sizes. Printer fonts and cartridge fonts are non-scalable.

You can tell whether a font is a printer or Type 1 font by checking the little icon that appears next to a font name in the Font Face list box in the Font dialog box (**Figure 2**). A P or printer icon will be displayed next to a printer font, and a T or T_1 will be displayed next to a Type 1 font.

To install the Type 1 fonts that come with the Personal Edition, you will have to launch WordPerfect as an administrator. For detailed instructions on installing these Type 1 fonts, turn to page 84.

Choosing a New Font and Font Size

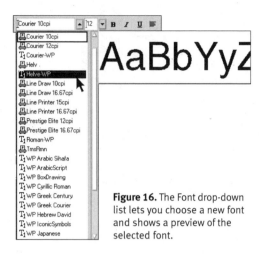

There are several ways you can add or change fonts and font sizes in a document. You can select a new font and/or font size, then type text, select text that you want to change to another font and/or size, or insert a *font code* in existing text, changing the typeface and/or size from that spot on until the end of the document (or until another font code is encountered).

Font sizes are set in *points*, an old system that predates computers and even typewriters. Just to give you an idea of relative sizes, 72 point type is 1" high (2.5 cm) and 18 point type is ¼" high (6 mm).

Figure 16. The Font drop-down list lets you choose a new font and shows a preview of the selected font.

To change fonts:

1. Select the text you want to change.

    or

    Position the insertion point where you want to change the font.

2. Use the Font drop-down list on the Property Bar to select a new font (**Figure 16**).

    or

    A. Choose Font from the Format menu (**Figure 1**) or press F9 on the keyboard. The Font dialog box will open (**Figure 2**).

    B. Use the Font Face list box to select a new font (**Figure 17**). You can see the font you've selected in the preview pane near the bottom left of the dialog box.

    C. Click OK.

Preview pane

Figure 17. Use the Font Face list box to select a new font. The font you choose is displayed in the preview pane.

CHANGE FONTS

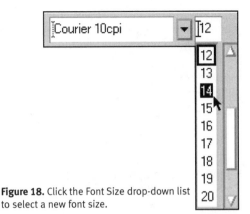

Figure 18. Click the Font Size drop-down list to select a new font size.

Figure 19. The Font Size list box lets you select a new font size.

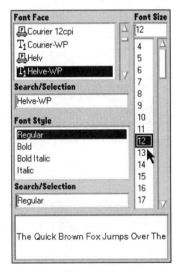

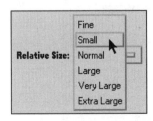

Figure 20. Choose a Relative Size from the drop-down list, then click OK.

To change font size:

1. Select the text you want to change or position the insertion point where you want to change the font.

2. Use the Font Size drop-down list on the Property Bar to select a new font size (**Figure 18**).

   or

   A. Choose Font from the Format menu (**Figure 1**) or press F9 on the keyboard. The Font dialog box will open (**Figure 2**).

   B. Use the Font Size list box to select a new font size (**Figure 19**). You can see the size you've selected in the preview pane near the bottom left of the dialog box.

   C. Click OK to close the dialog box.

Setting Relative Font Sizes

Instead of setting absolute font sizes in points, you can also change font size by setting sizes relatively smaller or larger than the currently selected font size. For instance, a setting of Extra Large is 200% bigger than the current font size and a setting of Fine is 60% smaller than the current font size.

To set a relative font size:

1. Select the text you want to make smaller or bigger or position the insertion point where you want to change the font.

2. Choose Font from the Format menu (**Figure 1**) or press F9 on the keyboard. The Font dialog box will open (**Figure 2**).

3. Use the Relative Size drop-down list to select a new size (**Figure 20**).

4. Click OK to close the dialog box.

Setting a New Default Font

Every document you create has a *document default font*. This is the font that WordPerfect uses for every document, unless you select another font. WordPerfect uses this font for the text in the body of the document as well as the text found in *headers* and *footers*. (For details on headers and footers, turn to Chapter 8, *Page and Document Setup*.)

To set a new default font for the current document:

1. With a document open, choose Font from the Format menu (**Figure 21**) or press F9 on the keyboard. The Font dialog box will open (**Figure 22**).

2. Click Initial Font. The Document Default Font dialog box will open (**Figure 23**).

3. Use the Font Face list box to select a font.

4. Use the Font Size list box to select a size.

5. When you have finished selecting the new default font, click OK to return to the Font dialog box.

6. Click OK to return to the document.

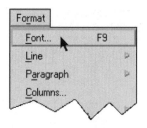

Figure 21. Choose Font from the Format menu.

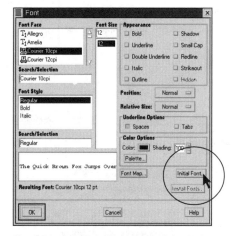

Figure 22. In the Font dialog box, click Initial Font.

Figure 23. The Document Default Font dialog box looks just like the left side of the Font dialog box. With this dialog box you can set the default font for the current document.

Figure 24. Use the Default Font dialog box to select a new font, font size, and Font Style as the default for all new documents.

To set a new default font for all new documents:

1. Choose Font from the Format menu (**Figure 21**) or press F9 on the keyboard. The Font dialog box will open (**Figure 22**).

2. Click Initial Font. The Document Default Font dialog box will open (**Figure 24**).

3. Use the Font Face list box to select a font.

4. Use the Font Size list box to select a size.

5. Make sure the box next to Set as Printer Initial Font is selected (**Figure 25**).

6. When you have finished selecting the new default font, click OK to return to the Font dialog box.

7. Click OK to return to the document. The next time you start a new document, the font you selected will be the default font.

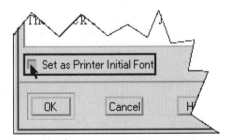

Figure 25. Make sure the box next to Set as Printer Initial Font is selected, then click OK.

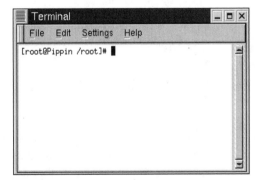

Figure 26. Open a terminal window, then move to the directory where WordPerfect is installed.

Where are All the Fonts?

The WordPerfect Personal Edition CD-ROM ships with 130 different fonts that you can use to create professional documents. In order to install any of the fonts, you need to start WordPerfect as an administrator (this is different than logging on to Linux as root). If you don't have the permissions to do this, you'll need to talk to your system administrator.

To install fonts:

1. Log on as root or su to root.

2. Insert the WordPerfect CD-ROM in your computer's CD-ROM drive.

3. Mount the CD-ROM drive (for directions on how to do this turn to page 21).

4. To launch WordPerfect as an administrator, open a terminal window (**Figure 26**). (Turn to page 22 for details on how to do this.

5. Move to the directory where WordPerfect is installed. In **Figure 27** the directory is /usr/wp.

6. Change to the wpbin directory.

7. Type ./xwp -adm (**Figure 27**), then press Enter on the keyboard. WordPerfect will launch.

8. Choose Font from the Format menu (**Figure 21**) or press F9 on the keyboard. The Font dialog box will open (**Figure 22**).

9. Click the Install Fonts button (**Figure 28**) (when you run WordPerfect normally, this button is not available and is grayed out). The Select Font Type dialog box will appear (**Figure 29**).

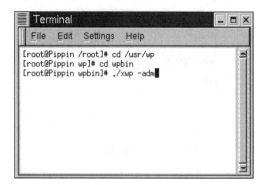

Figure 27. Change to the wpbin directory, then type ./xwp -adm to launch WordPerfect as an administrator.

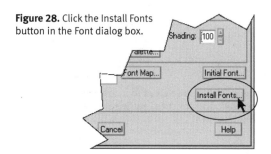

Figure 28. Click the Install Fonts button in the Font dialog box.

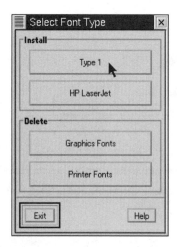

Figure 29. The Select Font Type dialog box is used to install new fonts.

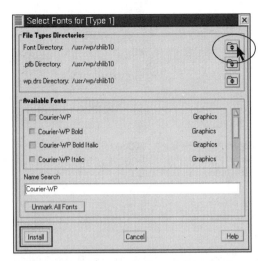

Figure 30. The Select Fonts for [Type 1] dialog box is used to tell WordPerfect where to find the new fonts, where to save them, and which fonts to install.

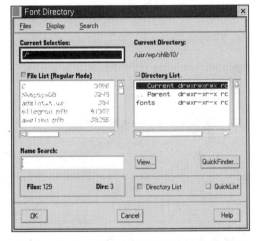

Figure 31. The Font Directory dialog box is used to tell WordPerfect where the fonts that will be installed are located.

Figure 32. Move through your computer's directories until you come to the fonts directory on the Word-Perfect CD-ROM. In this figure, the directory is /mnt/cdrom/fonts/.

10. In the Install area, click the Type 1 button. The Select Fonts for [Type 1] dialog box will open (**Figure 30**).

11. Click the list button to the right of Font Directory. The Font Directory dialog box will open (**Figure 31**). The current directory will probably read something such as /usr/wp/shlib10/. The shlib10 directory is the default WordPerfect font directory.

12. Use the Directory List box to move to the Font directory on the WordPerfect CD-ROM (**Figure 32**). In **Figure 32**, this directory is /mnt/cdrom/fonts/.

13. Click OK to close the Font Directory dialog box and return to the Select Fonts for [Type 1] dialog box. The directory you selected will appear to the right of Font Directory at the top of the dialog box in the File Types Directories area (**Figure 33**).

14. Click the list button to the right of the .pfb Directory. The Font Directory dialog box will open (**Figure 31**).

(continued)

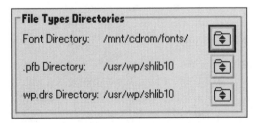

Figure 33. In the File Types Directories area of the Select Fonts for [Type 1] dialog box, the directory you selected appears to the right of Font Directory.

15. Use the Directory List box to move to the Font directory on the WordPerfect CD-ROM (**Figure 32**). In **Figure 32**, this directory is /mnt/cdrom/fonts/.

16. Click OK to close the Font Directory dialog box and return to the Select Fonts for [Type 1] dialog box. The directory you selected will appear to the right of .pfb Directory at the top of the dialog box in the File Types Directories area (**Figure 34**). The fonts on the CD-ROM will appear, selected in the Available Fonts area (**Figure 35**).

17. If you want to unselect all the fonts, click the Unmark All Fonts button. (This button toggles—once you have unmarked all fonts, the button will read "Mark All Fonts.")

18. Scroll down the Available Fonts list box, clicking the check box next to each font you want to install. (The number of fonts you can install is limited by the amount of space you have on your computer.)

19. When you have finished selecting fonts, click OK. A Location of Font Files dialog box will open (**Figure 36**), telling you that the directory where the computer has found the fonts on the CD-ROM is different than the directory where WordPerfect fonts are stored on your computer (of course it is!). The dialog box also asks if you want to copy the fonts to the directory where the WordPerfect fonts are stored on your computer (you do).

20. Click Yes. The fonts will be installed and a WordPerfect Font Install dialog box will appear when the installation is complete (**Figure 37**).

Figure 34. In the File Types Directories area of the Select Fonts for [Type 1] dialog box, the directory you selected appears to the right of .pfb Directory.

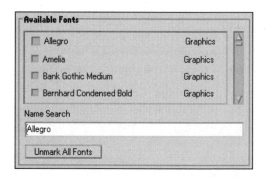

Figure 35. The fonts on the CD-ROM appear selected in the Available Fonts list box.

Figure 36. Click Yes to save the new fonts in your default WordPerfect font directory.

Figure 37. When WordPerfect has finished installing the new fonts, it will tell you so. Click Exit WPFI to finish the font installation or click Continue to install more fonts.

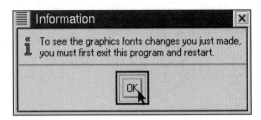

Figure 38. In order to see the new fonts you just installed, you'll need to restart WordPerfect.

Figure 39a. The fonts you installed appear in the Font Face list box.

21. When you are finished installing fonts, click Exit WPFI. (If you want to install more fonts, click Continue.) An Information dialog box will appear (**Figure 38**), telling you that you must restart WordPerfect in order to see the fonts that you just installed in the Fonts dialog box.

22. Click OK to return to the Font dialog box.

23. Click OK to close the Font dialog box.

24. Exit the WordPerfect program by pressing Ctrl+Shift+F4 on the keyboard, or by clicking the Close button on the program window.

25. Launch WordPerfect again (you don't need to run WordPerfect as an administrator this time, you can just launch WordPerfect the way you usually do).

26. Choose Font from the Format menu (**Figure 21**). The Font dialog box will open (**Figure 22**).

27. The fonts you installed will appear in the Font Face list box in the Font dialog box and the Font drop-down list on the Property Bar (**Figures 39a–b**). You can now use the fonts in your documents.

28. Make sure you unmount the CD-ROM (for details on how to do this, turn to page 28) and log off as root.

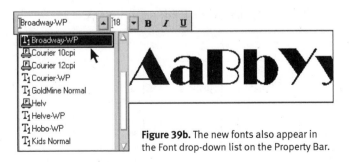

Figure 39b. The new fonts also appear in the Font drop-down list on the Property Bar.

Paragraph Formatting

Paragraph formatting (as the words imply) is applied to entire paragraphs of text. WordPerfect lets you change virtually every paragraph attribute you can think of, from justification, tabs, and indents to line and interparagraph spacing.

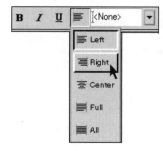

Figure 40. Choose a justification from the drop-down list on the Property Bar.

To set paragraph justification:

1. Position the insertion point where you want the justification to begin. (This will effect the paragraph the insertion point is in and any subsequent paragraphs.)

   or

   Select the paragraph(s) you want to justify.

2. Click the Justification button on the Property Bar to choose a justification from the drop-down list (**Figure 40**).

   or

   Choose a justification type from the Justification fly-out found on the Format menu (**Figure 41**).

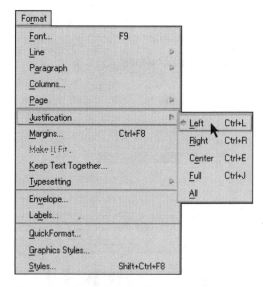

Figure 41. Choose a justification type from the Justification fly-out on the Format menu.

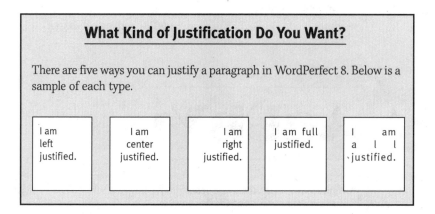

What Kind of Justification Do You Want?

There are five ways you can justify a paragraph in WordPerfect 8. Below is a sample of each type.

I am left justified.	I am center justified.	I am right justified.	I am full justified.	I am a l l justified.

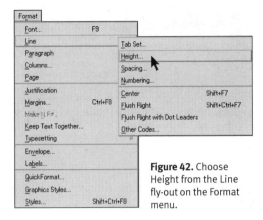

Figure 42. Choose Height from the Line fly-out on the Format menu.

Figure 43. Click the radio button next to Fixed, then enter an exact measurement in the text box.

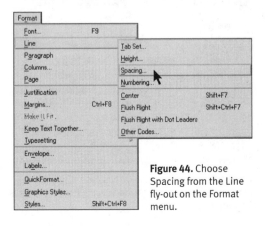

Figure 44. Choose Spacing from the Line fly-out on the Format menu.

Line Spacing

With WordPerfect, you can set the amount of space between lines in two ways: absolutely, using an exact measurement (this is known as *leading*), or automatically, where WordPerfect determines the line spacing by multiplying the line height by the line spacing value you set.

To set an exact line height:

1. Position the insertion point where you want the line height change to begin or select the paragraph(s) you want to change.

2. Choose Height from the Line fly-out on the Format menu (**Figure 42**). The Line Height dialog box will appear (**Figure 43**).

3. Click the radio button next to Fixed.

4. Enter an exact measurement in the Fixed text box.

5. Click OK to return to the document.

To set line spacing:

1. Position the insertion point where you want the line spacing change to begin or select the paragraph(s) you want to change.

2. Choose Spacing from the Line fly-out on the Format menu (**Figure 44**). The Line Spacing dialog box will appear (**Figure 45**).

3. Type the line spacing you would like in the Spacing text box.

4. Click OK.

✔ Tip

■ To change the line spacing for an entire document, press Ctrl+Home to move to the top of the document, then follow the steps listed above.

Paragraph Spacing

You can also set the amount of space between paragraphs.

To set the space between paragraphs:

1. Position the insertion point where you want the line spacing change to begin.

   or

   Select the paragraph(s) you want to change.

2. Choose Format from the Paragraph fly-out on the Format menu (**Figure 46**). The Paragraph Format dialog box will open (**Figure 47**).

3. Use the Spacing Between Paragraphs text box to set the number of lines you want between the paragraphs. A preview of the number of lines you've entered will appear in the preview pane.

4. Click OK to return to your document.

✔ Tip

■ If you want to change the paragraph spacing for an entire document, press Ctrl+Home on the keyboard to move to the top of the document, then follow the steps outlined above.

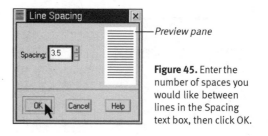

Figure 45. Enter the number of spaces you would like between lines in the Spacing text box, then click OK.

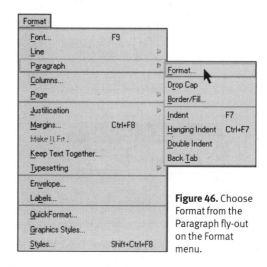

Figure 46. Choose Format from the Paragraph fly-out on the Format menu.

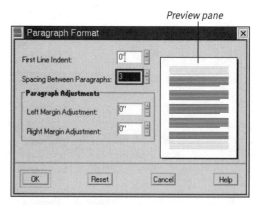

Figure 47. Enter the number of lines you would like between each paragraph in the Spacing Between Paragraphs text box.

SET THE SPACE BETWEEN PARAGRAPHS

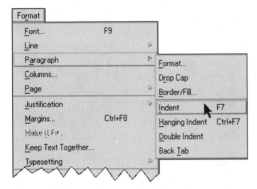

Figure 48. Choose the type of indent you want to use—Indent, Hanging Indent, or Double Indent—from the Paragraph fly-out on the Format menu.

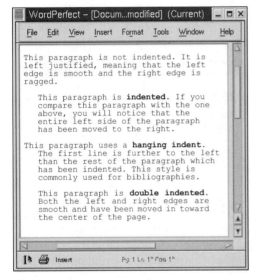

Figure 49. Depending upon the type of indentation you choose, the paragraph will be indented in one of the ways shown in this figure.

Shortcut Keys and Indents

There are a few keyboard shortcuts you can use to insert indents: F7 adds an indent and Ctrl+F7 adds a hanging indent.

Tabs and Indents

Tabs and indents are two different critters, though the two terms are commonly used interchangeably, making it all rather confusing.

A tab moves a single line of text over to the next *tab setting*. An indent moves the left or right side (or both) of an entire paragraph over to the next tab setting. As you can see, tabs and indents both use tab settings to determine where the line of text or paragraph will move to.

To insert a tab into a line of text:

1. Position the insertion point where you want to insert the tab (at the beginning of a paragraph is a typical place).

2. Press the Tab key on the keyboard.

To indent a paragraph:

1. Select the paragraph(s) you want to indent.

2. Choose the type of indent you want to use from the Paragraph fly-out on the Format menu (**Figure 48**). You can choose from Indent, Hanging Indent, or Double Indent (**Figure 49**).

or

1. Position the insertion point where you want the indented paragraph to start.

2. Choose the type of indent you want to use from the Paragraph fly-out on the Format menu (**Figure 48**). You can choose from Indent, Hanging Indent, or Double Indent (**Figure 49**).

3. Type your paragraph, then press Enter to end the indentation.

To indent the first line of every paragraph:

1. Select the paragraph(s) you want to indent.

   or

   Position the insertion point where you would like the indentation to start.

2. Choose Format from the Paragraph fly-out on the Format menu (**Figure 50**). The Paragraph Format dialog box will appear (**Figure 51**).

3. Type a measurement in the First Line Indent text box. A preview of the measurement you've entered will appear in the preview pane.

4. Click OK to close the dialog box and return to the document window.

✔ Tips

■ To indent the paragraphs in an entire document, press Ctrl+Home to move the insertion point to the top of the document, then follow the steps outlined above.

■ Using the Paragraph Format dialog box, you can also set how much the left and right sides of the paragraph(s) will be indented. To do so, enter the amount you want each side indented in the Left and Right Margin Adjustment text boxes in the Paragraph Adjustments area (**Figure 52**).

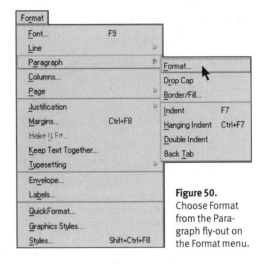

Figure 50. Choose Format from the Paragraph fly-out on the Format menu.

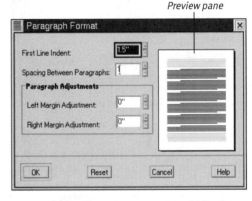

Figure 51. Type the exact amount you would like the first line of the paragraph(s) indented in the First Line Indent text box.

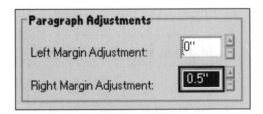

Figure 52. Use the Paragraph Adjustments area to set how far the left and right edges of a paragraph are indented.

Ruler Bar   Margin strip   Measurements

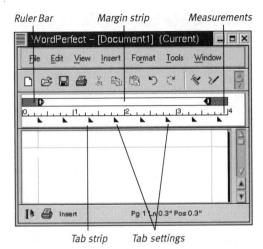

Tab strip   Tab settings

Figure 53. The Ruler Bar appears right below the toolbars.

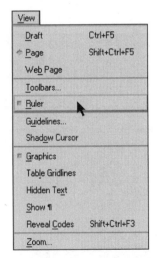

Figure 54. Choose Ruler from the View menu. A tiny square appears next to the menu item when it is displayed.

The WordPerfect Ruler Bar

To get started with changing tab settings, you will need to use the Ruler Bar.

The Ruler Bar shows you a lot of information in one little space. The Ruler Bar is made up of two horizontal strips, one above the numbered measurements and one below.

The margin strip is displayed above the numbered measurements (**Figure 53**). The small, black, sideways triangles display the positions of the left and right margins. You will use these triangles in Chapter 8, *Page and Document Setup*, when you find out how to set the page margins.

The tab strip is displayed below the numbered measurements (**Figure 53**). The tiny triangles indicate where the tabs are set. By default, WordPerfect places these tab settings every .5" (1.3 cm).

When you change the tab settings, the changes take effect from the paragraph where the insertion point is located on. To change tab settings for a specific paragraph, select that paragraph. To change tab settings for an entire document, press Ctrl+Home to move to the top of the document, then change the settings. Remember that tab settings effect both tabs and indents.

A complete list of the different types of tab settings can be found in the sidebar on page 97.

To view/hide the Ruler Bar:

Choose Ruler from the View menu (**Figure 54**). The Ruler Bar will appear right under the toolbars if it's not already displayed (**Figure 53**) or vanish if it is.

To move a tab setting:

1. Position the insertion point where you want to change the tab setting.

   or

   Select the paragraph(s) whose tab setting you want to change.

2. Position the mouse pointer over the tab setting you want to move.

3. Press the left mouse button and drag it to the new position (**Figure 55**). As you drag a vertical line will appear from the tab setting down through the document, giving you an indication of where the tab stop is in relation to the document page.

4. Release the mouse button when the tab setting is in the right place.

To create a new tab setting:

1. Position the insertion point where you want to change the tab setting.

   or

   Select the paragraph(s) whose tab setting you want to change.

2. Right click on a white area of the tab strip, between two tab settings. A QuickMenu will appear (**Figure 56**).

3. Choose the type of tab setting you would like to create from the QuickMenu. In **Figure 56** a right tab setting has been chosen.

4. Position the mouse pointer on the Ruler Bar where you want the tab setting to appear.

5. Click. The new tab setting will appear on the Ruler Bar (**Figure 57**).

   or

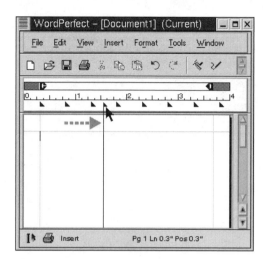

Figure 55. Press the left mouse button and drag the tab setting to its new position.

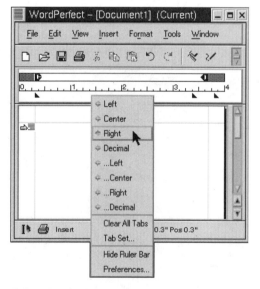

Figure 56. Right click on a white area of the tab strip and choose the type of tab setting you would like to use from the QuickMenu.

New tab setting

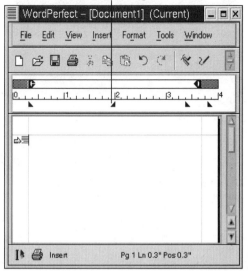

Figure 57. When you click the left mouse button, the new tab setting appears in the Ruler Bar. The right tab setting chosen on the QuickMenu in Figure 56 appears in this figure on the tab strip of the Ruler Bar.

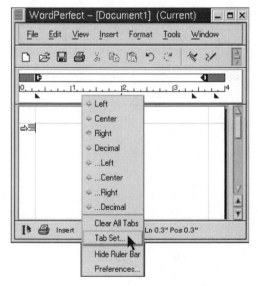

Figure 58. Choose Tab Set from the QuickMenu that appears when you right click on the tab strip.

1. Position the insertion point where you want to change the tab setting.

   or

   Select the paragraph(s) whose tab setting you want to change.

2. Right click on the tab strip and choose Tab Set from the QuickMenu that appears (**Figure 58**). The Tabs dialog box will appear (**Figure 59**).

   or

   Choose Tab Set from the Line fly-out on the Format menu (**Figure 60**). The Tabs dialog box will appear (**Figure 59**).

3. Use the Type drop-down list to select a the type of tab setting you want to add (**Figure 61**).

4. Use the Position text box to enter a measurement where the tab will appear.

5. Click Set. The tab setting will appear on the tab strip.

6. Create as many tab settings as you wish.

7. When you are finished, click OK to close the dialog box and return to the document.

CREATE A NEW TAB SETTING

95

To delete a tab setting:

1. Position the insertion point where you want to change the tab setting.

    or

    Select the paragraph(s) whose tab setting you want to change.

2. Position the mouse pointer over the tab setting you want to remove, press the left mouse button and drag the tab setting off the tab strip. When you release the mouse button, the tab setting will disappear.

To delete all tab settings:

1. Position the insertion point where you want to change the tab setting.

    or

    Select the paragraph(s) whose tab setting you want to change.

2. Right click on the tab strip and choose Clear All Tabs from the QuickMenu that appears (**Figure 62**).

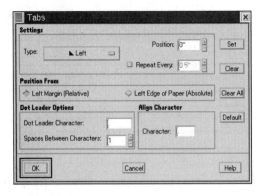

Figure 59. The Tabs dialog box is used to create new tab settings, and move and delete tab settings.

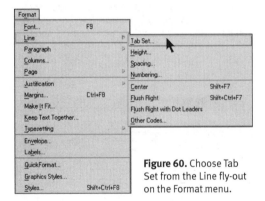

Figure 60. Choose Tab Set from the Line fly-out on the Format menu.

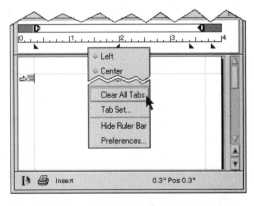

Figure 62. Choose Clear All Tabs from the QuickMenu.

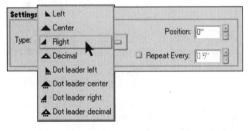

Figure 61. In the Settings area, choose a type of tab setting from the Type drop-down list.

Tab Setting Types

There are several different types of tab settings: left, right, center, decimal, and versions of these four types with *dot leaders*. Here's a brief description of each tab setting, including what it does and how it is displayed on the Ruler Bar.

 Left—On the Ruler Bar, this tab setting is displayed as a tiny triangle that points down and to the left. When a left tab setting is applied, text appears to the right of the tab setting position. The text is left aligned to the tab setting.

 Center—On the Ruler Bar, this tab setting is displayed as a tiny triangle that points up. When a center tab setting is applied, text appears centered on the tab setting position.

 Right—On the Ruler Bar, this tab setting is displayed as a tiny triangle that points down and to the right. When a right tab setting is applied, text appears to the left of the tab setting position. The text is right aligned to the tab setting.

 Decimal—On the Ruler Bar, this tab setting is displayed as a tiny triangle that points up with a small dot in the middle. This type of tab setting is used for numbers that contain decimal points such as currency amounts. When a decimal tab setting is applied, text is positioned with the decimal point at the tab setting position.

 Dot leaders—Along with the 4 tab setting types listed above, these types can also be displayed with a line of dots, a dot leader, that preceeds the text. This type of tab setting is commonly used for tables of contents.

Below is an example of each type of tab setting:

LEFT	CENTER	RIGHT	DECIMAL	LEFT WITH DOTS
Manicotti	Cheese	Red sauce	$13.95	.... Page 29
Pizza	Mushrooms	Garlic	125.69	.... Page 35
Ravioli	Spinach	Olive oil	£3.80	.... Page 75
Spaghetti	Artichoke	White sauce	12.50	.... Page 123
Tortellini	Red pepper	Pesto	¥890	.... Page 125

Hyphenation

WordPerfect will automatically divide words that are too long to fit on a line instead of wrapping the entire word to the next line. This is known as *hyphenation*. Hyphenation looks especially good when the paragraph text is full justified.

To turn hyphenation on:

1. Position the insertion point where you want the hyphenation to begin.

2. Choose Hyphenation from the Language fly-out on the Tools menu (**Figure 63**). The Line Hyphenation dialog box will open (**Figure 64**).

3. Select the check box next to Hyphenation On.

4. Click OK. The dialog box will close and hyphenation will be turned on.

✔ Tip

■ To turn hyphenation off, follow the steps above, but make sure the box next to Hyphenation On is unselected.

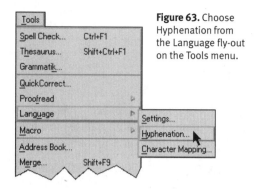

Figure 63. Choose Hyphenation from the Language fly-out on the Tools menu.

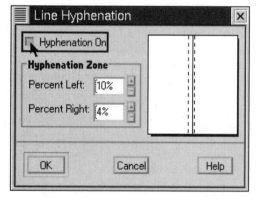

Figure 64. In the Line Hyphenation dialog box, select the check box next to Hyphenation On.

Summary

In this chapter you learned how to:

◆ Make text bold, italic, or underlined

◆ Add special formatting such as double-underlining

◆ Make text sub- or superscript

◆ Automatically change capitalization

◆ Change fonts and font sizes

◆ Set a relative font size

◆ Set a new default font

◆ Install the fonts that ship with the WordPerfect Personal Edition

◆ Set paragraph justification

◆ Change line spacing and height

◆ Use tabs and indents

◆ Turn on hyphenation

CLIPART, LINES, & CHARTS

Figure 1. Choose From File from the Graphics fly-out on the Insert menu.

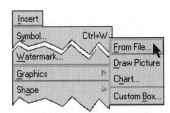

Clipart, shapes, and charts quickly add distinction, organization, and interest to your professional documents. The WordPerfect 8 Personal Edition ships with hundreds of clipart images on the CD-ROM. What a library of images to have at one's fingertips! Inserting images into documents is easy, so let's dive right in!

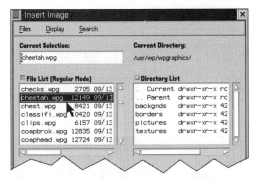

Figure 2. Select an image using the Insert Image dialog box.

Figure 3. The clipart image appears in the document window.

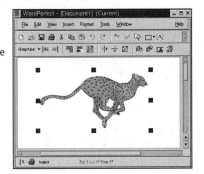

To insert clipart:

1. Position the insertion point where you would like the graphic to appear. (The shadow cursor is really handy for this if you want to place a graphic in an area of a document that does not have any text.)

2. Choose From File from the Graphics fly-out on the Insert menu (**Figure 1**). The Insert Image dialog box will open with the default WordPerfect graphics directory selected (**Figure 2**).

3. Highlight a clipart file in the File List box.

   or

   Use the Directory List box to move to another directory where clipart images are stored.

4. Click Insert in the Insert Image dialog box. The clipart image will appear, selected in the document (**Figure 3**).

To insert clipart from the Personal Edition CD-ROM:

1. Mount the CD-ROM (for directions on how to do this turn to page 21).

2. Position the insertion point where you would like the graphic to appear. (The shadow cursor is really handy for this if you want to place a graphic in an area of a document that does not have any text.)

3. Choose From File from the Graphics fly-out on the Insert menu (**Figure 1**). The Insert Image dialog box will open with the default WordPerfect graphics directory selected (**Figure 2**).

4. Use the Directory List box to move to the Clipart directory on the CD-ROM (**Figure 4**). In **Figure 4**, the directory is /mnt/cdrom/clipart/clipart/. Notice that there are many clipart directories in the Directory List box. The clipart is organized into categories by directory.

5. Double-click on a directory that matches the category of clipart image you would like to insert.

6. Highlight a clipart file in the File List box (**Figure 5**).

7. Click Insert. The clipart image will appear, selected in the document (**Figure 6**).

8. Unmount the CD-ROM.

✔ Tip

- If you want to delete an image, just select it in the document window, then press Delete on the keyboard.

Figure 4. The clipart on the CD-ROM is organized by category.

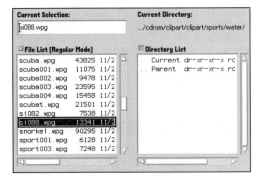

Figure 5. Highlight a clipart image using the File List box, then click Insert.

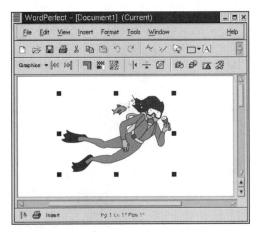

Figure 6. The CD-ROM clipart image appears selected in the document window.

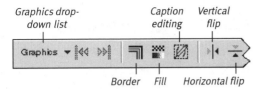

Figure 7. When a graphic is selected, special graphics commands appear on the Property Bar.

Figure 8. The handles at the left center and right center of a selected object affect the object's width.

Figure 9. The handles at the top center and bottom center of a selected object affect the object's height.

Figure 10. The handles at the corners of a selected object affect the object's height and width equally.

Using Image Boxes

Every image inserted into a WordPerfect document is contained in an image box. By default, an image box does not have a border, so text can be contoured around the box. However, if you want to add a border, you can. You can use image boxes to move and resize the graphic contained in the box and you can horizontally or vertically flip an image. When an image box is selected, the Property Bar automatically changes to display graphics command buttons (**Figure 7**) and eight black squares, *handles*, appear around the image.

Handles

Handles appear in a rectangular formation around an image when it is selected. These handles have various functions:

◆ The handles that appear to the right center and left center of the image effect the graphic's *horizontal scale*—they make the image narrower or wider (**Figure 8**).

◆ The handles that appear at the top center and bottom center of an image effect the graphic's *vertical scale*—they make the image shorter or taller (**Figure 9**).

◆ The handles that appear at the corners effect the graphic's *proportional scale*. These handles let you change the horizontal and vertical size of an object equally (**Figure 10**).

USING IMAGE BOXES; HANDLES

I Can't Access My Menus!

If you've been working with images and image boxes and you discover that most of the items on your menus are grayed out, don't worry! This just means that an image is still selected. Click in white space on the document, then check the menus again. The menu items will now be available.

To move an image:

Position the mouse pointer over the image, press the left mouse button, and drag the graphic to its new position.

To change an image's width:

1. Select the image. Eight handles will appear around it.

2. Position the mouse pointer over either the left center or right center handle (**Figure 11**).

3. Press the left mouse button and horizontally drag the handle. The handles disappear and a dashed rectangle, indicating the image box's edge, appears as you drag. In addition, the mouse pointer will change to a right or left pointing arrow next to a small vertical line. If you drag the handle toward the image, it will become narrower (**Figure 12**). If you drag the handle away from the image, it will become wider (**Figure 13**).

4. Release the mouse button when you are happy with the width.

Figure 11. Drag either the left or right handle to make an image wider or narrower.

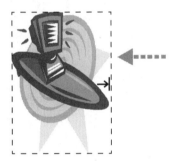

Figure 12. As you drag inward, the handles disappear and a rectangle appears on the screen, indicating the edge of the graphic as it gets narrower.

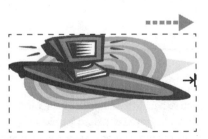

Figure 13. As you drag outward, the handles disappear and a rectangle appears on the screen indicating the edge of the graphic as it gets wider.

Press here

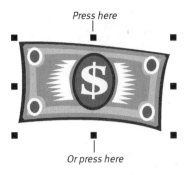

Or press here

Figure 14. To change an image's height use either the top center or bottom center handle.

Figure 15. As you drag toward the graphic, the handles disappear and a rectangle appears on the screen, indicating the edge of the graphic as it gets shorter.

Figure 16. As you drag away from the image, the handles disappear and a rectangle appears on the screen, indicating the edge of the graphic as it gets taller.

To change an image's height:

1. Select the image. Eight handles will appear around it.

2. Position the mouse pointer over either the top center or bottom center handle (**Figure 14**).

3. Press the left mouse button and vertically drag the handle. A dashed rectangle indicating the image box's edge appears as you drag. In addition, the mouse pointer will change to an up or down pointing arrow next to a small horizontal line. If you drag the handle toward the image, it will become shorter (**Figure 15**). If you drag the handle away from the image, it will become taller (**Figure 16**).

4. Release the mouse button when the image is the desired height.

CHANGE AN IMAGE'S HEIGHT

There's Always a Way Out!

If you end up in a dialog box you didn't mean to open, don't panic! Just click the Cancel button in the dialog box or press the Esc key on the keyboard to close the dialog box and return to your document.

To proportionally change an image's width and height:

1. Select the image. Eight handles will appear around it.

2. Position the mouse pointer over any one of the corner handles (**Figure 17**).

3. Press the left mouse button and diagonally drag the handle. A dashed rectangle indicating the image box's edge appears as you drag. In addition, the mouse pointer will change to a diagonal pointed arrow. If you drag toward the image, it will become smaller (**Figure 18**). If you drag away from the image, it will become larger (**Figure 19**).

4. Release the mouse button when you are happy with the image's new size.

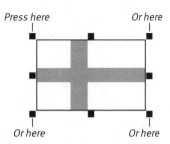

Figure 17. The handles at the corners of an image are used to proportionally resize the image's height and width.

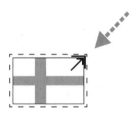

Figure 18. As you drag toward the image, the handles disappear and a rectangle appears on the screen, indicating the edge of the graphic as it gets proportionally smaller.

Making it Easier to See Images when You Move and Size Them

When you're moving and sizing images, it's easier to see where you are if you zoom out to a full page view.

To zoom out to a full page view:

1. Click on white space to deselect the image.

2. Click the Zoom button on the WordPerfect 8 Toolbar and select 100% from the drop-down list.

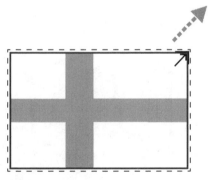

Figure 19. As you drag away from the image, the handles disappear and a rectangle appears on the screen, indicating the edge of the image as it gets proportionally larger.

Figure 20. When you select the image to be flipped, eight black handles appear around the object, indicating it's selected.

To flip an image vertically:

1. Select the image you want to flip (**Figure 20**).

2. Choose Flip Left/Right from the Graphics drop-down list on the Property Bar (**Figure 21**) or click the Vertical Flip button on the Property Bar. The image will flip vertically (**Figure 22**).

To flip an image horizontally:

1. Select the image you want to flip (**Figure 20**).

2. Choose Flip Top/Bottom from the Graphics drop-down list on the Property Bar (**Figure 23**) or click the Horizontal Flip button on the Property Bar. The image will flip horizontally (**Figure 24**).

Figure 21. Choose Flip Left/Right from the Graphics drop-down list on the Property Bar.

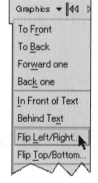

Figure 22. The object flipped vertically.

Figure 23. Choose Flip Top/Bottom from the Graphics drop-down list on the Property Bar.

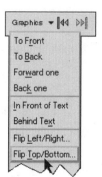

Figure 24. The object flipped horizontally.

FLIP AN OBJECT VERTICALLY AND HORIZONTALLY

To add a border around an image:

1. Select the image you want to add a border to.

2. Right click on the image and choose Border/Fill from the QuickMenu (**Figure 25**) or choose Border/Fill from the Graphics drop-down list on the Property Bar (**Figure 26**). The Box Border/Fill dialog box will open (**Figure 27**).

3. Click the button to the right of Border Style and choose a border from the list box. The border you choose will appear on the Border Style button.

4. Click OK to close the dialog box. The border you selected will appear around the object (**Figure 28**).

or

1. Select the image you want to add a border to.

2. Choose a border style from the Border drop-down box on the Property Bar (**Figure 29**). The border you selected will appear around the object (**Figure 28**).

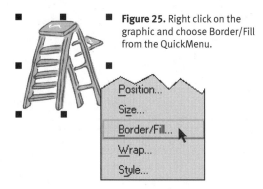

Figure 25. Right click on the graphic and choose Border/Fill from the QuickMenu.

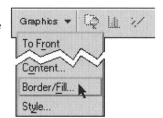

Figure 26. Choose Border/Fill from the Graphics drop-down list on the Property Bar.

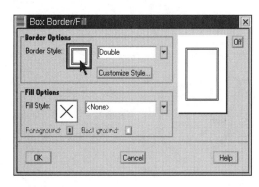

Figure 27. Click the Border Style button and select a border from the list box.

Figure 28. When you click OK, a border appears around the image.

Border button

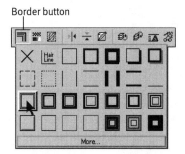

Figure 29. Click the Border button on the Property Bar, and then select a border from the drop-down list.

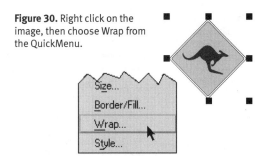

Figure 30. Right click on the image, then choose Wrap from the QuickMenu.

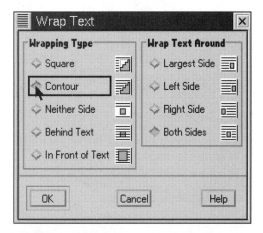

Figure 31. Select a radio button in both the Wrapping Type and Wrap Text Around areas, then click OK.

Figure 32. Depending on the text wrap style you chose, the text flows around the object. In this figure, the options selected in Figure 31 were used.

Setting Text Flow

You can set exactly how text will flow around, above, below, behind, or in front of an image.

To set text flow around an image:

1. Select the image that you want to change.

2. Right click on the image and choose Wrap from the QuickMenu (**Figure 30**). The Wrap Text dialog box will appear (**Figure 31**).

3. Choose the way you would like the text to flow by selecting a radio button in the Wrapping Type area and a radio button in the Wrap Text Around area. Your choices include:

    ◆ **Square**—the text flows around the borders of the Image box.

    ◆ **Contour**—the text follows the shape of the object as it flows.

    ◆ **Neither Side**—the text flows above and below an image, but not on either side.

    ◆ **Behind Text**—the text flows over the image, obscuring it.

    ◆ **In Front of Text**—the text flows under the image and is obscured by the image.

4. Click OK. The text will flow around the image using the options you have selected (**Figure 32**).

or

1. Select the image you want to change.

2. Choose a text flow option from the Wrap drop-down list on the Property Bar (**Figure 33**). The text will wrap around the object in the manner you selected.

Drawing Lines

In order to make your document more organized, you can insert horizontal and vertical lines to define areas or add emphasis. You can also draw *polylines*, lines that consist of a series of straight, connected segments.

To draw a horizontal line:

1. Position the insertion point where you would like the horizontal line to appear. If you are at the end of a paragraph, you can press Enter on the keyboard to move down to a blank line.

2. Choose Horizontal Line from the Shape fly-out on the Insert menu (**Figure 34**) or press Ctrl+F11 on the keyboard. The horizontal line will appear in the document, stretching from left margin to right margin (**Figure 35**).

✔ Tip

- A horizontal line between a header and the body of a newsletter or report can add structure and organization.

To draw a vertical line:

1. Position the insertion point where you would like the vertical line to appear. (Remember this line will go from the top of the page to the bottom.)

2. Choose Vertical Line from the Shape fly-out on the Insert menu (**Figure 36**). The vertical line will appear in the document, stretching from top margin to bottom margin (**Figure 37**).

✔ Tip

- Vertical lines look great between columns of text. (For details on creating columns, turn to Chapter 7, *Fun with Text.*)

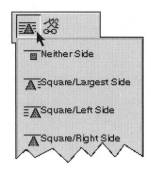

Figure 33. Click the Wrap button on the Property Bar, and then select a text wrapping option from the drop-down list.

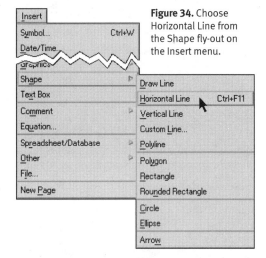

Figure 34. Choose Horizontal Line from the Shape fly-out on the Insert menu.

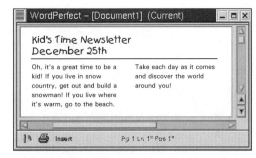

Figure 35. The horizontal line appears in the document.

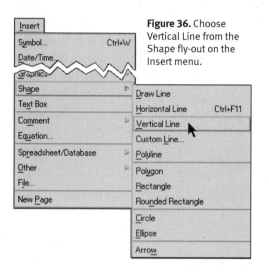

Figure 36. Choose Vertical Line from the Shape fly-out on the Insert menu.

To draw a custom line:

1. Choose Draw Line from the Shape fly-out on the Insert menu (**Figure 38**). The mouse pointer will change to a crosshair.

2. Position the crosshair where you would like the line to start.

3. Press the left mouse button and drag to the position where you would like the line to end. When you release the mouse button, the line appears selected in your Document (**Figure 39**). Notice that special line command buttons appear automatically on the Property Bar when a line is selected (**Figure 40**).

4. To change the thickness of the line, click the Thickness button on the Property Bar and select a new thickness from the drop-down list (**Figure 41**).

(continued)

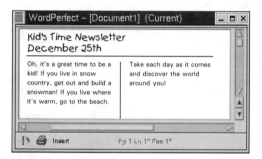

Figure 37. The vertical line appears in the document.

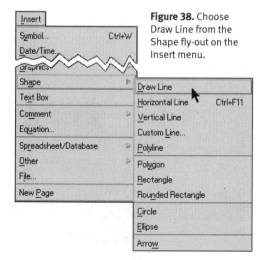

Figure 38. Choose Draw Line from the Shape fly-out on the Insert menu.

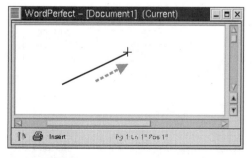

Figure 39. As you drag the mouse, the line appears in the document.

5. To change the color of the line, click the Color button on the Property Bar and select a new color from the drop-down palette (**Figure 42**).

6. To change the way the beginning and end of the line looks, click the Beginning Line and End Line buttons, respectively, and select a line cap from the drop-down list (**Figure 43**).

7. When you are finished editing your custom line, click on white space to deselect the line.

✔ Tips

■ A custom line is contained in an image box, like the graphics discussed earlier in this chapter. This means that you can do anything to a line that you would to a graphic, such as moving, resizing, adding a border, and setting text flow.

■ Just like text, lines can be cut, copied, and pasted.

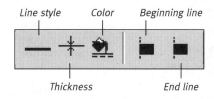

Line style   Color   Beginning line

Thickness   End line

Figure 40. When a custom line is selected, the Property Bar changes to include line commands.

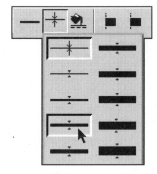

Figure 41. Click the Thickness button and select a new line width from the drop-down list.

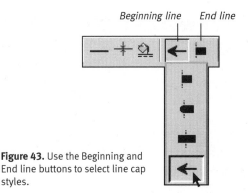

Beginning line   End line

Figure 43. Use the Beginning and End line buttons to select line cap styles.

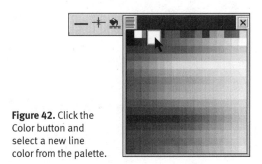

Figure 42. Click the Color button and select a new line color from the palette.

DRAW A CUSTOM LINE

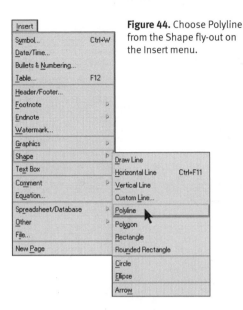

Figure 44. Choose Polyline from the Shape fly-out on the Insert menu.

To draw a polyline:

1. Choose Polyline from the Shape fly-out on the Insert menu (**Figure 44**). The mouse pointer will change to a crosshair.

2. Position the crosshair where you would like the polyline to start.

3. Click. (Don't press and drag.)

4. Move the mouse to the place where you want the first segment to end. As you move the mouse, a line will appear from the starting position, attached to the mouse crosshair.

5. Click again. The first segment will appear in the document (**Figure 45**).

6. Move the mouse to the next place where you would like a segment to end and click again (**Figure 46**).

7. Continue moving the mouse and clicking until you have created the line that you need.

8. Double-click to finish drawing the line. The line will appear selected in an image box (**Figure 47**).

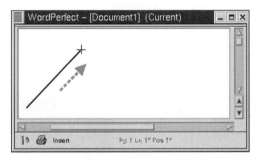

Figure 45. Position the mouse where you would like to start the line and click. Then, move the mouse where you would like the line segment to end and click again.

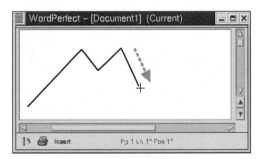

Figure 46. Continue moving the mouse and clicking to insert more line segments.

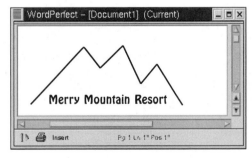

Figure 47. Double-click to finish drawing the polyline. The line appears selected in the document.

DRAW A POLYLINE

Drawing Shapes

WordPerfect almost feels like a drawing program! As well as inserting lines, you can also draw shapes—rectangles, circles, and ellipses right into your document.

To insert a shape:

1. Choose Rectangle, Rounded Rectangle, Circle, or Ellipse from the Shape fly-out on the Insert menu (**Figure 48**). The mouse pointer will change to a crosshair.

2. Position the crosshair at the upper left-hand corner of the area where you want to draw the shape.

3. Press the left mouse button and drag diagonally down to the right to create the shape (**Figure 49**). When you release the mouse button, the shape appears in the document, selected.

4. To change the fill color of a shape, click the Fill Color button on the Property Bar and select a new color from the palette (**Figure 50**).

5. To add a shadow to the shape, click the Shadow button on the Property Bar and choose a shadow from the drop-down list (**Figure 51**).

6. When you are finished creating the shape, click in white space to deselect the shape.

✔ Tip

- Shapes are contained in Image boxes, so they can be moved, resized, and flipped just like a graphic. You can also set the way text flows around shapes.

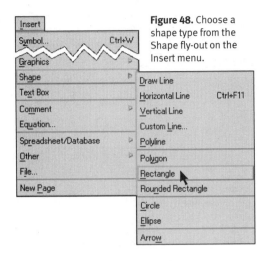

Figure 48. Choose a shape type from the Shape fly-out on the Insert menu.

Figure 49. Drag the mouse diagonally down to the right to draw the shape.

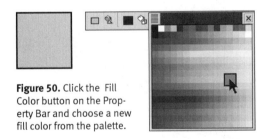

Figure 50. Click the Fill Color button on the Property Bar and choose a new fill color from the palette.

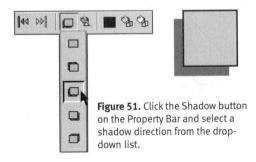

Figure 51. Click the Shadow button on the Property Bar and select a shadow direction from the drop-down list.

INSERT A SHAPE

Creating Charts

The WP Draw program that is connected to WordPerfect 8 lets you quickly and easily create a variety of 2D and 3D charts, including pie, bar, line, area, scatter, and hi-lo.

When creating a chart, WP Draw operates in a special chart mode, splitting its drawing window in two (**Figure 52**). At the upper part of the window is a *datasheet*, a spreadsheet where you can enter the data that you want to display on the chart. The lower part of the drawing window displays a preview of the chart being created. You can't enter data in the preview area, only in the datasheet. To the left of the WP Draw window is a Graph Toolbox that gives quick access to chart types. If you pass the mouse over a button on the Graph Toolbar, a description of what the button does appears in the WP Draw title bar.

Graph Toolbox   Datasheet   Chart legend   Chart title   Cells   Preview area

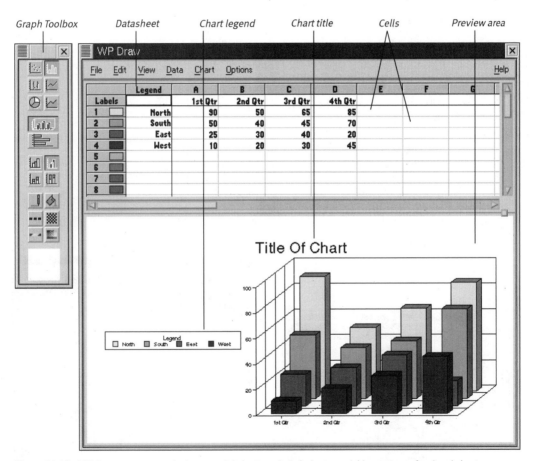

Figure 52. The WP Draw program works in a special chart mode to help you quickly create professional charts.

To insert a chart:

1. Choose Chart from the Graphics fly-out on the Insert menu (**Figure 53**). WP Draw will open with its drawing window split in two, showing a datasheet at the top and a chart preview at the bottom (**Figure 52**).

2. Choose the type of chart you would like to use from the Chart menu (**Figure 54**). That chart type will appear in the preview area (**Figure 55**).

3. To insert data, click on a *cell* in the datasheet to select it, then type the data.

4. To delete data from a cell:

   A. Select the cell, then press Delete on the keyboard. A Clear dialog box will open with Data selected in the Clear area (**Figure 56**).

   B. Click the radio button next to what you would like to clear, the data, formatting, or both.

   C. Click OK to close the dialog box and return to WP Draw.

5. Enter all your data in the cells.

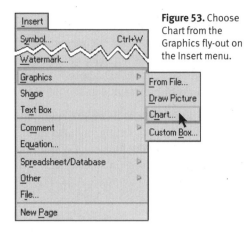

Figure 53. Choose Chart from the Graphics fly-out on the Insert menu.

Figure 54. Choose a chart type from the Chart menu.

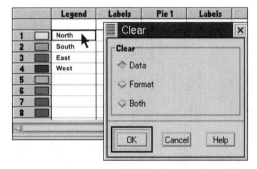

Figure 56. When deleting information from a cell, the Clear dialog box opens, asking whether you want to delete the cell's information, formatting, or both.

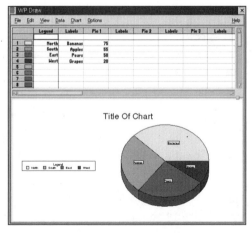

Figure 55. The chart style you select appears in the preview area.

INSERT A CHART

Figure 57. Choose Titles from the Options menu.

6. To add or change a chart title:

   A. Choose Titles from the Options menu (**Figure 57**). A Titles dialog box will open (**Figure 58**).

   B. Enter the title of the chart in the Title text box.

   C. If your chart has a subtitle or title for the x and y axes, enter that information in the appropriate text boxes.

   D. Click Preview to see the changes you have made in the preview area (**Figure 59**). If you like what you see, click OK to close the dialog box. Otherwise, you can continue working in the Titles dialog box.

   (continued)

Figure 58. Type the chart's title in the Title text box. Also enter a subtitle and titles for the x and y axes if you wish.

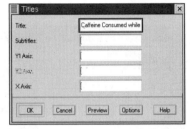

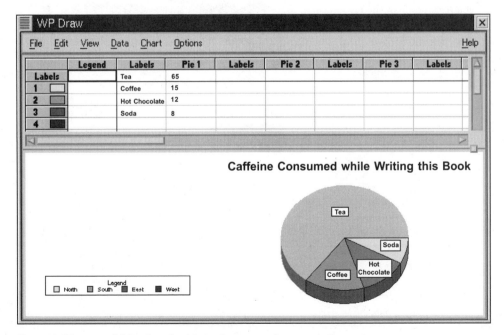

Figure 59. When you click Preview, the title you have entered appears in the preview area.

INSERT A CHART

7. To display or edit a legend:

A. Choose Legend from the Options menu (**Figure 60**). The Legend dialog box will open (**Figure 61**).

B. To display the legend, select the check box next to Display Legend. (To hide the legend, deselect the box.)

C. Set where the legend will appear using the Placement area and Position drop-down list (**Figure 62**).

D. Set whether the legend will display horizontally or vertically using the Orientation area (**Figure 63**).

E. Enter a title for the legend, if you wish, in the Name text box in the Title area (**Figure 64**). You can also select a font for the legend title by clicking the Font button.

F. Click Preview to see the changes you have made in the preview area (**Figure 65**). If you like what you see, click OK to close the dialog box. Otherwise, you can continue working in the Legend dialog box.

Figure 60. Choose Legend from the Options menu.

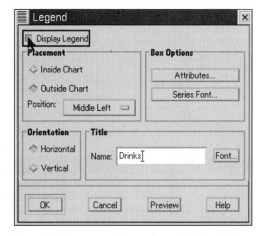

Figure 61. If you want to show a legend with your chart, make sure the check box next to Display Legend is selected.

Figure 63. Select whether you want the legend to appear horizontally (wider than it is tall) or vertically (taller than it is wide).

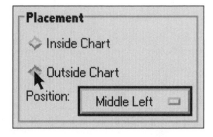

Figure 62. Select whether you want the legend placed inside or outside of the chart and the legend's position relative to the chart.

INSERT A CHART

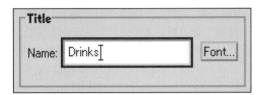

Figure 64. Enter a title for the legend in the Name text box.

8. When you are finished entering data, and setting up the title and legend, choose Exit and Return to [your document] (**Figure 66**). An Exit WP Draw dialog box will appear, asking whether you want to save changes (**Figure 67**).

(continued)

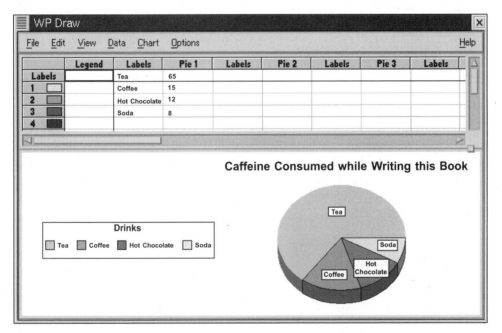

Figure 65. When you click Preview, the legend items you have entered appear in the preview area.

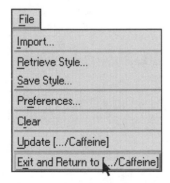

Figure 66. Choose Exit and Return to [your document] from the File menu. [your document] will contain the name of the document you are working on.

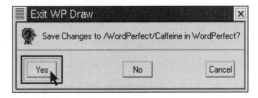

Figure 67. Click Yes to insert the chart in your document and save the changes.

9. Click Yes. WP Draw will close and your chart will appear in the document (**Figure 68**).

✔ Tips

■ To edit a chart, right click on the chart, and choose Edit Image from the QuickMenu (**Figure 69**).

■ A chart, like any other graphic, is contained in an Image box. This means that you can move it, resize it, and set text flow like any other graphic.

■ To delete a chart, select it, and then press Delete on the keyboard.

■ There are many more charting options available in WP Draw. Look around the drawing window and experiment. If you can imagine a chart, you can probably create it with WP Draw!

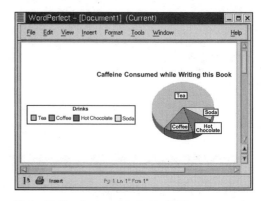

Figure 68. The chart you created in WP Draw appears in the WordPerfect document contained in an Image box. Just like any other image, you can move it, resize it, delete it, and change text flow around it.

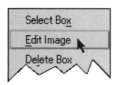

Figure 69. Choose Edit Image from the QuickMenu to edit a chart.

Summary

In this chapter you learned how to:

◆ Insert and move a clipart image

◆ Change image width and height

◆ Flip an image vertically and horizontally

◆ Set text flow around and image

◆ Add a border to an image

◆ Draw horizontal and vertical lines

◆ Create custom lines

◆ Draw polylines

◆ Draw shapes

◆ Create fabulous charts

INSERT A CHART

FUN WITH TEXT

Figure 1. Click the Font Color button on the Property Bar and choose a new color from the palette.

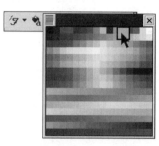

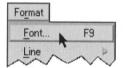

Figure 2. Choose Font from the Format menu.

C hapter 5, *Formatting Your Text*, showed you how to add text to documents. This chapter takes text one step further, adding advanced formatting techniques that bring organization, a professional look, and creative flair to your documents. Topics covered here range from changing text color and adding bullets and drop caps to setting columns and *styles*.

To change text color:

1. Select the text you want to change.

2. Click the Font Color button on the Property Bar and choose a color from the palette (**Figure 1**). The text will change to the color you selected.

or

1. Select the text you want to change.

2. Choose Font from the Format menu (**Figure 2**). The Font dialog box will open (**Figure 3**).

(continued)

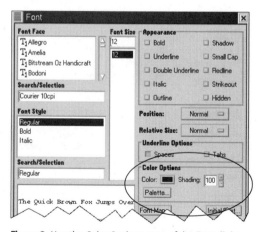

Figure 3. Use the Color Options area of the Font dialog box to change the text color.

3. In the Color Options area, click the button next to Color and choose a new color from the palette (**Figure 4**).

4. Use the Shading text box to set how intense or *saturated* the color will be (**Figure 5**). The higher the number the more saturated a color is. For instance, blue set to 100 shading will be a rich, bright blue. Blue set to 10 shading will be a very light blue.

5. Click OK to close the dialog box. The text will change to the color you selected.

✔ Tip

■ You can also change text color before you type the text by positioning the insertion point where you would like the colored text to start, choosing a new color using one of the methods outlined above, and then typing the colored text.

Highlighting

Just as if you were using a highlighting pen, WordPerfect lets you highlight the text in your documents.

To highlight text:

1. Choose On from the Highlight fly-out on the Tools menu (**Figure 6**). The mouse pointer will change to a tiny highlighting pen.

2. Position the mouse where you would like to start highlighting.

3. Press the left mouse button and drag until you are finished highlighting the text.

4. Release the mouse button.

✔ Tip

■ To turn highlighting off, just choose On from the Highlight fly-out on the Tools menu again.

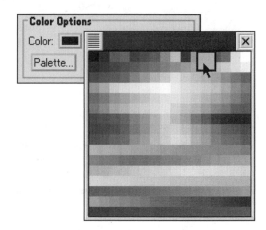

Figure 4. Select a new text color from the palette that appears when you click the button next to Color.

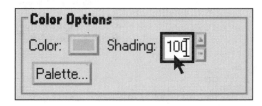

Figure 5. Use the Shading text box to set how intense a color is. The lower the number, the lighter the color.

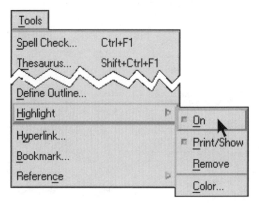

Figure 6. Choose On from the Highlight fly-out on the Tools menu.

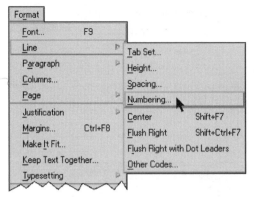

Figure 7. Choose Numbering from the Line fly-out on the Format menu.

Figure 8. Select the check box next to Turn Line Numbering On, then select the options you need.

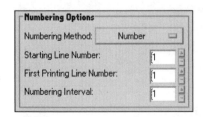

Figure 9. Use the Numbering Method drop-down list to select numbers, letters, or Roman numerals, then set the starting line number, which line will print first, and the interval between printed line numbers.

Line Numbering

Line numbering automatically numbers every line in a document. (This is different than inserting a numbered list which inserts a number for each paragraph.) You can set where the numbers appear on the page, and whether they continue through the entire document or stop and restart. (For details on creating a numbered list, turn to the section titled, *Bullets and Numbering*, on page 123.)

To add line numbering:

1. Position the insertion point where you want the line numbering to start.

2. Choose Numbering from the Line fly-out on the Format menu (**Figure 7**). The Line Numbering dialog box will appear (**Figure 8**).

3. Select the check box next to Turn Line Numbering On.

4. In the Numbering Options area, you can set (**Figure 9**):

    ◆   **Numbering Method**—using this drop-down list, you can set whether the line numbers will appear as numbers, letters, or Roman numerals.

    ◆   **Starting Line Number**—sets the number assigned to the first line of the paragraph if you want to use something other than 1.

    ◆   **First Printing Line Number**—sets the first line number that will print in a document. For instance, if you don't want line numbers before 9 to print, specify 9.

    ◆   **Numbering Interval**—this item sets the interval between printed line numbers. For instance, if you want a line number to print every fourth line, set this option to 4.

(continued)

ADD LINE NUMBERING

5. In the Position of Numbers area, you can choose one of two options (**Figure 10**):

♦ **From Left Edge of Page** prints the numbers an exact distance from the left edge the of the page. Enter an exact measurement in the text box.

♦ **Left of Margin** prints the numbers an exact distance from the left margin. Enter an exact measurement in the text box.

6. Using the three check boxes near the bottom of the Line Numbering dialog box (**Figure 11**), you can also set whether numbering is restarted on each page, blank lines are counted, and, if you are using columns, newspaper columns are counted.

7. If you want to select a font for the line numbering different from the one used for the document text, click the Font button near the upper-right corner of the Line Numbering dialog box. When the Line Numbering Font dialog box opens (**Figure 12**), select a new font, and then click OK to close the Line Numbering Font dialog box.

8. When you have finished making selections, click OK to close the Line Numbering dialog box. As you type your document, the line numbers will appear next to each line (**Figure 13**).

✔ Tips

■ Headers, footers, footnotes, and endnotes are not included in line numbering.

■ Line numbering is often used in legal documents, such as citations.

■ To turn line numbering off, open the Line Numbering dialog box, then deselect the box next to Turn Line Numbering On.

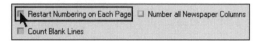

Figure 10. Select where the numbers will be positioned, then use the text box to set an exact measurement.

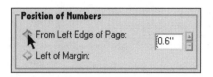

Figure 11. Set whether the numbering restarts on every page, whether blank lines are counted, and if you're using columns, whether columns are counted.

Figure 12. The Line Numbering Font dialog box works just like the regular Font dialog box. Choose a font and its attributes, then click OK.

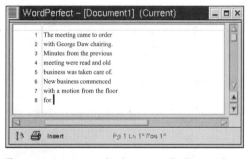

Figure 13. As you type the document, the line numbers appear down the page.

Figure 14. Choose Bullets & Numbering from the Insert menu.

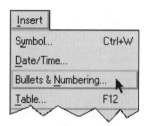

Figure 15. The Bullets & Numbers dialog box is used to select a bullet type and whether a new bullet appears when you press Enter on the keyboard.

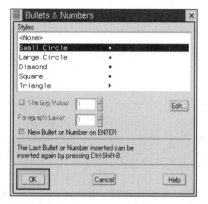

Figure 16. Select a bullet type in the Styles list box.

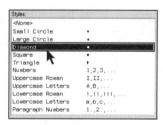

Figure 17. As the list is typed, bullets appear before each list item.

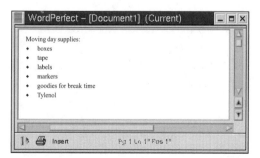

Bullets and Numbering

When the bullets or numbering feature is turned on, WordPerfect automatically places a bullet or number at the beginning of each paragraph. Bullets and numbers can be inserted as you type or added to text that has already been entered.

To create a bulleted list:

1. Position the insertion point where you want the bulleted list to start.

2. Choose Bullets & Numbering from the Insert menu (**Figure 14**). The Bullets & Numbers dialog box will open (**Figure 15**).

3. Highlight a bullet type in the Styles list box (**Figure 16**).

4. Select the box next to New Bullet or Number on ENTER if you want a new bullet to appear when you press the Enter key on the keyboard.

5. Click OK to close the dialog box. As you type your text, the bullets will appear in your document (**Figure 17**).

✔ Tips

■ To add bullets to existing text, select the text you would like to add bullets to, then follow steps 2–5 above.

■ You can also insert bullets into your document by pressing Ctrl+Shift+B on the keyboard. (This will insert the last selected bullet style.)

■ To turn bullets off, open the Bullets & Numbers dialog box and highlight <None> in the Styles list box, then click OK to close the dialog box.

To create a numbered list:

1. Position the insertion point where you want the numbered list to start.

2. Choose Bullets & Numbering from the Insert menu (**Figure 14**). The Bullets & Numbers dialog box will open (**Figure 15**).

3. Highlight a number type in the Styles list box (**Figure 18**).

4. Select the check box next to Starting Value and type a number in the text box (**Figure 19**).

5. Select the box next to New Bullet or Number on ENTER if you want a new bullet to appear when you press the Enter key on the keyboard.

6. Click OK to close the dialog box. As you type your text, the numbers will appear in your document (**Figure 20**).

✔ Tips

■ To add numbering to existing text, select the text you would like to add numbers to, then follow steps 2–6 above.

■ To turn numbering off, open the Bullets & Numbers dialog box and highlight <None> in the Styles list box, then click OK to close the dialog box.

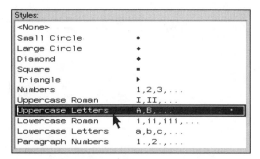

Figure 18. Select a numbered list type from the Styles list box.

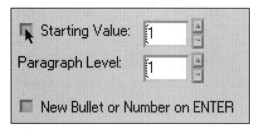

Figure 19. If you would like to set a starting value, select the check box, then enter a number in the text box. If you chose a lettering style in the Styles list box (one is chosen in Figure 18), then a value of 1 corresponds to A, 2 corresponds to B, etc.

Figure 20. As you type the numbered list, numbers appear next to each list item.

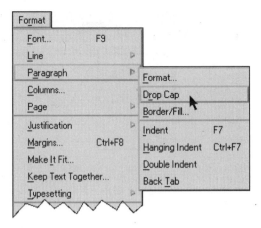

Figure 21. Choose Drop Cap from the Paragraph fly-out on the Format menu.

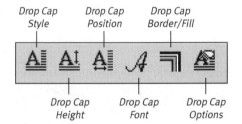

Drop Cap Style — Drop Cap Position — Drop Cap Border/Fill

Drop Cap Height — Drop Cap Font — Drop Cap Options

Figure 22. Special drop cap command buttons appear on the Property Bar.

Drop Cap Style

Figure 23. Click the Drop Cap Style button on the Property Bar and choose a drop cap type from the drop-down list.

Drop Caps

A drop cap is an enlarged letter or word at the beginning of a paragraph that draws a reader's attention in a visually inviting way. Drop caps can be created as you type or added to text that has already been entered.

To create a drop cap:

1. Position the insertion point at the beginning of the new paragraph where you would like the drop cap to appear.

   or

   Position the insertion point in an existing paragraph to which you would like to add a drop cap.

2. Choose Drop Cap from the Paragraph fly-out on the Format menu (**Figure 21**). The insertion point will enlarge, ready for you to type the drop cap. The Property Bar will change to display special drop-cap commands (**Figure 22**).

3. Click the Drop Cap Style button on the Property Bar and select a predefined drop cap style (**Figure 23**).

4. Click the Drop Cap Height button on the Property Bar and set how many lines high the drop cap will be (**Figure 24**).

   (continued)

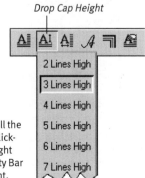

Drop Cap Height

Figure 24. Set how tall the drop cap will be by clicking the Drop Cap Height button on the Property Bar and selecting a height.

5. Click the Drop Cap Position button on the Property Bar and set where the drop cap will appear, next to the text, to the right of the margin, or in the margin (**Figure 25**).

6. To select a font for the drop cap:

A. Click the Drop Cap Font button on the Property Bar. The Drop Cap Font dialog box will open (**Figure 26**).

B. Select a typeface from the Font Face list box and set the other font attributes you would like.

C. Click OK to close the Drop Cap Font dialog box and return to the document.

Figure 25. Click the Drop Cap Position button on the Property Bar and select whether the drop cap appears with the text or alone in the margin.

7. To set a border around and add a fill behind the drop cap:

A. Click the Drop Cap Border/ Fill button on the Property Bar. The Drop Cap Border dialog box will open (**Figure 27**).

B. Click the Border Style button and select a border from the drop-down list.

C. Click the Fill Style button and select a fill from the drop-down list.

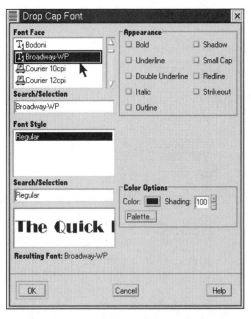

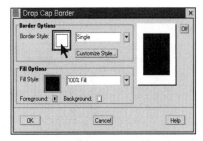

Figure 27. Use the Drop Cap Border dialog box to select a border and fill for the drop cap, if you want them. In this figure a single thin border and a solid black fill have been selected.

Figure 26. The Drop Cap Font dialog box works just like the regular Font dialog box. Select the font and attributes you want to use for the drop cap, then click OK.

CREATE A DROP CAP

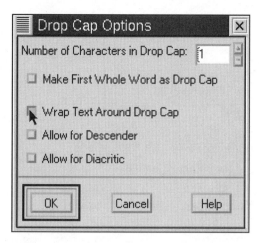

Figure 28. Select the drop cap options you would like, including how many characters are included in the drop cap and whether the text will wrap around the drop cap.

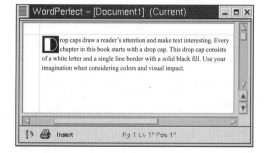

Figure 29. As you type, the drop cap appears, then the text returns to its normal size.

Figure 30. To remove a drop cap, click the No Drop Cap item on the Drop Cap Style drop-down list.

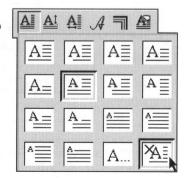

8. To set how many characters will be included in the drop cap:

   A. Click the Drop Cap Options button on the Property Bar. The Drop Cap Options dialog box will open (**Figure 28**).

   B. Type a number in the Number of Characters in Drop Cap text box.

      or

      Select the check box next to Make First Whole Word as Drop Cap.

   C. Click OK to close the dialog box and return to the document.

9. Type your drop cap. After you type the drop cap, WordPerfect automatically changes back to the regular document text so you can just continue typing (**Figure 29**).

✔ Tips

■ To remove a drop cap, position the insertion point before the drop cap, and then select the No Drop Cap item from the Drop Cap Style drop-down list on the Property Bar (**Figure 30**).

■ To create the black and white knockout drop cap shown in **Figure 29**, change the font color to white using the Drop Cap Font button on the Property Bar and add a black border and fill using the Drop Cap Border/Fill button also on the Property Bar.

Borders and Fills

With WordPerfect 8 you can quickly and easily add a border around a page, column, or paragraph. (For details on creating columns, turn to page 131.)

To add a page border and fill:

1. Position the insertion point on the page where you want the border to appear.

2. Choose Border/Fill from the Page fly-out on the Format menu (**Figure 31**). The Page Border dialog box will open (**Figure 32**).

3. Click the button next to Border Style and select a border from the drop-down list (**Figure 33**).

4. If you wish to add a fill, click the button next to Fill Options and select a fill from the drop-down list (**Figure 34**).

5. Make sure the check box next to Apply border to current page only is selected. Otherwise, a border will appear around every subsequent page.

6. Click OK. The border will appear around the page (**Figure 35**).

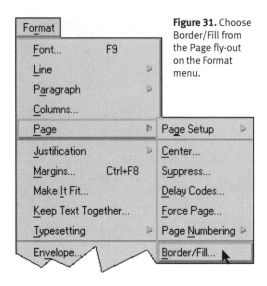

Figure 31. Choose Border/Fill from the Page fly-out on the Format menu.

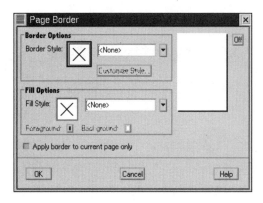

Figure 32. The Page Border dialog box is used to select a border and/or fill as the background for a page.

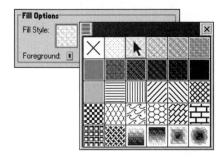

Figure 34. Click the Fill Style button and select a fill from the drop-down list. The fill you select appears on the Fill Style button.

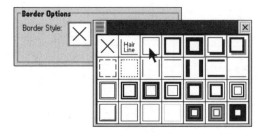

Figure 33. Click the Border Style button and select a border from the drop-down list. The border you select appears on the Border Style button.

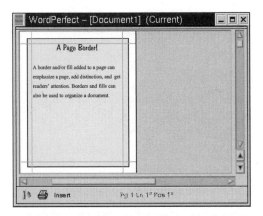

Figure 35. The border and fill you select appears on the page.

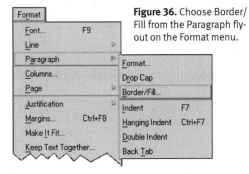

Figure 36. Choose Border/Fill from the Paragraph fly-out on the Format menu.

To add a paragraph border and fill:

1. Position the insertion point within the paragraph to which you want to add the border.

2. Choose Border/Fill from the Paragraph fly-out on the Format menu (**Figure 36**). The Paragraph Border dialog box will open (**Figure 37**).

3. Click the button next to Border Style and select a border from the drop-down list (**Figure 33**).

4. If you wish to add a fill, click the button next to Fill Options and select a fill from the drop-down list (**Figure 34**).

5. Make sure the check box next to Apply border to current paragraph only is selected. Otherwise, a border will appear around every subsequent paragraph in the document.

6. Click OK. The border will appear around the paragraph (**Figure 38**).

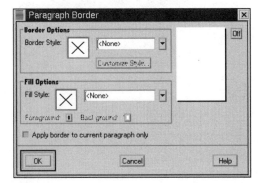

Figure 37. The Paragraph Border dialog box works just like the Drop Cap Border dialog box (Figure 27) and the Page Border dialog box (Figure 34). (It looks the same, too!)

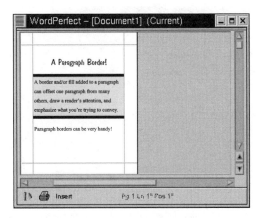

Figure 38. The paragraph border appears around the paragraph of text.

ADD A PARAGRAPH BORDER AND FILL

To add a border and fill to columns:

1. Position the insertion point anywhere within the columns. The border you select will surround every column in the document.

2. Choose Columns from the Format menu (**Figure 39**). The Define Columns dialog box will open (**Figure 40**).

3. Click the Border/Fill button. The Column Border dialog box will open (**Figure 41**).

4. Click the button next to Border Style and select a border from the drop-down list (**Figure 33**).

5. If you wish to add a fill, click the button next to Fill Options and select a fill from the drop-down list (**Figure 34**).

6. Make sure the check box next to Apply border to current column group only is selected. Otherwise, a border will appear around the columns on the current page and every subsequent column in the document.

7. Click OK. The border will appear around the columns (**Figure 42**).

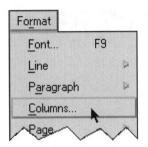

Figure 39. Choose Columns from the Format menu.

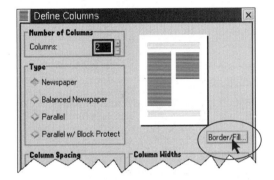

Figure 40. In the Define Columns dialog box, click the Border/Fill button to open the Column Border dialog box.

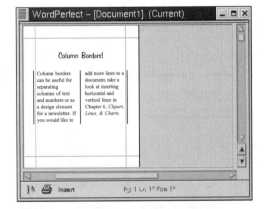

Figure 42. The column borders you selected appear around the columns in the document.

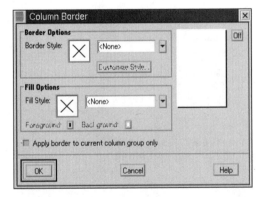

Figure 41. The Column Border dialog box works just like the Paragraph Border dialog box shown in Figure 37. Click the Border and Fill Style buttons to select a border and/or fill.

ADD A COLUMN BORDER AND FILL

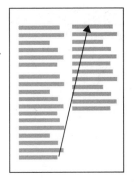

Figure 43. The text in newspaper columns flows down the page then up to the top of the next column.

Figure 44. The text in balanced newspaper columns flows down the page then up to the top of the next column just like regular newspaper columns but the bottom of each column is automatically lined up.

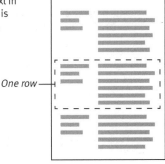

Figure 45. The text in parallel columns is grouped in rows.

One row

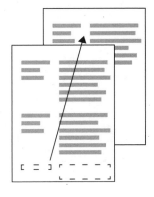

Figure 46. The text in parallel with block protect columns works like regular parallel columns, but rows are kept together on one page. If some of the text becomes too long for one page, then the entire row is moved to the next page.

Columns

Columns vertically divide text in a page, letting you create documents such as newsletters, lists, and inventories. You can define up to 24 columns on a page.

There are four types of columns:

◆ **Newspaper**—the text in a newspaper column flows down to the bottom of the page (or to a column break), then starts at the top again in the next column (**Figure 43**).

◆ **Balanced Newspaper**—this type of column is similar to normal newspaper columns, but WordPerfect automatically adjusts the bottom of the columns so they line up (**Figure 44**).

◆ **Parallel**—the text in parallel columns is grouped in rows across the page. The next row starts after the longest column in the previous row (**Figure 45**). This kind of column is handy for resumes.

◆ **Parallel with Block Protect**—this column type is similar to normal parallel columns, but rows are kept together on a page. If one row becomes too long to fit on that page, WordPerfect automatically moves the entire row to the next page (**Figure 46**).

Removing Borders and Fills

To remove page, paragraph, or column borders, just open the appropriate Border/Fill dialog box (they are shown in Figures 32, 37, and 41) and click the Off button found at the upper right.

To turn columns on:

1. Position the insertion point in the paragraph where you want the columns to start.

2. Choose Columns from the Format menu (**Figure 39**). The Define Columns dialog box will open (**Figure 47**).

3. In the Number of Columns area, type a number in the Columns text box.

4. Select a column type using the radio buttons in the Type area.

5. In the Column Spacing area, enter a measurement in the Spacing Between Columns text box. If you have selected Parallel or Parallel with Block Protect columns, also enter a measurement in the Line Spacing Between Rows in Parallel Columns text box.

6. In the Column Widths area, use the text boxes to set how wide the columns will be. WordPerfect automatically creates equal columns that span the page width, so if you don't want a custom column width or spacing, there's no need to set anything in this area.

7. Click OK. The column style you selected will appear in your document (**Figure 48**). Light gray *guidelines* will appear on the page, indicating where the columns are (these lines don't print).

✔ Tip

■ The column guidelines can be hidden. Turn to page 146 for details on how to do this.

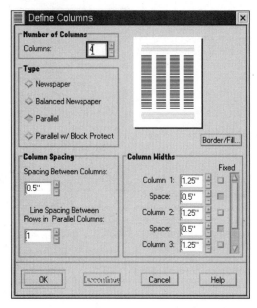

Figure 47. The Define Columns dialog box is used to set the number and type of columns, and how wide and far apart they are.

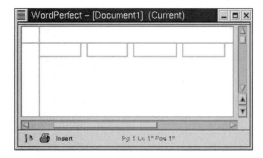

Figure 48. Light gray, non-printing guidelines appear in your document, indicating where the columns are.

Figure 49. Choose Ruler from the View menu.

TURN COLUMNS ON

Margin markers   Column width markers   Tab settings

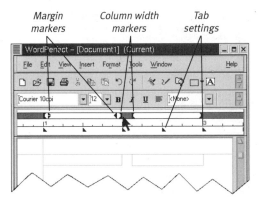

Figure 50. Reposition the column width markers on the Ruler Bar to change the width of the columns.

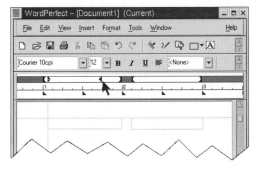

Figure 51. Drag the margin marker across the Ruler Bar to change the margin position.

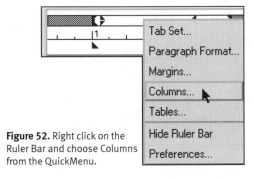

Figure 52. Right click on the Ruler Bar and choose Columns from the QuickMenu.

To edit columns using the Ruler Bar:

1. Position the insertion point within the columns you want to change.

2. Display the Ruler Bar if it isn't already available by choosing Ruler from the View menu (**Figure 49**).

3. Drag the column width markers to change how wide a column is (**Figure 50**). (You can also drag the tab settings to change their position in a column.)

4. Drag the margin markers to change where the left and right margins in a column are (**Figure 51**).

✔ Tip

■ To quickly open the Define Columns dialog box, right click on the Ruler Bar, and then choose Columns from the QuickMenu that appears (**Figure 52**).

To enter text in a column:

Position the insertion point in a column and type your text. To move to the next column, press Ctrl+Enter on the keyboard.

To move the insertion point from column to column:

Click the mouse in the column to which you want to move.

To turn columns off:

1. Position the insertion point where you want to turn the columns off.

2. Choose Columns from the Format menu (**Figure 39**). The Define Columns dialog box will open (**Figure 47**).

3. Click Discontinue. The dialog box will close.

Text Boxes

Just like the image boxes you used in Chapter 6, *Clipart, Lines, & Charts*, text boxes are also containers used to hold something. In this case, of course, text.

Text boxes can be placed anywhere on a document page, including margin areas. They are often used for text items, such as sidebars, callouts, or quotes, that need to be set off from the main body of the document. You can add borders and fills, set text wrapping, and add a caption to text boxes.

Figure 53. Choose Text Box from the Insert menu.

To insert a text box:

1. Use the shadow cursor to position the insertion point where you would like the text box to appear. (If you want to put a text box in the margin, position the insertion point as close as you can to that spot. You can move the text box once it's been created.)

2. Choose Text Box from the Insert menu (**Figure 53**). A text box will appear selected in the document and the insertion point will be inside the text box (**Figure 54**). Just like an Image box, eight black handles surround the selected text box in a rectangular formation.

3. Type your text just as you normally would, adding the formatting you need (**Figure 55**).

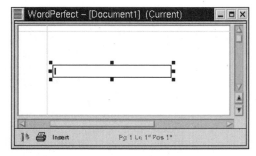

Figure 54. A text box appears selected in your document with the insertion point blinking inside it, ready for your text.

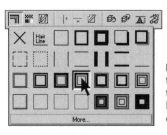

Figure 56. Click the Border button, then select a border from the drop-down list.

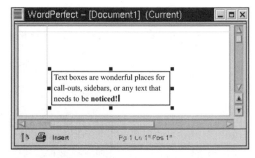

Figure 55. Type your text as you normally would, adding the formatting you need.

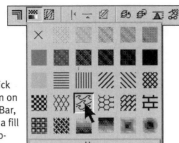

Figure 57. Click the Fill button on the Property Bar, then choose a fill from the drop-down list.

To add a border and fill to a text box:

1. Click the text box that you want to change to select it. You'll know it's selected when dashed lines appear around it.

2. Click the Border button on the Property Bar and select a border style from the drop-down list (**Figure 56**).

3. Click the Fill button on the Property Bar and select a fill from the drop-down list (**Figure 57**).

To resize a text box using the handles:

1. Click the text box that you want to change to select it. You'll know it's selected when dashed lines appear around it.

2. Position the mouse pointer over one of the eight handles.

3. Press the left mouse button and drag the handle to resize the box (**Figure 58**).

4. Release the mouse button when you are finished dragging the handle.

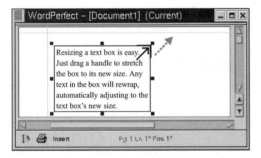

Figure 58. As you drag the handle, the text box stretches to its new shape. Any text in the box automatically rewraps to fit the new size of the text box.

✔ Tip

■ For more details on sizing text boxes using the handles, turn to pages 101–104 and follow the directions for sizing image boxes.

Figure 59. Right click on the text box and choose Size from the QuickMenu.

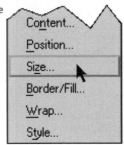

To resize a text box to exact measurements:

1. Click on white space to make sure nothing is selected in your document.

2. Right click on the text box you want to size and choose Size from the QuickMenu that appears (**Figure 59**). The Box Size dialog box will open (**Figure 60**).

3. In the Width and Height areas, you have the following options:

   ◆ **Set** makes the width or height of the text box exactly the measurement you type into the text box.

   ◆ **Full** stretches the text box the entire width (from left to right margins) or height (from top to bottom margins) of the page. If you select Full in both the Width and Height areas, the text box will cover the entire page.

   ◆ **Maintain proportions**—when this option is selected in one of the areas and an exact measurement is set in the other area, the text box will resize to keep its original width-to-height proportions.

4. When you have finished setting the width and height of the text box, click OK. The Box Size dialog box will close and the text box will change to its new size.

To move a text box:

1. Click the text box that you want to change to select it. You'll know it's selected when dashed lines appear around it.

2. Position the mouse pointer on the border of the text box.

3. Press the left mouse button and drag the text box to its new position (**Figure 61**).

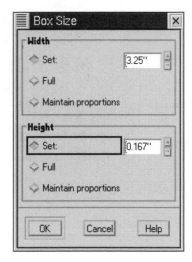

Figure 60. Use the Width and Height areas in the Box Size dialog box to set the exact dimensions of the text box.

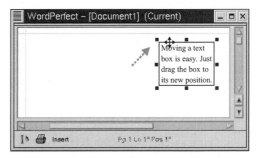

Figure 61. Position the mouse pointer over the border, press the left mouse button and drag the text box to its new position. When you are moving the text box, the mouse pointer changes to a four-headed arrow.

Figure 62. Right click on the text box and choose Caption from the QuickMenu.

RESIZE AND MOVE A TEXT BOX

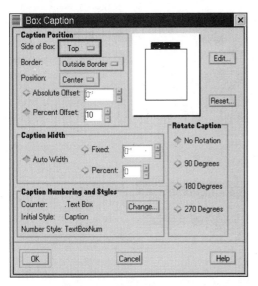

Figure 63. The Box Caption text box is used to set the caption's position, width, and text rotation.

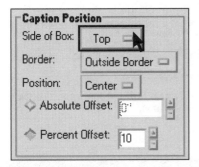

Figure 64. In the Caption Position area, set on which side of the text box the caption appears, whether it's inside, outside, or on the text box border, and whether it is left, center, or right justified.

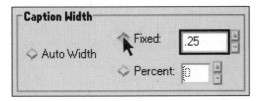

Figure 65. In the Caption Width area, you can set whether the caption is as wide as the text box, an exact measurement, or a percentage of the text box width.

To add a caption to a text box:

1. Click on white space to make sure nothing is selected in your document.

2. Right click on the text box and choose Caption from the QuickMenu that appears (**Figure 62**). The Box Caption dialog box will open (**Figure 63**).

3. In the Caption Position area (**Figure 64**), use the:

   ◆ **Side of Box** drop-down list to set where the caption will appear—top, bottom, left, or right.

   ◆ **Border** drop-down list to set whether the caption will appear outside, on, or in the border.

   ◆ **Position** drop-down list to left, center, or right justify the caption.

4. In the Caption Width area (**Figure 65**), select one of the following options:

   ◆ **Auto Width** sets the caption to the width of the text box.

   ◆ **Fixed** lets you set exactly how wide the caption is.

   ◆ **Percent** lets you set how wide the caption is in relation to the text box. A 50% setting means that the caption will be half the width of the text box.

5. In the Rotate Caption area you can select whether the text is not rotated, or is rotated 90, 180, or 270 degrees.

6. When you are finished selecting options, click Edit. The Box Caption dialog box will close, and the insertion point will be positioned in the new caption area.

7. To enter a caption, type your text.

8. When you are finished, click outside the caption to return to the document.

Styles

Styles let you quickly create consistently formatted documents by automatically setting text attributes. Styles also add a level of flexibility that you do not have if you format all your text "by hand." Changing a style *definition*, the text formatting that makes up a style, automatically changes all text in a document formatted with that style. For instance, instead of individually formatting each heading in a report, you could create a *style* for that report heading and apply it to all the headings. If you need to change the formatting of the headings, you merely revise the style.

There are two types of styles:

◆ **Character**—this type effects text formatting, such as font, font size, etc.

◆ **Paragraph**—this type effects paragraph formatting, such as justification, indentation, etc.

To create a style:

1. Format the text that you want to base your style on. (For instance, format one report heading the way you want all the report headings to look.)

2. Position the insertion point within that formatted text.

3. Choose Styles from the Format menu (**Figure 66**) or press Shift+Ctrl+F8 on the keyboard. The Style List dialog box will appear (**Figure 67**).

4. Click QuickStyle. The Styles QuickCreate dialog box will open (**Figure 68**).

5. Enter the name of your style in the Style Name text box.

6. Type a description of the style, if you wish, in the Description text box.

CREATE A STYLE

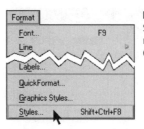

Figure 66. Choose Styles from the Format menu or press Shift+ Ctrl+F8 on the keyboard.

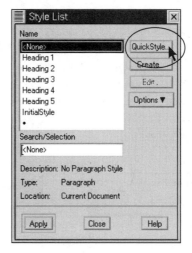

Figure 67. In the Style List dialog box, click the QuickStyle button.

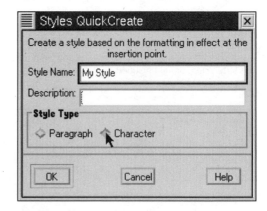

Figure 68. Enter a name for the style in the Style Name text box and set whether the style is a paragraph or character style.

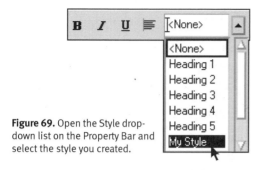

Figure 69. Open the Style drop-down list on the Property Bar and select the style you created.

Figure 70. Choose Make It Fit from the Format menu.

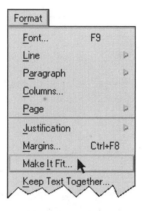

Figure 71. Set how many pages need to be filled and what formatting items should be adjusted.

7. In the Style Type area, select whether the style you are creating is a Paragraph or Character Style.

8. Click OK to close the Styles QuickCreate dialog box.

9. Click Close to close the Style List dialog box.

To use a style:

1. For a paragraph style, position the insertion point in the paragraph you want to format or for a character style, select the text you want to format.

2. Select your style from the Style drop-down list on the Property Bar (**Figure 69**).

Making Text Fit on the Page

The Make It Fit Expert is a wonderful, time-saving WordPerfect feature that will expand text to make it fit on the number of pages you specify or squash text to make it fit on just one page.

To use the Make It Fit Expert:

1. Open the document whose text you want to make fit.

2. Choose Make It Fit from the Format menu (**Figure 70**). The Make It Fit dialog box will appear (**Figure 71**).

3. In the Pages area, use the Desired Number of Filled Pages text box to set how many pages you would like to fill up with the document text.

4. In the Items to Adjust area, select the check boxes next to the formatting options you would like WordPerfect to use to make the text fit.

(continued)

USE A STYLE; THE MAKE IT FIT EXPERT

5. Click OK. The dialog box will close and the text and formatting options will be adjusted to fit the specified number of pages (**Figure 72**). In **Figure 72**, 6 lines of text have been adjusted to fit 1 entire page. As you can see, the results can be rather mixed sometimes.

✔ **Tip**

■ If you decide you do not like what the Make It Fit Expert has done to your document after you have applied it, immediately choose Undo from the Edit menu. Your document will return to its original form.

THE MAKE IT FIT EXPERT

Figure 72. The Make It Fit Expert comes up with interesting results sometimes. The heading in this figure has been enlarged to 30 point type and the text has been moved to the bottom of the page, far away from the header.

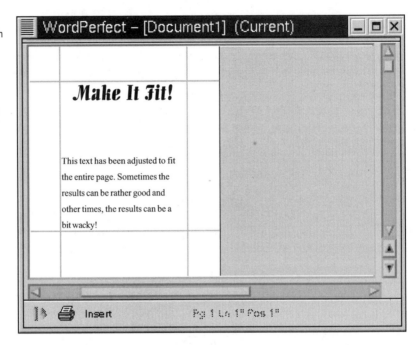

Summary

In this chapter you learned how to:

◆ Change text color

◆ Add highlighting

◆ Add line numbering

◆ Add bulleted and numbered lists

◆ Create drop caps

◆ Add borders and fills to pages, paragraphs, and columns

◆ Turn columns on and off

◆ Insert text boxes

◆ Create new styles

◆ Make text fit on a page

PAGE AND DOCUMENT SETUP

WordPerfect isn't your grandfather's word processor! (But wait! Did your grandfather have a word processor?) Besides being able to handle text and images in many ways, WordPerfect 8 includes desktop publishing capabilities. This means that besides creating just letters and reports, you can create many types of multi-page page publications such as brochures, flyers, and catalogs. In addition, you can create documents for any paper size that is used anywhere in the world. In the past, all this would have required separate desktop publishing software.

In this chapter you will learn how to set page size and orientation. Then you will set margins, view and hide margin guidelines, and set the text's vertical alignment on the page. From there you will add pages and page numbers to a document, move between pages, and insert a *subdocument* into a *master document*.

Which Way is My Page Oriented?

The term *page orientation* refers to the way a page is situated. If the page is taller than it is wide, it is in *portrait* orientation. If the page is wider than it is tall, it is in *landscape* orientation.

This is a portrait page.

This is a landscape page.

To select a page size and orientation:

1. Choose Page Size from the Page Setup fly-out on the Page fly-out on the Format menu (**Figure 1**). The Paper Size dialog box will open (**Figure 2**).

2. Select a paper size and orientation from the list box in the Available Paper Definitions area (**Figure 3**).

3. Click OK. The dialog box will close and the page in the document window will change to assume the size and orientation you selected.

✔ Tip

- If you don't see the paper size and/or orientation you need in the list box, you can create a new paper definition to suit your needs. See the next section for details on how to do this.

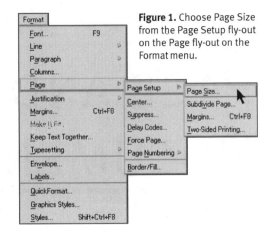

Figure 1. Choose Page Size from the Page Setup fly-out on the Page fly-out on the Format menu.

Figure 2. The Paper Size dialog box is used to select and create paper definitions.

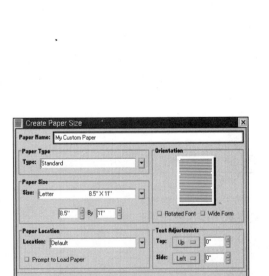

Figure 4. Use the Create Paper Size dialog box to set your own custom paper definition.

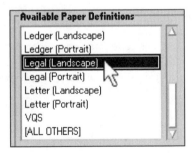

Figure 3. Select the paper definition that you want to use from the list box.

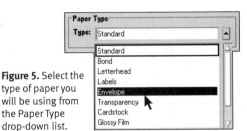

Figure 5. Select the type of paper you will be using from the Paper Type drop-down list.

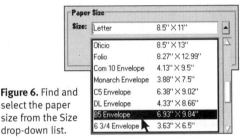

Figure 6. Find and select the paper size from the Size drop-down list.

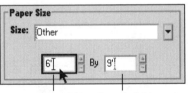

Paper width   Paper height

Figure 7. If you can't find the paper dimensions you need in the drop-down list, select Other, and then enter the paper measurements in the text boxes.

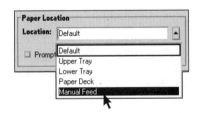

Figure 8. From the Location drop-down list, select where you will be feeding the paper into the printer.

To create a new paper definition:

1. Choose Page Size from the Page Setup fly-out on the Page fly-out on the Format menu (**Figure 1**). The Paper Size dialog box will open (**Figure 2**).

2. Click Create. The Create Paper Size dialog box will open (**Figure 4**).

3. Type a descriptive name for your paper in the Paper Name text box.

4. In the Paper Type area, use the Type drop-down list to select the kind of paper you will be using, such as letterhead, envelope, or cardstock (**Figure 5**).

5. In the Paper Size area, use the Size drop-down list to select the paper dimensions that match what you need (**Figure 6**). If you don't see exactly what you want, scroll to the bottom of the list and select Other.

6. If you selected Other, use the text boxes below the Size drop-down list to enter the exact measurements you need (**Figure 7**). The left text box sets the width and the right text box sets the height of the paper.

7. In the Paper Location area, use the Location drop-down list to select which printer paper feed location you want to use (**Figure 8**).

8. If you want WordPerfect to ask you to load the paper in the printer, make sure the box next to Prompt to Load Paper is selected in the Paper Location area.

9. To set where the text prints on your custom page, use the Top and Side drop-down lists and text boxes in the Text Adjustments area to set what you need. This can be very handy to make sure that text is printed within a specific area since all printers have an unprintable zone.

(continued)

10. To set the way the paper is loaded into the printer and whether the text is rotated, use the Orientation area (**Figure 9**). Depending upon the capabilities of your printer, you can feed the narrow edge of the paper into the printer or rotate the paper 90 degrees and feed the wide edge into the printer. In addition, WordPerfect can print a page with the text oriented the way one reads or with the text rotated 90 degrees. The four possible text and paper orientation combinations are displayed in **Figures 10a–d**.

If you need to use a special text and paper orientation, select the check box(es) next to Rotated Font and/or Wide Form.

11. Click OK. The Create Paper Size dialog box will close and the paper definition you just created will appear in the list box in the Available Paper Definitions area of the Paper Size dialog box (**Figure 11**).

12. To use your new paper definition, highlight it in the list box, then click OK. The Paper Size dialog box will close and your document will assume the custom paper size, changing to the newly specified dimensions.

✔ Tip

■ If you are sharing a printer with other folks, you will need to log on as an administrator to create a new paper definition.

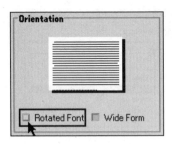

Figure 9. The Orientation area is used to set whether the font and paper are rotated.

Figure 10a. No font rotation, no form rotation.

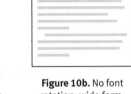

Figure 10b. No font rotation, wide form.

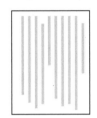

Figure 10c. Font rotation, no form rotation.

Figure 10d. Font rotation, wide form.

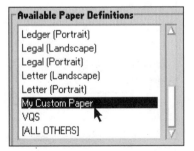

Figure 11. The custom paper definition you created appears in the Available Paper Definitions list box, ready for use.

CREATE A NEW PAPER DEFINITION

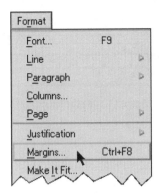

Figure 12. Choose Margins from the Format menu.

Margin strip

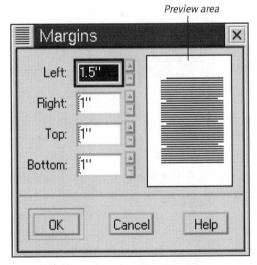

Figure 13. Right click on the margin strip at the top of the Ruler Bar and choose Margins from the QuickMenu.

Preview area

Figure 14. Enter a measurement in the appropriate text box in the Margins dialog box. The setting you enter is displayed in the preview area.

Page Margins and Margin Guidelines

Margins are the white spaces between the edges of the page and the text. The width of the margins is shown on the page as gray, non-printing *guidelines*. The WordPerfect margin default is 1" on all sides—top, bottom, left, and right. You can use the Margins dialog box to set any of the page margins or the Ruler Bar to set the left and right margins.

To set all page margins:

1. For side margins, select the paragraphs you want to change.

   or

   Position the insertion point anywhere on the page whose top and/or bottom margins you want to change.

2. Choose Margins from the Format menu (**Figure 12**) or press Ctrl+F8 on the keyboard or right click on the margin strip on the Ruler Bar and choose Margins from the QuickMenu (**Figure 13**). The Margins dialog box will appear (**Figure 14**).

3. Type a measurement into the text box(es) next to the margin(s) you want to change. The tiny page in the preview area will display the settings you have entered.

4. Click OK. The Margins dialog box will close and the margins in the document will change.

✔ Tip

■ If you want to use the Ruler Bar and it's not displayed, choose Ruler from the View menu.

To set the left and right margins using the Ruler Bar:

1. Select the paragraphs whose left and/or right margins you want to change.

2. On the margin strip at the top of the Ruler Bar, drag the left or right margin marker to a new position (**Figure 15**). The left or right margin in the document will move to the new position.

To display or hide margin guidelines:

1. Choose Guidelines from the View menu (**Figure 16**). The Guidelines dialog box will appear (**Figure 17**).

2. To display margin guidelines, select the check box next to Margins. To hide margin guidelines, deselect the check box next to Margins.

3. Click OK. The margin guidelines will display or hide depending upon whether you selected the check box or not.

SET LEFT/RIGHT MARGINS; DISPLAY MARGINS

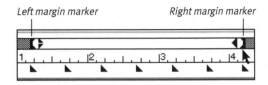

Left margin marker   Right margin marker

Figure 15. Drag the left or right margin marker to a new position.

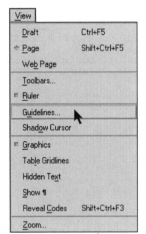

Figure 16. Choose Guidelines from the View menu.

Displaying Guidelines

The Guidelines dialog box (**Figure 17**) can be used to set whether table, margin, column, or header/footer guidelines are visible as you work on a document. If there are guidelines you always want to view, select them in the Turn Guidelines On area, then select the check box next to Use as Default. Every time you use WordPerfect, the guidelines you selected will be visible.

Figure 17. Use the Guidelines dialog box to set whether the margin guidelines are visible or not.

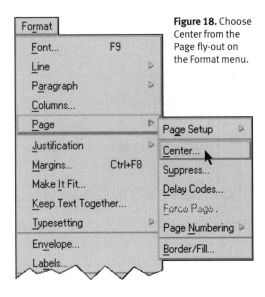

Figure 18. Choose Center from the Page fly-out on the Format menu.

Vertical Text Alignment

After setting the top and bottom margins, you can also tell WordPerfect to vertically center the text on a page.

To center text between the top and bottom margins:

1. Position the insertion point on the page that contains the text you want to center.

2. Choose Center from the Page fly-out on the Format menu (**Figure 18**). The Center Page(s) dialog box will appear (**Figure 19**).

3. In the Center area, you can select a radio button to set WordPerfect to:

   ◆ Center the text on the current page

   ◆ Center the text on the current page and any pages after the current page

   ◆ Not center the text on the page

4. When you have selected an option, click OK. The dialog box will close and the text will move to the vertical center of the page (**Figure 20**).

✔ Tip

■ To turn vertical text centering off on a page, position the insertion point on that page, open the Center Page(s) dialog box, and then select the No Centering option in the Center area.

Figure 19. Use the Center area to set whether the text is centered on the current page, subsequent pages, or not centered.

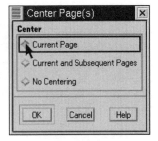

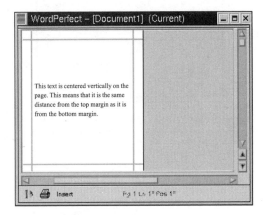

Figure 20. The text is centered vertically on the page.

Headers and Footers

Headers and footers are commonly used to place dates, page numbers, titles, or a company name at the top or bottom of each page, or on alternating pages, in a document.

WordPerfect lets you use two different headers—*Header A* and *Header B*—and two different footers—*Footer A* and *Footer B*—at any place in a document. Only two headers and two footers can be active at one time on a page.

To create a header or footer:

1. Position the insertion point in the first paragraph on the page where you want the header or footer to first appear.

2. Choose Header/Footer from the Insert menu (**Figure 21**). The Headers/Footers dialog box will open (**Figure 22**).

3. In the Select area, click the radio button next to the header or footer you want to create.

4. Click Create. The dialog box will close and header or footer guidelines will appear at the top or bottom of the document (**Figure 23**). The insertion point will be positioned within the header or footer, ready for typing. Special header/footer command buttons will appear on the Property Bar (**Figure 24**).

5. Type your header or footer text as you normally would, using any formatting or editing features that you would like.

6. Click the Header/Footer Distance button on the Property Bar. The Distance dialog box will open (**Figure 25**). Use the Distance Between Text and Header (or Footer) text box to set the exact distance.

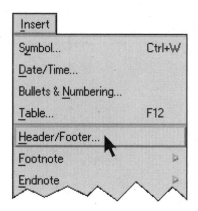

Figure 21. Choose Header/Footer from the Insert menu.

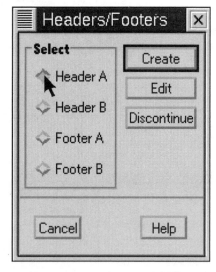

Figure 22. Select the header or footer you want to create using the radio buttons, then click Create.

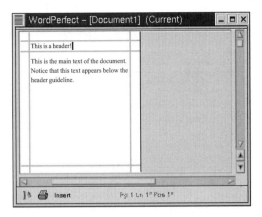

Figure 23. Depending upon whether you are creating a header or footer, guidelines will appear indicating the position of the header or footer. In this figure, a header is being created.

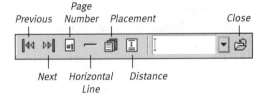

Figure 24. When the insertion point is positioned within a header or footer, header/footer specific command buttons appear on the Property Bar.

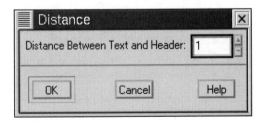

Figure 25. Enter a measurement in the Distance Between Text and Header text box, then click OK.

7. Click OK to close the Distance dialog box. The header or footer guideline will move to indicate the distance measurement you set.

8. Click the Header/Footer Placement button on the Property Bar. The Placement dialog box will open (**Figure 26**).

9. Use the radio buttons in the Place On area to set whether the header or footer will appear on odd or even pages or on every page.

10. Click OK to close the Placement dialog box.

11. When you are finished creating the header or footer, click the Close Header/Footer button on the Property Bar or click in the document window outside of the header or footer area. The insertion point will return to the main body of the document.

Figure 26. Use the Placement dialog box to set how often a header or footer appears—on odd or even pages or on every page.

To quickly move between headers and footers:

Position the insertion point in a header or footer, then click the Previous Header/Footer button.

or

The Next Header/Footer button on the Property Bar.

To edit a header or footer:

1. Click anywhere inside the header or footer you want to edit.

2. Edit the header or footer text as you would normally edit text (**Figure 27**).

3. Click the Close Header/Footer button on the Property Bar or click in the document window outside of the header or footer area. The insertion point will return to the main body of the document.

To turn off a header or footer:

1. Position the insertion point on the page where you want to turn off the header or footer. (Don't place the insertion point in the header or footer.)

2. Open the Headers/Footers dialog box (**Figure 28**) by choosing Header/Footer from the Insert menu (**Figure 21**).

3. Use the Select area to choose which header or footer to turn off.

4. Click Discontinue.

5. Click OK. The dialog box will close and the header or footer will no longer appear on any page beyond the current one.

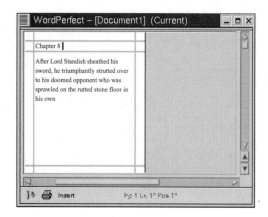

Figure 27. Edit the header or footer text just as you would normal body text, including changing typefaces and formatting.

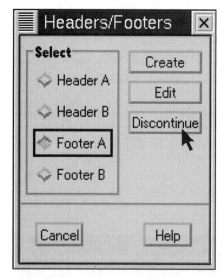

Figure 28. Select the header or footer you want to turn off using the radio buttons, then click Discontinue.

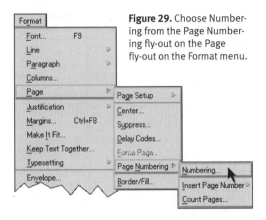

Figure 29. Choose Numbering from the Page Numbering fly-out on the Page fly-out on the Format menu.

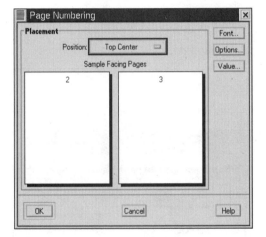

Figure 30. Set where the page numbers appear on the page using the Position drop-down list.

Figure 31.
You can select a special font for the page numbers using the Page Numbering Font dialog box.

To add the date to a header or footer:

Create a new header or footer or edit an existing one, position the insertion point where you want to place the date, and then press Ctrl+D on the keyboard.

To add page numbers:

1. Position the insertion point on the page where you want the numbering to begin.

2. Choose Numbering from the Page Numbering fly-out on the Page fly-out on the Format menu (**Figure 29**). The Page Numbering dialog box will appear (**Figure 30**).

3. Use the Position drop-down list to set where the page number will appear on the page. A preview of the positioning will appear in the preview area below the drop-down list.

4. To set a font for the page numbering that is different than the default document font, click the Font button and use the Page Numbering Font dialog box (**Figure 31**).

5. Click OK. The page numbers will appear in your document.

Inserting Page Numbers while Working in Headers or Footers

You can quickly add page numbers to a document when you are working in a header or footer. With the insertion point positioned inside a header or footer, click the Page Number button on the Property Bar (**Figure 24**).

The Suppress Command

You can use the Suppress command to tell WordPerfect to hide headers, footers, or a page number on a specific page.

To hide headers, footers, or a page number on a specific page:

1. Move the insertion point to the page where you want to hide the headers, footers, or page number.

2. Choose Suppress from the Page fly-out on the Format menu (**Figure 32**). The Suppress dialog box will open (**Figure 33**).

3. Use the Suppress On Current Page area to set which items you want to hide— headers, footers, or page numbering.

4. Click OK. The items you selected will be hidden on that specific page.

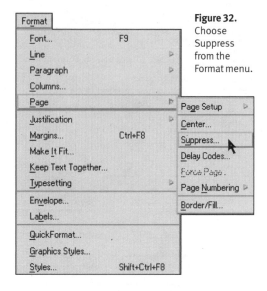

Figure 32. Choose Suppress from the Format menu.

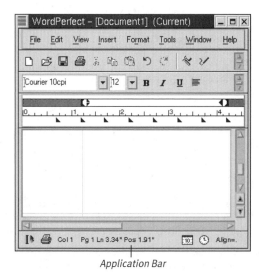

Application Bar

Figure 34. The Application Bar is located at the bottom of the document window.

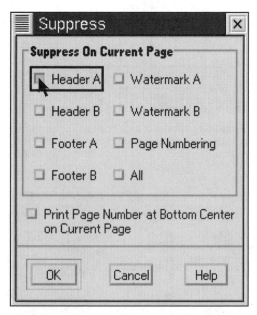

Figure 33. Select the items you want to hide on the current page. You can also print a centered page number by selecting Print Page Number at Bottom Center on Current Page.

Figure 35. Choose Toolbars from the View menu to open the Toolbars dialog box.

Figure 36. Select or deselect Application Bar depending upon whether you want to show or hide it.

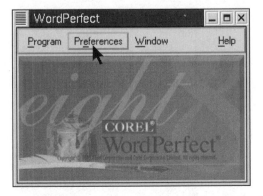

Figure 37. Choose Preferences in the program window.

The Application Bar

The Application Bar is displayed at the bottom of the document window (**Figure 34**). It lets you quickly see information related to the document on which you are working. By default, the Application Bar shows the font you are using, the position of the insertion point, information about columns, mergers, or tables, if you are using any of these features, and whether you are in insert or typeover mode.

You can show or hide the Application Bar as you please and customize the information it displays, as well.

To show/hide the Application Bar:

1. Choose Toolbars from the View menu (**Figure 35**). The Toolbars dialog box will appear (**Figure 36**).

2. To show the Application Bar, select the check box next to Application Bar in the Available toolbars list box. To hide the Application Bar, deselect the Application Bar item.

3. Click OK. The Application Bar will appear or disappear.

To customize Application Bar information:

1. In the program window, choose Preferences (**Figure 37**). The Preferences dialog box will open (**Figure 38**).

2. Click Application Bar. The Application Bar Preferences dialog box will appear (**Figure 39**).

3. Use the Select items to appear on the bar list box to set which items will be displayed.

4. Click OK. The Application Bar Preferences dialog box will close, returning you to the Preferences dialog box.

5. Click Close to close the Preferences dialog box and return to the document window. The items you selected to appear on the Application Bar will display (**Figure 40**).

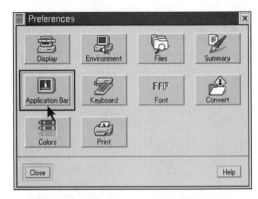

Figure 38. Click the Application Bar button in the Preferences dialog box.

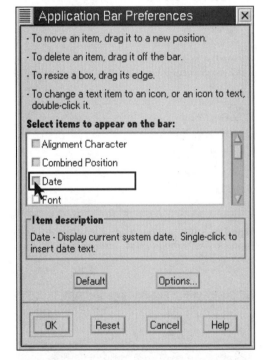

Figure 39. From the list box, select the items that you want to appear on the Application Bar.

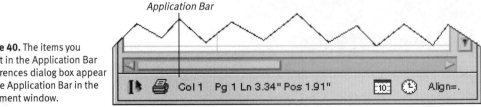

Figure 40. The items you select in the Application Bar Preferences dialog box appear on the Application Bar in the document window.

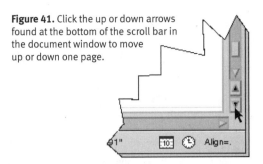

Figure 41. Click the up or down arrows found at the bottom of the scroll bar in the document window to move up or down one page.

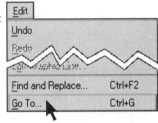

Figure 42. Choose Go To from the Edit menu or press Ctrl+G on the keyboard.

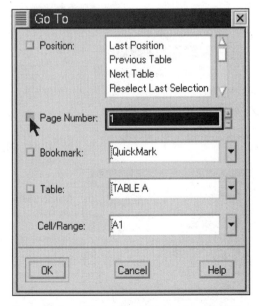

Figure 43. Enter the number of the page you would like to go to in the Page Number text box, then click OK.

Go Where You Want to Go

You can quickly move through a document using the up and down arrows on the scroll bar at the bottom right of the document window or the Go To command.

To move from page to page using the scroll bar arrows:

At the bottom right of the document window, click the up arrow to move up one page or click the down arrow to move down one page (**Figure 41**).

To go to a specific page:

1. Choose Go To from the Edit menu (**Figure 42**) or press Ctrl+G on the keyboard. The Go To dialog box will appear (**Figure 43**).

2. Make sure the check box next to Page Number is selected, then enter the number of the page in the corresponding text box.

3. Click OK. The insertion point will be moved to the top of the page you specified.

✔ Tip

■ If text is selected or if the insertion point is in a column or table, the Go To dialog box options will automatically change to let you move around those areas.

Master Documents and Subdocuments

As you probably know, it is easier to edit a small document than it is to edit a very big one (imagine editing the single document that would make up a 900-page book!)

Master documents are used to manage large documents. Instead of creating one monster-sized document, a large project can be split up into smaller, more manageable *subdocuments* that are *linked* to a master document (**Figure 44**).

When a subdocument is linked to a master document, that link is displayed in the master document. Master documents can be *expanded* in order to print or display the entire document. Once you've printed or displayed the entire document, the master document can then be *condensed* back to its previous form.

To create a master document and insert a subdocument:

1. Open the document you want to use as the master document.

2. Position the insertion point where you want to insert a subdocument.

3. Choose Subdocument form the Document fly-out on the File menu (**Figure 45**). The Include Subdocument dialog box will open (**Figure 46**).

4. Click the list button to the right of the Subdocument Name text box. The Select File dialog box will appear (**Figure 47**).

5. Use the Directory List box to move to the directory where the document you want to include is stored.

6. Highlight the document in the File List box.

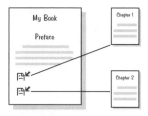

Master document   Subdocuments

Figure 44. When subdocuments are inserted into a master document, they are linked to the master document. A tiny icon appears in the master document indicating where the subdocument is inserted.

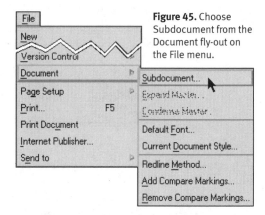

Figure 45. Choose Subdocument from the Document fly-out on the File menu.

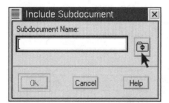

Figure 46. Click the list button to browse for a subdocument file.

Figure 47. Use the Directory and File List boxes to select a subdocument file.

Figure 48. The full path of the file you selected appears in the Subdocument Name text box.

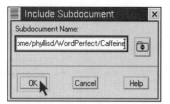

7. Click Select. The Select File dialog box will close and the full pathname of the file you selected will appear in the text box in the Include Subdocument dialog box (**Figure 48**).

8. Click OK. The Include Subdocument dialog box will close and a tiny subdocument icon will appear in the left margin of the master document.

Figure 49. Click the tiny subdocument icon to view the full pathname.

✔ Tip

■ To view the path and document name of a subdocument, click on the subdocument icon in the left margin of the master document. A balloon will appear displaying the full path (**Figure 49**).

To expand a master document:

1. Open the master document you want to expand.

2. Choose Expand Master from the Document fly-out on the File menu (**Figure 50**). The Expand Master Document dialog box will open (**Figure 51**).

3. In the Subdocuments list box, select the check boxes next to the subdocuments you want expanded into the master document. To select all subdocuments in a master document, click Mark All.

4. Click OK. The Expand Master Document dialog box will close and the subdocuments you selected will appear in the master document.

Figure 50. Choose Expand Master from the Document fly-out on the File menu.

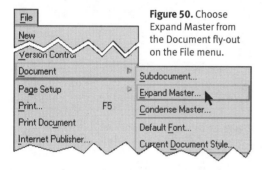

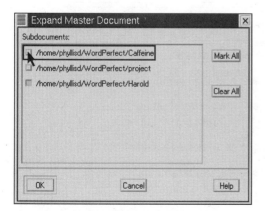

Figure 51. Select the subdocuments you want to expand in the list box, then click OK. By default, all subdocuments are selected.

To condense a master document:

1. If it's not already displayed in the document window, open the master document you want to condense.

2. Choose Condense Master from the Document fly-out on the File menu (**Figure 52**). The Condense/Save Subdocuments dialog box will appear (**Figure 53**).

3. In the Subdocuments list box, deselect the subdocuments you would like to condense. By default, all subdocuments are selected.

4. Click OK. The master document returns to its pre-expanded form.

✔ Tip

■ If you make any changes to a subdocument while it is expanded in the master document, you can save those changes using the Condense/Save Subdocuments dialog box. Just select the check boxes next to the subdocuments marked Save, then click Save All.

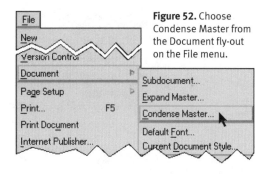

Figure 52. Choose Condense Master from the Document fly-out on the File menu.

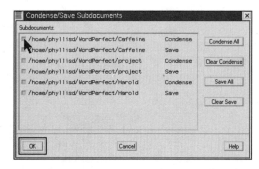

Figure 53. Select the subdocuments you want to condense, then click OK. By default, all subdocuments are selected.

Summary

In this chapter you learned how to:

◆ Set page size and orientation

◆ Create a new custom paper definition

◆ Set margins

◆ View/hide margin guidelines

◆ Create headers and footers

◆ Edit headers and footers

◆ Add page numbers to a document

◆ Change Application Bar information

◆ Move between pages

◆ Insert subdocuments into a master document

◆ Expand and condense a master document

CHECK YOUR WORK

Good grammar and spelling are as important in the creation of a professional document as good layout. WordPerfect comes with five tools that help you quickly find and fix the mistakes in your documents.

In this chapter you will learn how to use several tools:

- **QuickCorrect** automatically replaces common spelling errors and mistyped words. It can also be used to expand abbreviations. For instance, when writing this book, I needed to type "dialog box" several hundred times. Instead of typing both words out every time, I would type "db" and QuickCorrect would automatically change it to "dialog box."

- **Spell-As-You-Go** gives immediate access to Word-Perfect's dictionary. If it finds a word that is possibly misspelled, diagonal red stripes appear beneath the word.

- **Spell Check** is used to search documents for misspelled words, words that have been duplicated, and capitalization errors.

- **Grammar-As-You-Go** lets you check your grammar as you type. If it finds a word or phrase that may have a grammatical error, diagonal blue stripes appear beneath the word or phrase.

- **Grammatik** is used to check documents for spelling, punctuation, grammar, and stylistic mistakes. With Grammatik, you can set up custom writing styles, depending upon the types of writing you do. A few of the predefined styles are advertising, fiction, memo, and technical.

QuickCorrect

Besides automatically replacing spelling mistakes, mistyped words, and abbreviations, QuickCorrect can also be used to insert *SmartQuotes*—typographer's quotation marks—in place of straight single and double quotes, and fix such problems as two spaces between words and two uppercase letters at the beginning of a sentence.

Another QuickCorrect option is called *Format-As-You-Go*. Format-As-You-Go helps you insert formatting elements, such as bulleted and numbered lists, ordinal numbers, and lines, as you type.

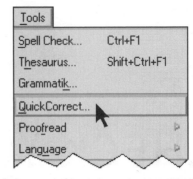

Figure 1. Choose QuickCorrect from the Tools menu.

To turn QuickCorrect on or off:

1. Choose QuickCorrect from the Tools menu (**Figure 1**). The QuickCorrect dialog box will appear with the QuickCorrect radio button selected at the top (**Figure 2**).

2. To turn QuickCorrect on, make sure the check boxes next to Replace words as you type and Correct other mis-typed words when possible are selected. To turn QuickCorrect off, deselect the check boxes.

3. Click OK. The QuickCorrect dialog box will close and will be on or off depending upon whether you selected the check boxes or not.

✔ Tip

■ By default, QuickCorrect is turned on when you launch WordPerfect for the first time.

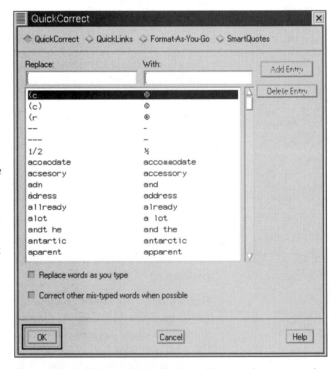

Figure 2. The QuickCorrect dialog box is used to set replacement words for misspelled words or abbreviations, automatically insert SmartQuotes, and set Format-As-You-Go options.

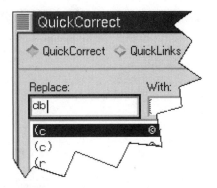

Figure 3. Type the misspelled word or abbreviation in the Replace text box.

To add a new entry to QuickCorrect:

1. Choose QuickCorrect from the Tools menu (**Figure 1**). The QuickCorrect dialog box will appear with the QuickCorrect radio button selected at the top (**Figure 2**).

2. In the Replace text box, enter the incorrect spelling of a word you usually misspell, or type an abbreviation for a word or several words that you would like replaced as you type (**Figure 3**).

3. In the With text box, enter the correct spelling for the word or the word(s) you would like replaced by the abbreviation (**Figure 4**).

4. Click Add Entry.

5. Continue adding as many words or abbreviations as you would like in the Replace and With text boxes, following the steps 2–4 above.

6. When you are finished entering words, click OK. The QuickCorrect dialog box will close. The next time you type one of the misspelled words or abbreviations you entered, QuickCorrect will replace the text after you press the space bar on the keyboard.

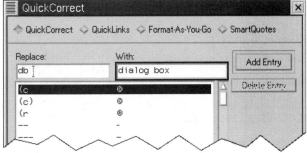

Figure 4. Type the correctly spelled word or the word(s) that will replace the abbreviation.

✔ Tip

■ Make sure the check box next to Replace words as you type is selected in the QuickCorrect dialog box (**Figure 5**). Otherwise, QuickCorrect will be turned off.

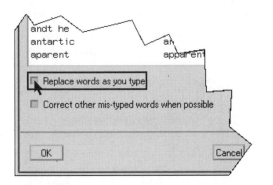

Figure 5. Make sure the check box next to Replace words as you type is selected, otherwise, QuickCorrect will be turned off.

ADD A NEW ENTRY TO QUICKCORRECT

To turn on SmartQuotes:

1. Choose QuickCorrect from the Tools menu (**Figure 1**). The QuickCorrect dialog box will appear with the QuickCorrect radio button selected at the top (**Figure 2**).

2. Select the SmartQuotes radio button. The QuickCorrect dialog box will change to display SmartQuote options (**Figure 6**).

3. In the Select quotation marks area, select the check boxes next to the options you would like to turn on:

   ◆ **Use double quotation marks as you type** replaces straight double quotation marks with typographer's double quotes.

   ◆ **Use single quotation marks as you type** replaces straight single quotation marks with typographer's single quotes.

   ◆ **Use straight quotation marks after numbers**. This is handy if you are typing measurements and don't want to have to turn SmartQuotes off every time you need a straight quote to indicate inches or feet.

4. Click OK. The QuickCorrect dialog box will close. The next time you type a single or double quote, it will automatically be replaced with a typographer's quote.

✔ Tip

■ You can set the type of typographer's quotes that are used by clicking the drop-down list button next to the Open and Close text boxes in the Select quotation marks area (**Figure 7**).

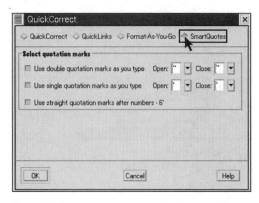

Figure 6. Click the SmartQuotes radio button at the upper right of the dialog box to display SmartQuote options.

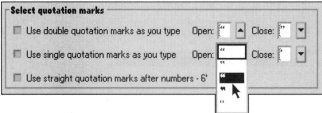

Figure 7. Use the drop-down lists next to Open and Close to select the types of quotation marks you would like as the automatic replacements.

WordPerfect's Proofreading Tools are Good, but...

...there's no substitute for reading a document carefully to manually check for mistakes. While WordPerfect's Spell Check and Grammatik tools are a great way to help you quickly find and fix errors, they aren't perfect. Computers help us do many things, but they are still tools and no substitute for humans!

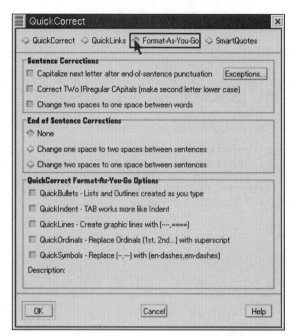

Figure 8. Click the Format-As-You-Go radio button near the top of the QuickCorrect dialog box to access Format-As-You-Go options.

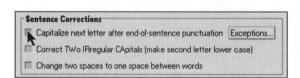

Figure 9. In the Sentence Corrections area, select the check boxes next to the options you would like to turn on—capitalize the letter after a period, make the second capital letter lowercase when two capitals appear together, or change two spaces to one space between words.

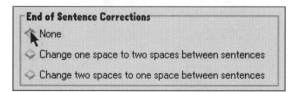

Figure 10. In the End of Sentence Corrections area, select the radio button that suits your needs—no corrections, change one space to two spaces between sentences, or change two spaces to one space between sentences.

To turn SmartQuotes off:

1. Choose QuickCorrect from the Tools menu (**Figure 1**). The QuickCorrect dialog box will appear with the QuickCorrect radio button selected at the top (**Figure 2**).

2. Select the SmartQuotes radio button and deselect the boxes in the Select quotation marks area (**Figure 6**).

3. Click OK to close the QuickCorrect dialog box.

To turn on Format-As-You-Go:

1. Choose QuickCorrect from the Tools menu (**Figure 1**). The QuickCorrect dialog box will appear with the QuickCorrect radio button selected at the top (**Figure 2**).

2. Select the Format-As-You-Go radio button. The QuickCorrect dialog box will change to display Format-As-You-Go options (**Figure 8**).

3. In the Sentence Corrections area (**Figure 9**), select the check boxes next to the options to capitalize the next letter after a period, make the second capital letter lowercase when two capital letters appear together, or change two spaces to one between words.

4. In the End of Sentence Corrections area (**Figure 10**), select a radio button to set no corrections, change one space to two between sentences, or change two spaces to one between sentences.

(continued)

5. In the QuickCorrect Format-As-You-Go Options area (**Figure 11**), select the check boxes next to the options to use:

◆ **QuickBullets**—automatically adds bullets or numbers to lists as you type. To start a bulleted list, type a lowercase o, then press the Tab key. To start a numbered list, type a number followed by a period, then press the Tab key. To end the list, press Enter after the last list item, then press the Backspace key.

◆ **QuickIndent**—adds an indent to a paragraph if the tab key is pressed at the beginning of any line except the first one in a paragraph.

◆ **QuickLines**—inserts a single or double horizontal line from the left to right margins by typing four hyphens (-) or equal signs (=) at the beginning of a line, and then pressing Enter.

◆ **QuickOrdinals**—automatically converts an ordinal number to superscript. For example 2nd, becomes 2nd.

◆ **QuickSymbols**—replaces 2 hyphens (--) with an en-dash (–) and 3 hyphens (---) with an em-dash (—).

6. When you have finished selecting Format-As-You-Go options, click OK. The QuickCorrect dialog box will close. The next time type a Format-As-You-Go item, such as an ordinal number, WordPerfect will automatically format it for you.

To turn Format-As-You-Go off:

Open the QuickCorrect dialog box, select the Format-As-You-Go radio button, then deselect all check boxes in the dialog box.

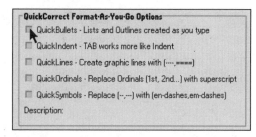

Figure 11. In the QuickCorrect Format-As-You-Go Options area, select the check boxes next to the items you want to turn on—QuickBullets, QuickIndent, Quick-Lines, QuickOrdinal, or QuickSymbols. Everything in this area is very quick!

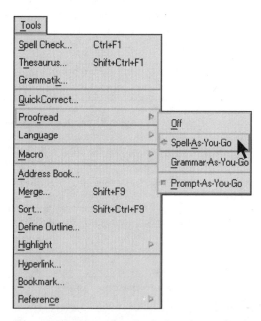

Figure 12. Choose Spell-As-You-Go from the Proofread fly-out on the Tools menu.

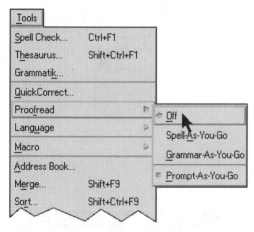

Figure 13. Choose Off from the Proofread fly-out on the Tools menu to turn Spell-As-You-Go off.

Figure 14. Choose the correctly spelled word from the Spell-As-You-Go menu, or if you know the word is spelled correctly but isn't in the WordPerfect dictionary, click Add to enter the word to the dictionary, or click Skip in Document to pass over future occurrences of the word.

Spell-As-You-Go

As you type, Spell-As-You-Go automatically checks your words, looking for any misspellings. If Spell-As-You-Go finds a word that it thinks is incorrect or is not included in the WordPerfect dictionary, diagonal red stripes appear beneath the word.

To turn on Spell-As-You-Go:

Choose Spell-As-You-Go from the Proofread fly-out on the Tools menu (**Figure 12**). When Spell-As-You-Go is on, a tiny diamond appears to the left of the menu item.

✔ Tips

■ Spell-As-You-Go and Grammar-As-You-Go cannot be turned on at the same time.

■ To turn Spell-As-You-Go off, choose Off from the Proofread fly-out on the Tools menu (**Figure 13**).

To correct possible misspellings:

1. Position the mouse pointer over the word underscored with red diagonal stripes and click the right mouse button. The Spell-As-You-Go menu will open, showing a list of possible alternative words (**Figure 14**).

2. Choose the correct spelling from the list.

   or

   If you know the word is spelled correctly, this means that it is not in the Word-Perfect dictionary. Choose Add to enter the word into the dictionary or Skip in Document to have the speller ignore the word for the rest of the document.

   The Spell-As-You-Go menu will disappear and the word's spelling will be corrected.

Spell Check

You can spell check an entire document at once using WordPerfect's Spell Check feature.

To spell check a document:

1. Open the document you want to spell check.

2. Choose Spell Check from the Tools menu (**Figure 15**) or press Ctrl+F1 on the keyboard. The Spell Checker dialog box will open (**Figure 16**) and several things will happen:

   ◆ The first word the Spell Checker finds wrong will be underlined.

   ◆ The misspelled word will appear next to Not found in the Spell Checker dialog box.

   ◆ The Spell Checker's first suggested replacement will appear in the Replace With text box.

   ◆ A list of other possible spellings or words will appear in the Suggestions list box.

3. You can:

   ◆ Click Replace to substitute the misspelled word with the word in the Replace With text box.

   ◆ Highlight one of the words in the Suggestions list box, then click Replace.

   ◆ Click Skip Once or Skip Always to pass over the word this one time or for the entire document.

   ◆ Click Add to add the word next to Not found to the WordPerfect dictionary.

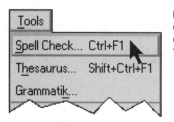

Figure 15. Choose Spell Check from the Tools menu.

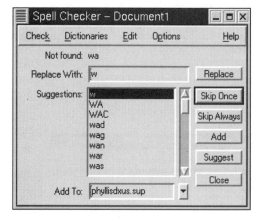

Figure 16. The Spell Checker dialog box opens and spell checking automatically begins. The first possible error is displayed next to Not found and a possible replacement is displayed in the Replace With text box.

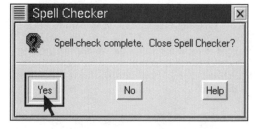

Figure 17. When the Spell Checker has finished running through your document, a dialog box will open, asking if you want to close the Spell Checker. Click Yes.

SPELL CHECK A DOCUMENT

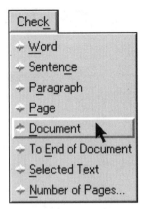

Figure 18. Open the Check menu, then choose the part of your document you would like spell checked—all the way from the entire document down to one word.

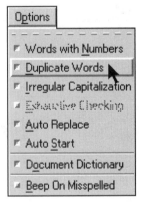

Figure 19. Open the Options menu, then choose which items you don't want spell checked.

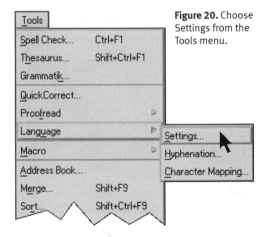

Figure 20. Choose Settings from the Tools menu.

◆ Click Suggest to see additional words or phrases in the Suggestions list box.

◆ Click Close to stop checking spelling before the Spell Checker has run through the entire document.

4. When the Spell Checker has gone through the entire document, a Spell Checker dialog box will appear telling you that the spell check is finished (**Figure 17**).

5. Click Yes to close the Spell Checker.

✔ Tips

■ To spell check a part of your document, position the insertion marker in the text you want to spell check (for instance, inside the word, sentence, or paragraph), then choose the part that you want to check from the Check menu in the Spell Checker dialog box (**Figure 18**).

■ You can turn off spell checking for various options such as words with numbers, duplicate words, and irregular capitalization. To do so, choose the Options menu in the Spell Checker dialog box and deselect the items you don't want spell checked (**Figure 19**).

■ If you write in several languages, you can spell check those languages by choosing Settings from the Language fly-out on the Tools menu (**Figure 20**). The Language dialog box will open (**Figure 21**). From the list box, choose the language you want to spell check, then click OK. Spell check your document following the steps outlined on these two pages.

Grammar-As-You-Go

Grammar-As-You-Go checks your sentences for grammar mistakes as you type. A word or phrase that is possibly incorrect is underlined with diagonal blue stripes.

To turn Grammar-As-You-Go on or off:

Choose Grammar-As-You-Go from the Proofread fly-out on the Tools menu (**Figure 22**). When Grammar-As-You-Go is on, a tiny diamond appears to the left of the menu item.

✔ Tips

- Grammar-As-You-Go and Spell-As-You-Go cannot be turned on at the same time.

- To turn Grammar-As-You-Go off, choose Off from the Proofread fly-out on the Tools menu (**Figure 13**).

To correct possible grammar mistakes:

1. Position the mouse pointer over the word or phrase underscored with blue diagonal stripes and click the right mouse button. The Grammar-As-You-Go menu will open, showing a list of possible alternatives (**Figure 23**).

2. Choose the correct word or phrase from the list.

   or

   Choose Ignore to pass over the possible grammar error.

   The Grammar-As-You-Go menu will disappear and the word or phrase will change depending upon what you selected.

Figure 21. Select the language you would like to spell check, then click OK.

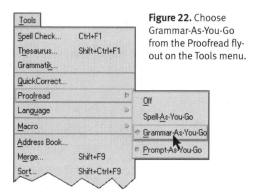

Figure 22. Choose Grammar-As-You-Go from the Proofread fly-out on the Tools menu.

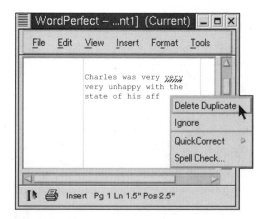

Figure 23. Choose the suggestion from the Grammar-As-You-Go menu or choose Ignore to skip over the possible grammar error.

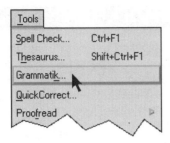

Figure 24. Choose Grammatik from the Tools menu.

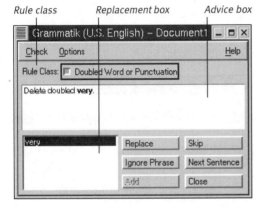

Figure 25. The Grammatik dialog box offers advice on how to fix possible grammar errors.

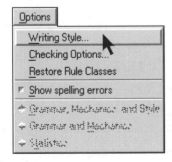

Figure 26. Choose Writing Style from the Options menu to open the Writing Style dialog box.

Grammatik

You can proofread an entire document at one time using WordPerfect's Grammatik feature.

To proofread a document:

1. Open the document you want to proofread.

2. Choose Grammatik from the Tools menu (**Figure 24**). The Grammatik dialog box will appear (**Figure 25**) and the first error Grammatik finds will be underlined in your document.

3. Choose Writing Style from the Options menu (**Figure 26**). The Writing Style dialog box will open (**Figure 27**).

4. Select a style from the Writing Style list box.

5. In the Formality Level area, select the radio button that best describes how formal your document is—standard, formal, or informal.

6. Click OK. The Writing Style dialog box will close, returning you to the Grammatik dialog box (**Figure 25**). With the first possible grammar or spelling error that Grammatik has found, the dialog box will display several things:

   ◆ Rule Class, near the top of the dialog box, displays what type of error is underlined, such as spelling, capitalization, correct use of speech, passive voice, or clichés.

   ◆ Advice Box explains the possible writing error and how it can be fixed.

   ◆ Replacement Box shows a list of possible corrections.

(continued)

7. You can click:

◆ **Replace** to substitute the incorrect word or phrase with the one that is highlighted in the Replacement box.

◆ **Skip** to pass over the possible error and move to the next one.

◆ **Next Sentence** to ignore any other errors in the current sentence and move to the next sentence.

◆ **Ignore Word/Phrase** to pass over that specific word or phrase for the rest of the document.

◆ **Add** to enter the word or phrase in Grammatik.

◆ **Close** to stop grammar checking before Grammatik has run through the entire document.

8. When the grammar check is finished Grammatik will open a dialog box asking if you want to close Grammatik (**Figure 28**).

9. Click Yes to close Grammatik and return to your document.

Figure 27. Select the writing style you are using from the list box, then select one of the formality level radio buttons.

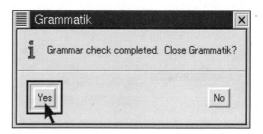

Figure 28. When Grammatik has finished checking your document, it will tell you so. Click Yes to close the grammar checker.

Summary

In this chapter you learned how to:

◆ Automatically replace misspelled words or abbreviations as you type using QuickCorrect

◆ Insert SmartQuotes in place of straight quotation marks

◆ Set up automatic formatting using the Format-As-You-Go feature

◆ Correct misspelled words on-the-fly using Spell-As-You-Go

◆ Spell check a document

◆ Check your grammar as you type using Grammar-As-You-Go

◆ Proofread an entire document using Grammatik

10

ADDING TABLES

*T*ables are used to present information in an organized way. They are made up of *rows* and *columns* of *cells* which let you position information accurately (**Figure 1**). Cells can contain text and images. If you create a table and discover that you need to add or delete cells or change cell size, WordPerfect makes it easy to customize an existing table.

You can format text inside cells just like any other text. Using the Property Bar, you can set the font, font size, font style, and alignment—left, right, center, or full justification. In fact, if you've created a special text style for the table, you can use that, too.

WordPerfect's table feature even lets you insert functions that you would normally see in a spreadsheet program, such as automatically adding up the sums of selected columns or incrementing a numerical pattern.

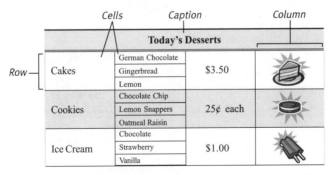

Figure 1. A table is made up of cells that are organized into rows and columns. Shading, borders, and other formatting can be applied to tables to give them a customized look.

To create a table:

1. Position the insertion point where you would like the table to appear.

2. On the WordPerfect 8 Toolbar, position the mouse pointer over the Table button and press the left mouse button. A tiny grid will appear (**Figure 2**).

3. Drag the mouse pointer down and to the right to highlight the number of rows and columns on the grid.

4. Release the left mouse button. The table will appear in your document with the insertion point blinking in the first cell (**Figure 3**).

or

1. Position the insertion point where you would like the table to appear.

2. Choose Table from the Insert menu (**Figure 4**) or press F12 on the keyboard. The Create Table dialog box will open (**Figure 5**).

3. In the Create area, select the Table radio button.

4. In the Table Size area, use the Columns and Rows text boxes to set how many columns and rows your table will contain.

5. Click OK. The Create Table dialog box will close and the table will appear in your document with the insertion point blinking in the first cell (**Figure 3**).

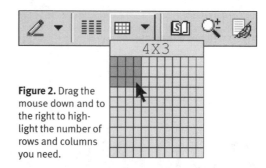

Figure 2. Drag the mouse down and to the right to highlight the number of rows and columns you need.

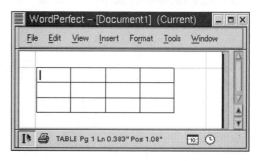

Figure 3. The table appears in the document with the insertion point positioned in the first cell.

Figure 4. Choose Table from the Insert menu.

Figure 5. Select the Table option in the Create area, then enter the number of rows and columns in the text boxes in the Table Size area.

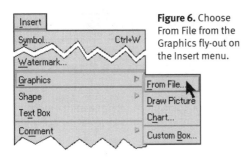

Figure 6. Choose From File from the Graphics fly-out on the Insert menu.

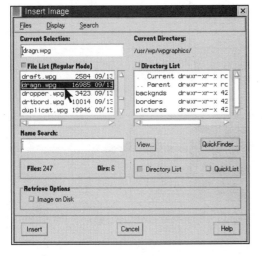

Figure 7. Use the Insert Image dialog box to move to the directory where the image file is stored and select it.

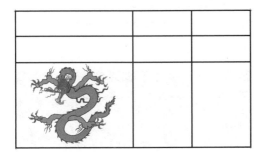

Figure 8. The table exands to accommodate the image you insert.

To add text to a table:

Position the insertion point within a cell and type your text. The cell will automatically expand to accommodate the text.

✔ Tips

- You can quickly move from one cell to the next in a table by pressing the Tab key or using the arrow keys on the keyboard.

- To quickly add another row to a table, position the insertion marker in the lower-right cell and press the Tab key.

- To insert a tab in a cell to indent text, hold down the Ctrl key, then press the Tab key.

To insert an image into a table:

1. Position the insertion point in the cell where you want to add the image.

2. Choose From File from the Graphics fly-out on the Insert menu (**Figure 6**). The Insert Image dialog box will open (**Figure 7**).

3. Use the Directory List and File List boxes to select an image file.

4. Click Insert. The Image will appear in the table (**Figure 8**).

✔ Tip

- For more information about inserting images in your documents, turn to pages 99–100.

ADD TEXT AND INSERT AN IMAGE INTO A TABLE

173

Selecting Table Elements

Being able to select a cell, row, column, or table can be a little tricky until you discover just how to do it.

To select a cell:

1. Move the mouse pointer towards the top of the cell you want to select. The mouse pointer will change to an upwards facing arrow (**Figure 9**).

2. Click. The cell will be selected (**Figure 10**).

To select a column:

1. Move the mouse pointer towards the top of the upper cell you want to select. The mouse pointer will change to an upwards facing arrow (**Figure 9**).

2. Press the left mouse button and drag down to select the column (**Figure 11**).

To select a row:

1. Move the mouse pointer towards the top of the leftmost cell you want to select. The mouse pointer will change to an upwards facing arrow (**Figure 9**).

2. Press the left mouse button and drag right to select the row (**Figure 12**).

To select a table:

1. Move the mouse pointer towards the top of the first cell in the table. The mouse pointer will change to an upwards facing arrow (**Figure 9**).

2. Press the left mouse button and drag diagonally down to the right to select the entire table (**Figure 13**).

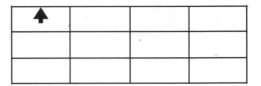

Figure 9. Move the mouse pointer towards the top of the cell you want to select until the pointer changes to an upward arrow.

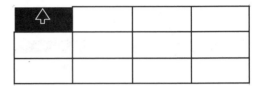

Figure 10. When you click, the cell is highlighted, indicating that it's selected.

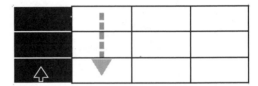

Figure 11. Drag downwards to select an entire column.

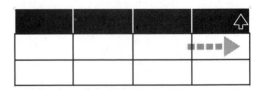

Figure 12. Drag across to select an entire row.

Figure 13. Drag diagonally down to the right to select an entire table.

Figure 14. Choose Insert from the Table menu on the Property Bar.

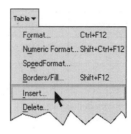

Figure 15. Right click on the table and choose Insert from the QuickMenu.

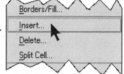

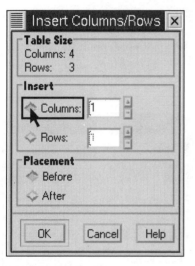

Figure 16. Select either Columns or Rows in the Insert area, then enter the number you want to add in the appropriate text box.

New column

Col 1		Col 2	Col 3	Col 4

Figure 17. The new column or row appears next to the cell where the insertion point is located.

Changing the Table's Shape

Many times the information displayed in a table expands as the table is created. New columns or rows could be needed or the information is difficult to fit in the standard table setup and cells need to be *split* or *joined*. In fact, if you need to, you can even split an entire table.

To add rows or columns to a table:

1. Position the insertion point in the column or row next to the place where you want to add the columns or rows.

2. Click the Table menu on the Property Bar and choose Insert (**Figure 14**).

    or

    Right click on the table and choose Insert from the QuickMenu (**Figure 15**).

    The Insert Columns/Rows dialog box will open (**Figure 16**).

3. In the Insert area, select either the Columns or Rows radio button, then in the appropriate text box enter the number of columns or rows you would like to insert.

4. In the Placement area, select a radio button to set whether the rows or columns will appear before or after the row or column where the insertion point is located.

5. Click OK. The Insert Columns/Rows dialog box will close and the new columns or rows will be added to the table (**Figure 17**).

✔ Tip

■ When you're working in the Insert Columns/Rows dialog box, the current size of your table is displayed in the Table Size area.

To insert a new row above the current row:

Position the insertion point in the row *below* where you want the new one. Click the Insert Row button on the Property Bar.

Lamps	Shades	Cords	Bulbs
2	5		1	2

Figure 18. Place the insertion point in the cell you want to split.

To split a cell:

1. Place the insertion point in the cell you want to split (**Figure 18**).

2. Click the Table menu on the Property Bar and choose Cell from the Split fly-out (**Figure 19**). The Split Cell dialog box will open (**Figure 20**).

3. Select the radio button next to Columns or Rows and use the appropriate text box to enter the number of columns or rows you would like the cell split into.

4. Click OK. The Split Cell dialog box will close and the cell will split as you specified (**Figure 21**).

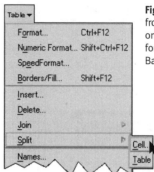

Figure 19. Choose Cell from the Split fly-out on the Table menu found on the Property Bar.

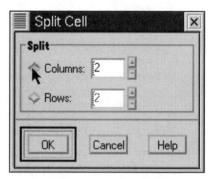

Figure 20. In the Split area, select whether you want to split the cell horizontally into columns or vertically into rows, then enter a number in the appropriate text box.

Nancy	Julian	Harold	Fairweather

Figure 22. Select the cells you want to join. The cells must be next to one another.

Lamps	Shades	Cords	Bulbs
2	5		1	2

Figure 21. The cell splits into rows or columns depending upon the settings you selected.

SPLIT A CELL

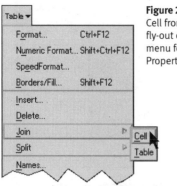

Figure 23. Choose Cell from the Join fly-out on the Table menu found on the Property Bar.

Nancy	Julian	Harold	Fairweather

Figure 24. The selected cells join together.

Beets	Carrots	Celery	Snap Peas
Oranges	Lemons	Limes	Grapefruit

Figure 25. Position the insertion point in the row that will become the top row of the new table.

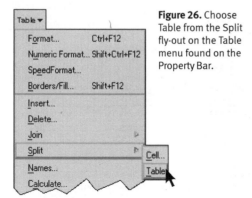

Figure 26. Choose Table from the Split fly-out on the Table menu found on the Property Bar.

To join cells:

1. Select the cells you want to join (**Figure 22**). (The cells must be right next to each other.)

2. Click the Table menu on the Property Bar and choose Cell from the Join fly-out (**Figure 23**). The cells will join together (**Figure 24**).

To split a table:

1. Position the insertion point in the row that you want to become the top row of the new table (**Figure 25**).

2. Click the Table menu on the Property Bar and choose Table from the Split fly-out (**Figure 26**). The table will split into two (**Figure 27**).

Beets	Carrots	Celery	Snap Peas

Oranges	Lemons	Limes	Grapefruit

Figure 27. The table splits into two separate tables.

To delete a row or column:

1. Select the row or column you want to delete.

2. Click the Table menu on the Property Bar and choose Delete (**Figure 28**). The Delete dialog box will open (**Figure 29**).

3. In the Delete area select what you want to delete—the column or row you have selected, or simply its contents.

4. Click OK. The row or column or its contents will disappear from the table.

✔ Tip

■ If you only want to delete the contents of the selected row or column, select the Cell Contents radio button in the Delete area.

To delete a table:

1. Select the table you want to delete.

2. Click the Table menu on the Property Bar and choose Delete (**Figure 28**) or press the Delete or Backspace key on the keyboard. The Delete Table dialog box will appear (**Figure 30**).

3. In the Delete area, select either Entire Table, Table Contents, or Table Structure.

4. Click OK. The Delete Table dialog box will close and the delete option you selected will be applied to the table.

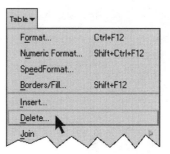

Figure 28. Choose Delete from the Table menu found on the Property Bar.

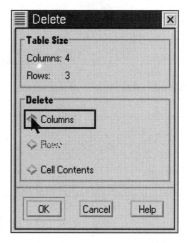

Figure 29. In the Delete area, select what you want to delete—the row or column you have selected, or simply its contents.

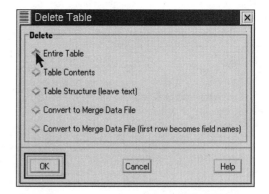

Figure 30. Use the Delete area to select which part of the table you will delete—the entire table, only the table's contents, or the table framework.

DELETE A ROW, COLUMN, OR TABLE

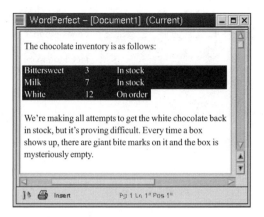

Figure 31. Select the text you would like to convert to a table.

Figure 32. In the Convert Table dialog box, select the radio button that describes the text you selected, then click OK.

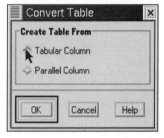

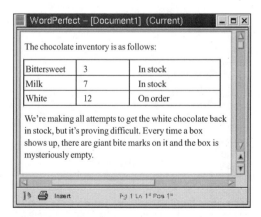

Figure 33. The text you selected is placed into a table.

Converting Text into a Table

WordPerfect makes it easy to convert text that has been set in columns using tabs or parallel columns into a table. (For a discussion about tabs and tab settings, turn to pages 93–97; to find out more about parallel columns, turn to page 131.)

To convert text into a table:

1. Select the tabbed text or parallel columns you want to convert (**Figure 31**).

2. Choose Table from the Insert menu (**Figure 4**). The Convert Table dialog box will appear (**Figure 32**).

3. Select either the Tabular Column or Parallel Column radio button depending upon the type of text you selected.

4. Click OK. The Convert Table dialog box will close and the text will be converted into a table (**Figure 33**).

Changing Column Width

As you can see in **Figure 33**, the table in which the text is placed is not necessarily well balanced. In **Figure 33**, the third column is much wider than the other two—a little tweaking is in order.

WordPerfect makes it easy to change a column's width. All you have to do is drag the column's border to a new position.

1. Position the mouse pointer over a column border until it changes to a double-headed arrow.

2. Press the left mouse button and drag the column border to its new position.

Formatting your Table

WordPerfect lets you quickly set how text is positioned and formatted in the cells, using cell, row, and column attributes. Then, with the special table command buttons on the Property Bar and *SpeedFormatting* you can set how the table and its elements—cells, rows, and columns—look.

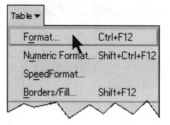

Figure 34. Choose Format from the Table menu found on the Property Bar.

To set cell attributes:

1. Position the insertion point in the cell whose attributes you want to change.

   or

   Select the cells whose attributes you want to change.

2. Click the Table menu on the Property Bar and choose Format (**Figure 34**) or press Ctrl+F12 on the keyboard. The Format dialog box will open with the Cell radio button selected (**Figure 35**).

3. In the Alignment area (**Figure 36**), use the drop-down lists to set the text's vertical alignment in the cell—top, center, or bottom—and horizontal alignment, or justification, in the cell—left, right, center, full, all, or decimal aligned justification.

4. In the Cell Attributes area (**Figure 37**) you can set whether a cell is *locked* and if it is to be ignored when performing calculations. Information in locked cells cannot be changed.

5. Use the Appearance and Text Size areas to set the text's appearance, if you want to use special formatting.

6. Click OK. The Format dialog box will close and the text in the cell(s) you selected will assume the new formatting you set.

Figure 35. With the Cell radio button selected, the Format dialog box displays the possible settings for a cell.

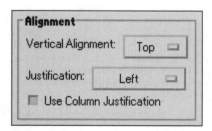

Figure 36. In the Alignment area, use the drop-down lists to set the text's vertical and horizontal alignment in a cell.

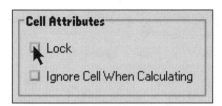

Figure 37. In the Cell Attributes area, set whether the cell is locked and/or ignored when performing calculations.

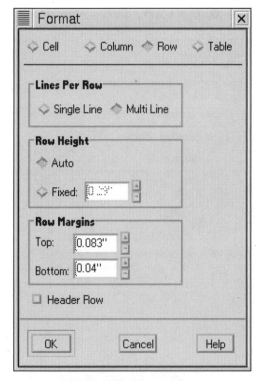

Figure 38. When the Row radio button is selected in the Format dialog box, all row commands and options are available for you to set.

To set row attributes:

1. Select the row(s) whose attributes you want to change.

2. Click the Table menu on the Property Bar and choose Format (**Figure 34**) or press Ctrl+F12 on the keyboard. The Format dialog box will open with the Row radio button selected (**Figure 38**).

3. In the Lines Per Row area, set whether the cells are allowed to have more than one line of text. By default Multi Line is selected. If you select Single Line, the cell *will not* expand to accommodate more than one line of text.

4. Use the Row Height area to set whether cells in the row automatically expand to fit their contents or are an exact height.

5. In the Row Margins area, use the text boxes to set the top and bottom margins for the cells in the selected row(s).

6. If you would like the row(s) you have selected to become *Header Rows*, then select the box next to that item. Header rows appear at the top of a table every time the table moves to a new page.

7. Click OK. The Format dialog box will close and the row(s) you selected will assume the new formatting.

To set column attributes:

1. Select the column(s) whose attributes you want to change.

2. Click the Table menu on the Property Bar and choose Format (**Figure 34**) or press Ctrl+F12 on the keyboard. The Format dialog box will open with the Column radio button selected (**Figure 39**).

3. In the Alignment area (**Figure 40**), use the drop-down lists to set the text's justification alignment in the cell—left, right, center, full, all, or decimal aligned—and how far the cell is aligned from the page's right margin.

4. In the Column Margins area (**Figure 41**), use the text boxes to set the left and right margins in the cells that are selected.

5. Use the Appearance and Text Size areas to format the text in the selected column(s).

6. In the Column Width area (**Figure 42**), use the text box to set the width of the column. If you select the Fixed Width check box, the column will remain the specified width no matter what changes go on in the columns around it.

7. Click OK. The Format dialog box will close and the column(s) you selected will assume the new formatting.

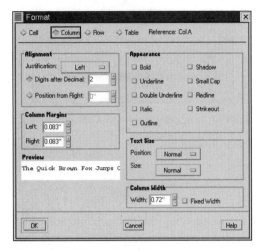

Figure 39. With the Column radio button selected in the Format dialog box, you have access to all column commands and settings.

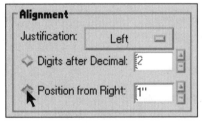

Figure 40. In the Alignment area, set the text justification, the number of digits displayed after a decimal, or how far the column is from the right margin.

Figure 42. In the Column Width area, you can set the exact width of the column. If you select Fixed Width, the column will not expand no matter how much text or how many images are put in it.

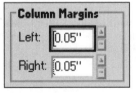

Figure 41. Use the Column Margins area to set the left and right margins in the selected cells.

SET COLUMN ATTRIBUTES

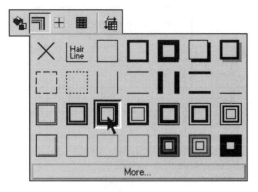

Figure 43. Use the Borders drop-down list to select a border for the cell, row, column, or table.

sand	*The Beach*	water
bucket		waves
shovel		surf
sieve	*Summer!*	tide

Figure 44. The selected border appears around the table element. In this case, the entire table was selected, so the border appears around the table.

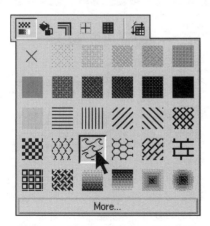

Figure 45. Use the Fill Style drop-down list to select a fill for the cell, row, column, or table.

To add borders to a cell, row, column, or table:

1. Select the cell, row(s), column(s), or table to which you want to add borders.

2. Click the Borders button on the Property Bar and choose a border style from the drop-down list (**Figure 43**). The drop-down list will close and the border will appear around the table elements you selected (**Figure 44**).

To add shading to a cell, row, column, or table:

1. Select the cell, row(s), column(s), or table to which you want to add shading.

2. Click the Fill Style button on the Property Bar and choose a fill from the drop-down list (**Figure 45**). The drop-down list will close and the shading will appear in the table elements you selected (**Figure 46**).

Backgrounds can be Busy!

As you can see in **Figure 46**, the background in the center cell is very busy and obscures the swimmer. Use background patterns sparingly. They can draw attention, but they can also hide your message.

sand	*The Beach*	water
bucket		waves
shovel		surf
sieve	*Summer!*	tide

Figure 46. The fill appears in the selected table element. In this case, it's the large cell in the center of the table.

To format an entire table using SpeedFormat:

1. Position the insertion point anywhere in the table you want to format (**Figure 47**).

2. Click the Table menu on the Property Bar and choose SpeedFormat (**Figure 48**). The Table SpeedFormat dialog box will appear (**Figure 49**).

3. Use the Available Styles list box to select a SpeedFormat. When you select a SpeedFormat a sample of the style you have selected appears in the preview area.

4. If you have added any previous formatting that you want to get rid of, select the box next to Clear Current Table Settings Before Applying.

5. Click Apply. The Table SpeedFormat dialog box will close and the table will assume the new formatting (**Figure 50**).

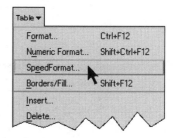

SODA SALES (in cases)			
	East	West	Total
root beer	157	328	
cream soda			
Total			

Figure 47. Position the insertion point anywhere in the table you would like to format.

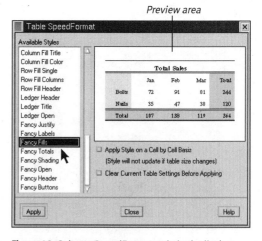

Figure 48. Choose SpeedFormat from the Table menu found on the Property Bar.

Preview area

Figure 49. Select a SpeedFormat style in the list box, then click Apply. A preview of the style you select appears in the preview area.

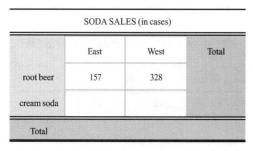

SODA SALES (in cases)			
	East	West	Total
root beer	157	328	
cream soda			
Total			

Figure 50. The SpeedFormat style you select transforms any table.

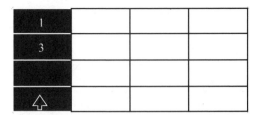

Figure 51. Select the row or column that contains the numbers you wish to turn into a series.

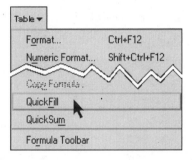

Figure 52. Choose QuickFill from the Table menu found on the Property Bar.

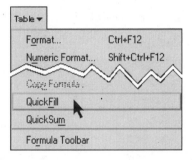

Figure 53. WordPerfect automatically completes the selected row or column, using the incremental number pattern.

Two "Quick" Calculations

WordPerfect includes two features that help you quickly add numbers in a row or column, or create a numerical series.

The *QuickFill* feature will continue a pattern of increasing values down a column or across a row for you. For instance, if two cells in a column contain the numbers 1 and 3, QuickFill will continue the pattern with 5, 7, 9, etc., filling the remaining selected cells.

The *QuickSum* feature lets you add up a column of numbers in a table.

To use QuickFill:

1. Select the row or column that contains the number pattern you want to increase in specified increments (**Figure 51**).

2. Click the Table menu on the Property Bar and choose QuickFill (**Figure 52**). The pattern will appear in the remaining cells (**Figure 53**).

Tables and Formulas

WordPerfect 8 for Linux comes equipped with very powerful spreadsheet capabilities. Unfortunately, there's not enough room in this book to get into the many functions and formulas that you can use in a table. In fact, there's so much available that it could become a book in itself!

If you want to learn more about formulas and how they work in tables, take a look at the *WordPerfect 8 User's Guide* that comes with the Personal Edition. Pages 555–569 and 660–686 will give you a pretty good idea of what is available and get you started.

To perform a QuickSum:

1. Position the insertion point in the cell below the column where you would like the sum to appear (**Figure 54**).

2. Click the Table menu on the Property Bar and choose QuickSum (**Figure 55**). The column of numbers will be added up and the result will appear in the text box (**Figure 56**).

Oranges	26		
Lemons	75		
Limes	35		
Total Fruit			

Figure 54. Position the insertion point in the cell below the column of numbers you want to add up.

Oranges	26		
Lemons	75		
Limes	35		
Total Fruit	136		

Figure 56. The sum appears in the cell at the bottom of the column.

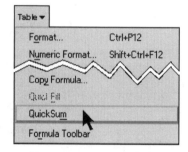

Figure 55. Choose QuickSum from the Table menu found on the Property Bar.

Summary

In this chapter you learned how to:

- Create a table
- Add text to a table
- Insert an image into a table
- Select a cell, column, row, or table
- Add rows or columns to a table
- Split or join cells

- Split a table
- Delete rows, columns, or tables
- Convert text into a table
- Set cell, column, and row attributes
- Use SpeedFormat
- Perform a QuickFill and a QuickSum

MERGING AND SORTING

*C*an you imagine typing 500 personalized form letters and envelopes? That would be a most onerous task indeed! Thankfully, WordPerfect's *Merge* command takes the burden out of such a task. All you need to do is type out one form letter and then use the Merge command to create personalized letters for everyone on your list.

In order to perform a merge, two types of files need to be created:

◆ A *data file*—all the names and addresses of the people you are sending the letter to; and

◆ A *form file*—this is the actual form letter.

After the data file and form file are completed, the merge is performed, generating a third document containing the 500 merged, personalized form letters. You can then print the form letters.

But, merging is not limited to form letters! Any type of document that uses repeated information—such as reports, contracts, mailing labels, telephone lists, and envelopes—can be merged.

This chapter will take you through the merge process, from creating the data file to creating the form file, then on to performing the actual merge. From there, you'll discover how to create an envelope merge (you've got to send those letters out somehow!). Then, you'll learn how to perform a simple alphabetical or numerical sort on a document. Finally, you'll find out how to perform a simple sort. This can be handy if you have a large data file that you want to sort in a particular way—perhaps by zip code or telephone number.

Creating the Data File

A data file contains the information—such as names, addresses, and telephone numbers—that is merged into a form file.

Data files can be created in either *text* or *table* format. Information in a *data text file* is arranged into *fields* and *records*. The fields and records in a *data table file* are arranged into columns (fields) and rows (records).

A field is the individual piece of information such as a person's name. Another field could be that same person's address. A third field could be that person's telephone number. If you are missing the information that would go into a field for a particular person, you can leave the field blank. Fields can be as small as one character or several lines long.

A record is a group of related fields, such as the information about a person, including her name, address, and telephone number.

To create the data file:

1. Choose Merge from the Tools menu (**Figure 1**) or press Shift+F9 on the keyboard. The Merge dialog box will open (**Figure 2**).

2. In the Data File area:

   Click Data to create a data text file.

   or

   Select the box next to Place Records in a Table, then click Data to create a data table file.

   The Create Merge File dialog box will open (**Figure 3**). (The Create Merge File dialog box will not appear if you have a new document open in the document window. If this is the case, the Create Data File dialog box (**Figure 4**) and the Merge Toolbar (**Figure 5**) will appear. Skip to step 5.)

Figure 1. Choose Merge from the Tools menu.

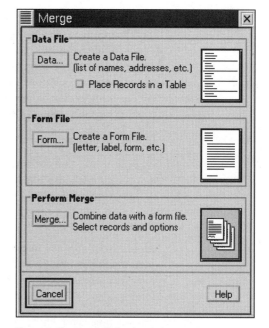

Figure 2. The Merge dialog box helps you create and organize the data and form files, and perform the merge.

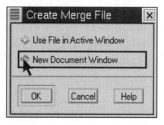

Figure 3. In the Create Merge File dialog box, set where you want to place the data file—either in the current document or in a new one.

CREATE THE DATA FILE

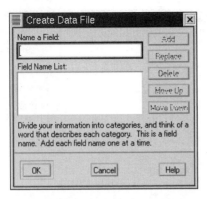

Figure 4. The Create Data File dialog box is used to create the fields in which information will be placed.

Merge Toolbar

Figure 5. The Merge Toolbar appears below the Property Bar.

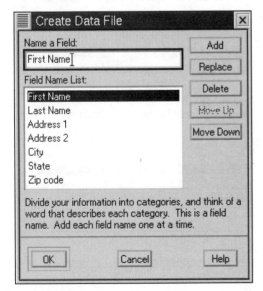

Figure 6. Type the name of a field in the text box, then click Add. The new field appears in the Field Name List box.

3. Select Use File in Active Window to create the data file in the document that is currently open.

or

Select New Document Window to create the data file in a new document. (This is recommended since you are creating a new data file that you will probably want to use over and over again.)

4. Click OK. The Create Merge File dialog box will close and several things will happen:

◆ The Create Data File dialog box will appear, ready to help you create your list of fields (**Figure 4**).

◆ The Merge Toolbar will appear at the top of the document window just under the Property Bar (**Figure 5**).

5. To create a field:

A. Type the name of the field in the Name a Field text box (**Figure 6**).

B. Click Add. The field will appear in the Field Name List box. (If you don't give a field a name, WordPerfect will automatically assign a number to it.)

(continued)

6. Repeat step 5 until you have created all the fields you will need, then click OK. The Create Data File dialog box will close and two things will happen:

   ◆ The Quick Data Entry dialog box will appear (**Figure 7**). This dialog box is used to easily fill in the fields.

   ◆ If you are using a data text file, the fields that you created using the Create Data File dialog box will appear at the top of the document after the *merge code* FIELDNAMES (**Figure 8**).

   ◆ If you are using a data table file, the fields that you created will appear at the top of a table in the document (**Figure 9**).

7. In the Record area of the Quick Data Entry dialog box, enter the information for one record into the text box next to each field. To move from one text box to the next, either click Next Field or press Enter or Tab on the keyboard. If you want to put more than one line into a field, press Ctrl+Enter on the keyboard.

8. When you have completely filled in all the fields, click New Record. The fields that you entered for the first record will appear at the top of the data file document or at the top of the data text table, and the Quick Data Entry dialog box text boxes will clear, ready for the next record.

9. Continue entering records, following steps 7–8, until you have completed your list.

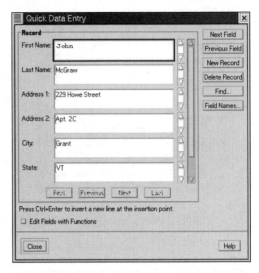

Figure 7. The Quick Data Entry dialog box makes it easy to enter information into fields and create records.

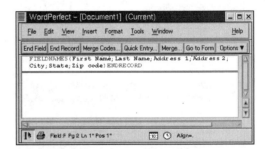

Figure 8. If you are using a data text file, the fields you created appear at the top of the document between the merge codes FIELDNAMES and ENDRECORD.

Figure 9. If you are using a data table file, the fields you created appear at the top of a data table in the document.

Figure 10. Click Yes to save the data file.

Figure 11a. Each record in a data text file is separated by a double horizontal line.

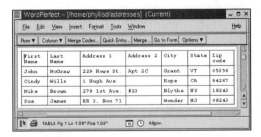

Figure 11b. The fields in a data table file are organized neatly into columns, making it easy to see the information.

10. Click Close. The Quick Data Entry dialog box will close and a Merge dialog box will appear (**Figure 10**), asking whether you want to save the data file document (you do).

11. Click Yes. The Save Data File As dialog box will appear.

12. Use the Directory List box to move to the directory where you want to keep the data file, then type the file's name in the Filename/Current Selection text box.

13. Click OK. The Save Data File As dialog box will close. Congratulations! You've just created a data file (**Figures 11a–b**).

✔ Tips

■ If you don't name a field, WordPerfect will automatically assign a number for you.

■ If you need to insert a new record into a data text file, position the insertion point in the document where you would like the record to appear, then click Quick Entry on the Merge Toolbar. Use the Quick Entry dialog box as described in steps 7–8 above.

■ If you need to insert a new record into a data table file, insert a row into the table where you would like the record to appear, then type the information in the fields in the table. (For details on how to insert rows into a table, turn to pages 175–176, in Chapter 10, *Adding Tables*.)

■ Data table files are inherently easier to look through and use than data text files because the table format organizes the data into columns.

Creating the Form File

The next step in performing a merge is to create the document that the data file will be merged into. The fields that you created when you made the data file will be inserted into the document you want personalized, such as a form letter, contract, or mailing label. Each field is inserted into the appropriate position in the form file as a *field code*.

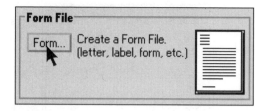

Figure 12. Click Form in the Form File area of the Merge dialog box.

To create the form file:

1. Start a new document.

2. Choose Merge from the Tools menu (**Figure 1**). The Merge dialog box will appear (**Figure 2**).

3. In the Form File area, click Form (**Figure 12**). The Create Form File dialog box will open (**Figure 13**).

4. Make sure the radio button next to Associate a Data File is selected, then click the list button next to the text box. The Select Data File dialog box will open (**Figure 14**).

5. Use the Directory List box to move to the location where the data file is stored, then use the File List box to select the file.

6. Click OK. The Select Data File dialog box will close and you will return to the Create Form File dialog box. The full path of the data file will be in the text box (**Figure 13**).

7. Click OK. The Create Form File dialog box will close and the Merge Toolbar will appear below the Property Bar in the document window. Now, it's time to create the document that the data file will be merged into.

Figure 13. Use the Create Form File dialog box to link the data file that you created with the form file you are about to create.

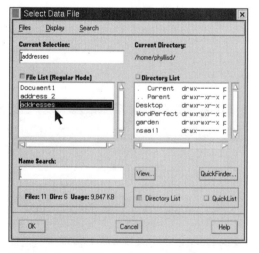

Figure 14. Use the Directory List and File List boxes to select the data file you created, then click OK.

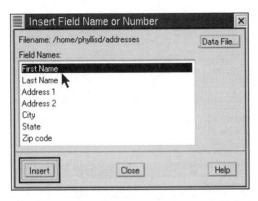

Figure 15. Select the field that you want to insert in the form file document, then click Insert.

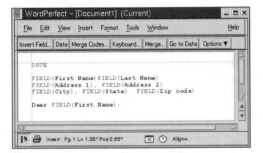

Figure 16. Insert the field codes into the document where you would like the personalized information. For instance, in this figure the field code for First Name has been inserted after the letter's salutation.

Figure 17. Continue inserting field codes and typing the document until it's completed.

8. Start typing your form file, for instance a form letter or contract.

9. When you come to a place where you want to insert a field code—for instance, a person's first name after the greeting in a letter—click Insert Field on the Merge Toolbar. The Insert Field Name or Number dialog box will appear (**Figure 15**).

> **Insert Field...**

10. In the Field Name list box, select the field that you want to insert.

11. Click Insert. The field code will be inserted into your document (**Figure 16**). The Insert Field Name or Number dialog box will remain open, ready for you to insert another field code.

12. Continue typing your document and inserting field codes as described in steps 9–11 above until the document is finished.

13. When you have finished inserting field codes, click the Close button to close the Insert Field Name or Number dialog box.

14. Save the form file. (For details on how to save a file, turn to page 43.) Your form file is now ready to be merged with the data file (**Figure 17**).

✔ Tips

■ When inserting field codes into the form file document using the Insert Field Name or Number dialog box, be a little careful about which window is active. Otherwise, you may end up inserting a few extra field codes that you did not intend to. If this happens, just select the errant field code and press Delete on the keyboard.

■ To insert a date field in your document (this will automatically insert today's date when you use the document) click the Date button on the Merge Toolbar.

CREATE THE FORM FILE

Performing the Merge

Now that you have created both the data file and the form file, it's time to perform the merge and create a third file that contains all the personalized copies of the form file.

To perform the merge:

1. Choose Merge from the Tools menu (**Figure 1**). The Merge dialog box will open (**Figure 2**).

2. In the Perform Merge area (**Figure 18**), click Merge. The Perform Merge dialog box will appear (**Figure 19**).

3. To select the form file:

   A. Click the list button next to the Form File text box and choose Select File from the drop-down list (**Figure 20**). The Select Form File dialog box will appear (**Figure 21**).

   B. Use the Directory List and File List boxes to select the form file that you created.

   C. Click OK. The Select Form File dialog box will close, returning you to the Perform Merge dialog box.

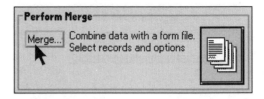

Figure 18. Click Merge in the Perform Merge area of the Merge dialog box.

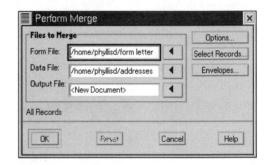

Figure 19. The Perform Merge dialog box is used to set the form and data files that will be merged and where the resulting document will go.

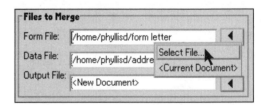

Figure 20. Click the list button, then choose either Select File or <Current Document> from the drop-down list.

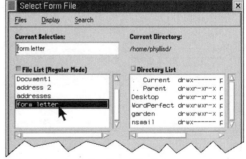

Figure 21. In the Select Form File dialog box, select the form file you want to use for the merge.

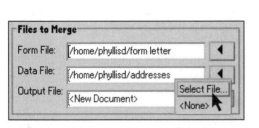

Figure 22. Click the list button, then choose Select File from the drop-down list.

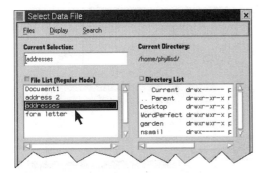

Figure 23. Use the Select Data File dialog box to find and select the data file that you created, then click OK.

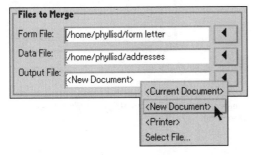

Figure 24. Click the list button, then choose either <Current Document>, <New Document>, <Printer>, or Select File from the drop-down list.

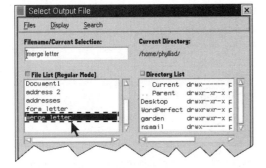

Figure 25. Use the Select Output File dialog box to find and select the file where the results of the merge will be placed.

4. To select the data file:

A. Click the list button next to the Data File text box and choose Select File from the drop-down list (**Figure 22**). The Select Data File dialog box will open (**Figure 23**).

B. Use the Directory List and File List boxes to select the data file that you created.

C. Click OK. The Select Data File dialog box will close, returning you to the Perform Merge dialog box.

5. To set where the merged file will be placed:

A. Click the list button next to the Output File text box and choose either Current File, New Document, Printer, or Select File from the drop-down list (**Figure 24**). If you choose Select File, the Select Output File dialog box will open (**Figure 25**).

B. If you are using the Select Output File dialog box, Use the Directory List and File List boxes to select the form file that you created, then click OK. The Select Output File dialog box will close, returning you to the Perform Merge dialog box.

(continued)

PERFORM THE MERGE

6. When you have entered the full path of each file in the Form, Data, and Output File text boxes, click OK. The Perform Merge dialog box will close and WordPerfect will perform the merge (**Figure 26**), placing the merged documents in the place you specified—either the current document, a new document, or the document you selected—or it will send the merged documents directly to the printer.

✔ Tips

■ You can cancel a merge that is in progress by pressing the Esc key on the keyboard.

■ If your form file is password protected, the merged document will have the same password as the form file.

■ To create mailing labels, you will need to select the type of label you are using from the Labels dialog box (**Figure 27**) before you create the form file. Choose Labels from the format menu (**Figure 28**), then choose the label style you are using from the Available Labels list box in the Labels dialog box. Click OK to close the dialog box, then insert the field codes onto the label to set it up for merging as you would any other form file.

Figure 26. When the data and form files are merged, the result is a personalized document. The three windows above are showing three pages of the same merged form letter document. Each page is a personalized letter.

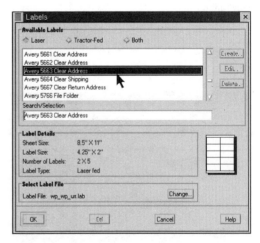

Figure 27. Select the label you are going to use from the list box in the Labels dialog box. The label is just another page size definition, though a specialized one.

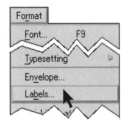

Figure 28. Choose Labels from the Format menu.

PERFORM THE MERGE

Figure 29. Click Form in the Form File area of the Merge dialog box.

Figure 30. Use the Create Form File dialog box to link the data file that you created with the form file you are about to create.

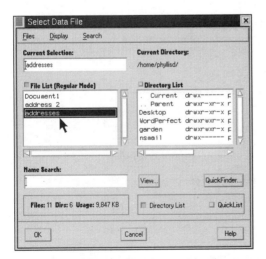

Figure 31. Use the Directory List and File List boxes to select the data file you created, then click OK.

Creating an Envelope Merge

Creating an envelope merge works the same way as the merge described in the previous sections, except the form file is an envelope instead of a form letter, contract, or label.

To create an envelope form file:

1. Start a new document.

2. Choose Merge from the Tools menu (**Figure 1**). The Merge dialog box will open (**Figure 2**).

3. In the Form File area (**Figure 29**), click Form. The Create Form File dialog box will open (**Figure 30**).

4. Make sure the radio button next to Associate a Data File is selected, then click the list button next to the text box. The Select Data File dialog box will open (**Figure 31**).

5. Use the Directory List box to move to the location where the data file is stored, then use the File List box to select the file.

6. Click OK. The Select Data File dialog box will close and you will return to the Create Form File dialog box. The full path of the data file will be in the text box (**Figure 30**).

7. Click OK. The Create Form File dialog box will close and the Merge Toolbar will appear below the Property Bar in the document window.

(continued)

8. Choose Envelope from the Format menu (**Figure 32**). The Envelope dialog box will open (**Figure 33**).

9. In the Return Address area, enter a return address in the text box if you wish to do so.

10. Position the insertion point in the Mailing Addresses text box, then click Field in the Envelopes area (**Figure 34**). The Insert Field Name or Number dialog box will open (**Figure 15**).

11. Select the field you want to insert in the Field Names list box, then click Insert. The Insert File Name or Number dialog box will close and the field code will appear in the Mailing Addresses text box.

12. Repeat step 11 until you have entered all the relevant address field codes (**Figure 35**). A preview of the envelope will appear in the preview area (**Figure 36**).

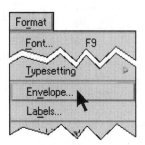

Figure 32. Choose Envelope from the Format menu.

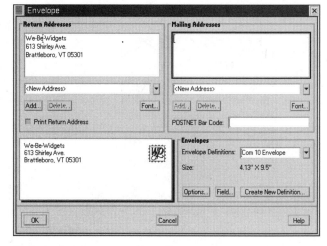

Figure 33. Type in a return address if you want to use one, then position the insertion marker in the Mailing Addresses text box.

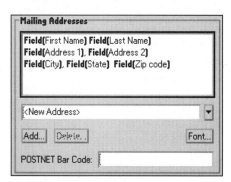

Figure 35. Insert the field codes you need to personalize the envelopes. As you enter the codes, type in any other characters you want to use, for example, commas and spaces.

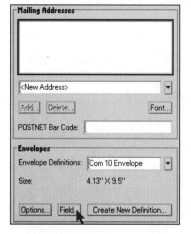

Figure 34. Click Field in the Envelopes area to start inserting field codes into the Mailing Addresses text box.

Figure 36. As you enter the form fields, a preview of the envelope appears in the preview area.

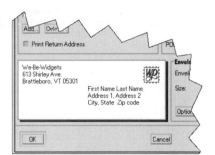

Figure 37. In the USPS Bar Code Options area, set the bar code to appear either above or below the address.

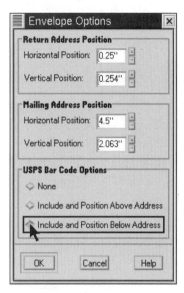

13. To insert a USPS Bar Code:

    A. Click the Options button in the Envelopes area (**Figure 34**). The Envelope Options dialog box will appear (**Figure 37**).

    B. In the USPS Bar Code Options area, either set the bar code to appear above the address or below the address (this is usually better).

    C. Click OK. The Envelope Options dialog box will close, returning you to the Envelope dialog box.

    D. Position the insertion point in the POSTNET Bar Code text box (**Figure 34**).

    E. Click Field, then from the Insert Field Name or Number dialog box, choose the zip code field you have created (**Figure 15**).

    F. Click OK to close the Insert Field Name or Number dialog box and return to the Envelope dialog box.

14. Click OK. The Envelope dialog box will close and the envelope with its field codes will appear in the document window (**Figure 38**).

15. Save the envelope form file.

16. Perform the merge as described starting on page 194. Your envelopes will appear in the document window, ready for printing, or you can send the merged document straight to the printer.

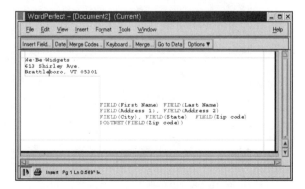

Figure 38. The envelope form file has everything it needs to create personalized envelopes with a merge.

Sorting Things Out

The Sort command is used to arrange text in a document alphabetically or numerically. Sorts are performed on five types of document elements: lines, paragraphs, merge data files, parallel columns, and table rows. An example of a simple sort is alphabetizing a list of name and phone numbers.

To sort a document:

1. Open the document you want to sort (**Figure 39**). (Or if the document is already open, make sure it has been saved.)

2. To sort an entire document, press Ctrl+Home on the keyboard to position the insertion point at the top of the document.

    or

    To sort part of a document, select that portion.

    or

    To sort a table or parallel column, position the insertion point within the table or parallel column.

3. Choose Sort from the Tools menu (**Figure 40**) or press Shift+Ctrl+F9 on the keyboard. The Sort dialog box will open (**Figure 41**).

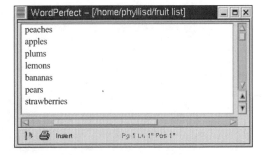

Figure 39. Open the document you want to sort.

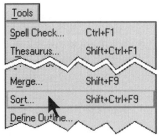

Figure 40. Choose Sort from the Tools menu.

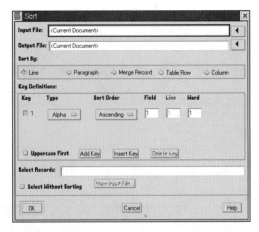

Figure 41. The Sort dialog box is used to set which document will be sorted, where the result will be placed, and how the sort will be performed.

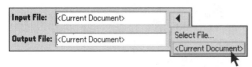

Figure 42. Click the list button, then choose either Select File or ‹Current Document› from the drop-down list.

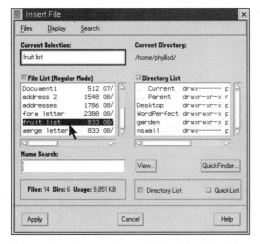

Figure 43. Use the Insert File dialog box to select the file that will be sorted.

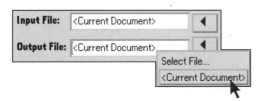

Figure 44. Click the list button, the choose either Select File or ‹Current Document› from the drop-down list.

4. Set the Input File by:

   A. Clicking the list button next to the Input File text box and choosing Select File or ‹Current Document› from the drop-down list (**Figure 42**). If you choose Select File, the Insert File dialog box will appear (**Figure 43**).

   B. If you are using the Insert File dialog box, use the Directory List and File List boxes to select the form file that you created, then click OK. The Insert File dialog box will close, returning you to the Sort dialog box.

5. Set the file where the sorted information will be placed by:

   A. Clicking the list button next to the Output File text box and choosing Select File or ‹Current Document› from the drop-down list (**Figure 44**). If you choose Select File, the Insert File dialog box will appear (**Figure 43**).

   B. If you are using the Insert File dialog box, use the Directory List and File List boxes to select the form file that you created, then click OK. The Insert File dialog box will close, returning you to the Sort dialog box.

6. Choose a radio button in the Sort By area to set the type of sort by line, paragraph, merge record, table row, or column (**Figure 45**).

(continued)

Figure 45. Use the radio buttons in the Sort By area to set whether the sort will be performed by line, paragraph, merge record, table row, or column.

SORT A DOCUMENT

7. In the Key Definitions area (**Figure 46**):

   A. Use the Type drop-down list to set whether the sort is alphabetic or numeric.

   B. Use the Sort Order drop-down list to set whether the sort is ascending (A to Z, 1 to 10) or descending (Z to A, or 10 to 1).

8. If you want to place uppercase letters first in an alphabetical sort (for instance, Coffee would come before coffee), select the check box next to Uppercase First.

9. Click OK. The sort will be performed and the result will appear in the document window (**Figure 47**).

✔ Tips

■ If you decide that you didn't want to sort the items after all, click the Undo button on the WordPerfect 8 Toolbar or choose Undo from the Edit menu.

■ There are many more sorting features available in WordPerfect, but they go well beyond the scope of this book (it's quite an advanced topic). To find out more about sorting, turn to pages 464–472 in the *WordPerfect 8 User's Guide* that comes with the Personal Edition.

Figure 46. Use the Key Definitions area to set whether the sort is alphabetic or numeric, and whether the sort will be performed in an ascending or descending order.

Figure 47. When you click OK in the Sort dialog box, the contents of the document are sorted and displayed in their new order.

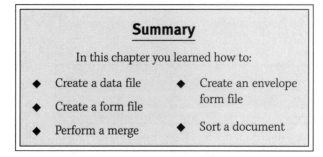

Summary

In this chapter you learned how to:

◆ Create a data file

◆ Create a form file

◆ Perform a merge

◆ Create an envelope form file

◆ Sort a document

MACROS
MADE EASY

Macros are mini-programs that perform keystrokes and commands automatically. They can save a lot of time and mouse clicking if a task needs to be performed over and over. For instance, suppose you want to end your business letters with the closing "Sincerely," then your name a few spaces below that. You could create a macro that would move the insertion point to the bottom of the document, automatically insert "Sincerely," and then move down the allotted space and insert your name.

WordPerfect macros do not use a specialized macro editor. To edit a macro, you simply need to open it in WordPerfect, just as you would any other document.

There are two ways to *record* macros. You can:

◆ Create the macro by performing the actions that you want the macro to execute. Think of it as a cassette recorder being used to record keystrokes and commands instead of sounds. WordPerfect records the commands for you.

◆ Type in the actual commands themselves. For this, you will need a knowledge of the WordPerfect macro language and its syntax.

This chapter deals with the first of these recording methods. The second is well beyond the scope of this book. If you are interested in learning about macro commands and syntax, take a look at the online Macro manual that comes with the Personal Edition. To access it, choose Macros from the Help menu.

There are 17 macros that ship with the WordPerfect Personal Edition. Their functionality ranges from capitalizing the first letter in a selected word to using graphics to create decorative borders.

Recording Macros

Recording macros is very simple. All you need to do is turn on the macro recorder (much like pressing the record button on a tape player or VCR) and perform the keystrokes you want repeated. You might want to practice the keystrokes first for your little "performance." If you make a mistake, don't worry, you can just start recording the macro from the beginning again.

As you type the commands and keystrokes, WordPerfect automatically records what you type. You should know, however, that while the macro recorder is recording, you won't be able to use the mouse to position the insertion point in the document. If you want to move the insertion point, you will have to use the keyboard. Some of the most frequently used keystrokes are listed on page 57.

To record a macro:

1. Choose Record from the Macro fly-out on the Tools menu (**Figure 1**) or press Ctrl+F10 on the keyboard. The Record Macro dialog box will open (**Figure 2**).

2. Click the list button next to the Macro Name text box. The Select File dialog box will appear (**Figure 3**).

3. Use the Select File dialog box to move to the directory where you want to save the macro.

4. Type the name of your macro with a .wcm file extension in the Filename/ Current Selection dialog box. Make sure to type the .wcm extension. This tells WordPerfect that the file is a macro. (The directory where the macros that ship with WordPerfect are stored is /wp/wpmacros. You might what to put the macro there or create your own macro directory.)

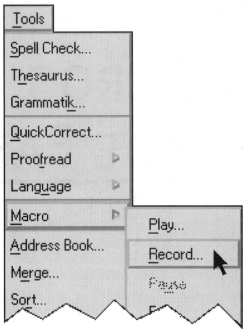

Figure 1. Choose Record from the Macro fly-out on the Tools menu.

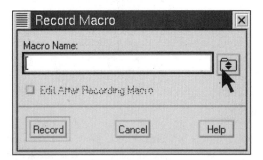

Figure 2. Click the list button in the Record Macro dialog box to set the location where the macro will be saved and what it will be named.

Figure 3. Use the Select File dialog box to set where the macro is stored. Enter the name of your new macro in the Filename/Current Selection text box, then click OK to return to the Record Macro dialog box.

Figure 4. When the location of the macro to be recorded and its name are set in the Macro Name text box, click Record.

5. Click OK. The Select File dialog box will close, returning you to the Record Macro dialog box. The text box will be filled with the full path of the macro you are about to record (**Figure 4**).

6. Click Record. The Record Macro dialog box will close, returning you to the document window, and the macro recorder will be turned on.

7. Enter the keystrokes and commands that you want executed by the macro.

8. When you are finished recording your macro, turn the macro recorder off by choosing Record from the Macro fly-out on the Tools menu (**Figure 1**).

✔ Tips

- It does seem confusing to use a Select File dialog box to set the name and location of a macro that hasn't been recorded yet. But, don't let the dialog box title throw you, it still works the way it should.

- Make sure a filename is entered in the text box in the Record Macro dialog box before you click Record. Otherwise, WordPerfect will create a *temporary macro* that will be deleted when you exit WordPerfect.

RECORD A MACRO

To play a macro:

1. Choose Play from the Macro fly-out on the Tools menu (**Figure 5**) or press Shift+Ctrl+F10 on the keyboard. The Play Macro dialog box will appear (**Figure 6**).

2. Click the list button next to the right of the Macro Name text box. The Select File dialog box will open with the WordPerfect default macro directory open (**Figure 7**).

3. Use the Directory List box to move to the directory where the macro is stored, then use the File List box to select the macro.

4. Click OK. The Select File dialog box will close, returning you to the Play Macro dialog box. The full path of the macro file you selected will be entered in the text box.

5. Click Play. The Play Macro dialog box will close and the macro will execute its recorded keystrokes and commands.

✔ Tips

- If you are using a macro that will make changes to a selected word, line, or paragraph, make sure you use the mouse to select the text before playing the macro.

- If you play a macro and don't get the results you expected, you can undo the macro's actions by clicking the Undo button on the WordPerfect 8 Toolbar or selecting Undo from the Edit menu.

- The WordPerfect Personal Edition ships with 17 macros, ready for you to use. You will find them in the /wp/wpmacros directory. To find out what each of these macros does, open the online Macro manual by choosing Macros from the Help menu, and then click the Shipping Macros link on the help page that opens.

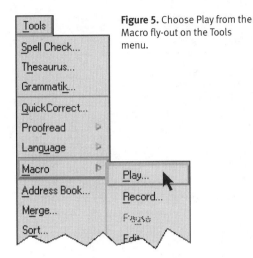

Figure 5. Choose Play from the Macro fly-out on the Tools menu.

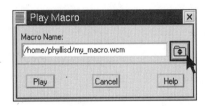

Figure 6. Click the list button in the Play Macro dialog box to locate the macro in the directory where it is stored.

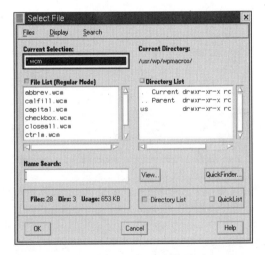

Figure 7. Use the Directory List and File List boxes to locate and select the macro you want to play.

PLAY A MACRO

Figure 8. Choose Toolbars from the View menu.

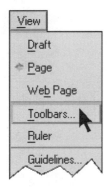

Making Your Macros Easy to Play

There are two places you can put a macro to make it easy to find and play. You can add a macro to a toolbar or assign a keyboard shortcut. This means that every time you want to play the macro, all you have to do is click a toolbar button or press the appropriate keys on the keyboard.

To add a macro to a toolbar, you will first need to display the toolbar you want to add the macro button to, then edit that toolbar.

To display a toolbar:

1. Choose Toolbars from the View menu (**Figure 8**). The Toolbars dialog box will open (**Figure 9**).

2. From the Available toolbars list box, select the toolbar you want to view.

3. Click OK. The toolbar will appear at the top of the document window.

or

Right click on a toolbar and choose the toolbar you want to open from the QuickMenu that appears (**Figure 10**). The toolbar will appear at the top of the document window.

Figure 9. From the Available toolbars list box, select the check box next to the toolbar you want to view.

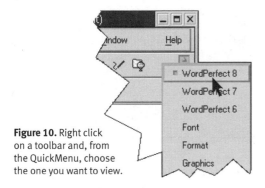

Figure 10. Right click on a toolbar and, from the QuickMenu, choose the one you want to view.

DISPLAY A TOOLBAR

To add a macro button to a toolbar:

1. Right click on the toolbar to which you want to add a macro button.

2. Choose Edit from the QuickMenu (**Figure 11**). The Toolbar Editor dialog box for that toolbar will open with the Activate a Feature option button selected (**Figure 12**).

3. Select the radio button next to Play a Macro. The dialog box will change to show an Add Macro button (**Figure 13**).

4. Click Add Macro. The Select Macro dialog box will appear (**Figure 14**).

5. Click the list button next to the Macro Name text box. The Select File dialog box will open with the WordPerfect default macro directory open (**Figure 7**).

6. Use the Directory List box to move to the directory where the macro is stored, then use the File List box to select the macro.

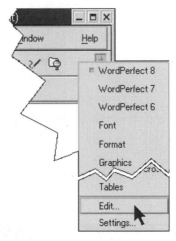

Figure 11. Right click on the toolbar that you want to add the button to, then choose Edit from the QuickMenu.

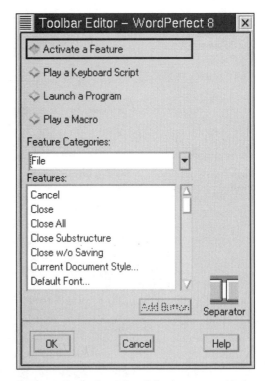

Figure 12. The Toolbar Editor dialog box opens with the Activate a Feature radio button selected.

Figure 13. When you click the Play a Macro radio button, an Add Macro button appears in the dialog box.

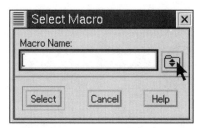

Figure 14. Click the list button next to the Macro Name text box to select the macro that you want to assign to the toolbar.

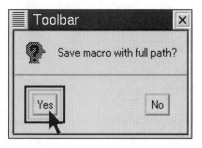

Figure 15. Click Yes to save the macro with its full path. This is necessary if the macro is located in a directory other than the WordPerfect default directory, /wp/wpmacros.

Macro button

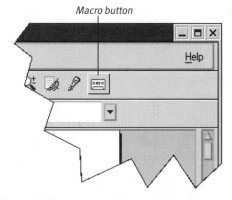

Figure 16. The new macro button appears on the toolbar, ready for you to click. Try it out! Position the insertion point, if you need to, then click the macro button and watch the macro play!

7. Click OK. The Select File dialog box will close, returning you to the Select Macro dialog box. The full path of the macro file you selected will be entered in the text box.

8. Click Select. A Toolbar dialog box will open, asking whether you want to save the macro with its full pathname (**Figure 15**).

9. Click Yes. The Toolbar and Select Macro dialog boxes will close, returning you to the Toolbar Editor dialog box. A button with a cassette tape icon on it will appear on the toolbar (**Figure 16**).

10. Click OK to close the Toolbar Editor dialog box and return to the document window. Your custom macro button is ready to go!

✔ Tips

■ In step 5, if you select a macro that is saved in the WordPerfect default directory (/wp/wpmacros), the Toolbar dialog box (**Figure 15**) will not appear.

■ You can also use the Toolbar Editor to add buttons for virtually every WordPerfect command to any toolbar that you want to customize. This can be a big help if you use a particular command many times.

ADD A MACRO BUTTON TO A TOOLBAR

To assign a macro to a keyboard shortcut:

1. Choose Preferences in the program window (**Figure 17**). The Preferences dialog box will open (**Figure 18**).

2. Click Keyboard. The Keyboard Preferences dialog box will open (**Figure 19**). The keyboard you are using will be selected in the Keyboards list box.

3. Click Create. The Create Keyboard dialog box will appear (**Figure 20**).

4. Type a name for your custom keyboard into the New Keyboard Name dialog box. You could use your name, for instance, or a name that describes the personalized nature of the keyboard.

5. Click OK. The Create Keyboard dialog box will close and the Keyboard Editor dialog box will open (**Figure 21**).

6. In the Choose a Key to Assign or Unassign area, use the drop-down list to select a keystroke combination that will play the macro. This list box is divided into two columns (**Figure 22**). The left column shows the keystroke and the right column shows what is assigned to that keystroke. If there is nothing in the column to the right of a keystroke, that keystroke is unassigned. Make sure you select an unassigned keystroke. For this example, F12+Ctrl has been selected because it is an unassigned keystroke.

Figure 17. Choose Preferences in the program window.

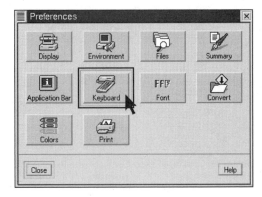

Figure 18. Click Keyboard in the Preferences dialog box.

Figure 19. Select the keyboard you are using from the list box, then click Create. You will be creating a new keyboard, based on the one selected in the list box.

Figure 20. Type a name for the custom keyboard in the text box, then click OK.

Figure 21. The Keyboard Editor dialog box is used to assign keystrokes. You can customize your keyboard to help you quickly perform the commands you use most.

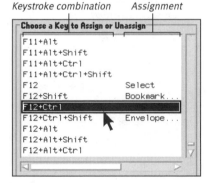

Figure 22. The list box is divided into two columns, the left for the keystroke combination and the right for its current assignment. For this example F12+Ctrl has been selected because it is unassigned.

7. In the Assign Key To area, select the radio button next to Play a Macro. The Assign Key To area will change to display an Assign Macro button (**Figure 23**).

8. Click Assign Macro. The Select Macro dialog box will appear (**Figure 14**).

9. Click the list button next to the Macro Name text box. The Select File dialog box will open with the WordPerfect default macro directory open (**Figure 7**).

10. Use the Directory List box to move to the directory where the macro is stored, then use the File List box to select the macro.

11. Click OK. The Select File dialog box will close, returning you to the Select Macro dialog box. The full path of the macro file you selected will be entered in the text box.

12. Click Select. A Select Macro dialog box will open, asking whether you want to save the macro with its full pathname (**Figure 24**).

13. Click Yes. The two Select Macro dialog boxes will close, returning you to the Keyboard Editor dialog box. The macro you selected will appear with its full pathname to the right of the keystroke combination you selected in the list box (**Figure 25**).

(continued)

Figure 23. Select the radio button next to Play a Macro, then click the Assign Macro button.

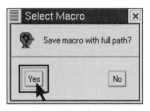

Figure 24. Click Yes to save the macro with its full path.

14. Click OK. The Keyboard Editor dialog box will close, returning you to the Keyboard Preferences dialog box. The name of the new keyboard you created will appear in the Keyboards list box (**Figure 26**).

15. Make sure the new keyboard is selected in the Keyboards list box, then click Select. The Keyboards Preferences dialog box will close, returning you to the Preferences dialog box.

16. Click Close to close the Preferences dialog box and return to the WordPerfect document window. Try out your new macro keyboard shortcut. Position the insertion point, if you need to, then press the keyboard combination and watch the macro play!

✔ Tips

- ■ If you make a mistake and assign the macro to a keyboard combination you didn't intend to, just select the keyboard combination from the Choose a Key to Assign or Unassign area, then click the Unassign button.

- ■ If you play a macro and don't get the results you wanted, just click the Undo button on the WordPerfect 8 Toolbar, or choose Undo from the Edit menu.

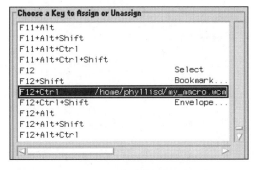

Figure 25. The macro and its full path appear in the assignment column. In this example, the keystroke combination F12+Ctrl is now assigned to my_macro.wcm and will play that macro when pressed.

Figure 26. Select your new custom keyboard in the Keyboards list box, then click Select.

Summary

In this chapter you learned how to:

- ◆ Record a macro
- ◆ Play a macro
- ◆ Display a toolbar
- ◆ Assign a macro to a toolbar button
- ◆ Assign a macro to a keyboard shortcut

ASSIGN A MACRO TO A KEYBOARD SHORTCUT

CREATING WEB DOCUMENTS

Now that you know how to use most of WordPerfect's document creation tools, it's time to take your expertise to the World Wide Web. Believe it or not, creating Web pages is easy with WordPerfect's *Internet Publisher*. The Internet Publisher works with a special *Web Editor* that contains all the Web formatting options you will need.

This chapter will take you through everything you need to know to create a Web page. First, you will open the Web Editor, specify a *title*, create headings, and add text. Then, you will insert bulleted and numbered lists. Next, you'll find out how to create *hypertext links* and *image links*. Finally, you will save your document in *HTML format*, ready for browsing on the Web.

World Wide Web Terms

◆ **Browser**—the program that decodes the information coming from a Web server, turning it into the Web pages you see on your computer monitor. One of the predominant browsers is Netscape Navigator.

◆ **HTML** (Hypertext Markup Language)— a computer language used for describing the contents of Web pages. The Web Editor takes care of writing the HTML files for you. You don't need to know HTML to use the Web Editor.

◆ **Hyperlink**—an image or text that is clicked by the user to jump to another Web page in the same Web site or to another Web site.

◆ **ISP** (Internet Service Provider)—a business that provides the service of connecting users to the Internet.

◆ **URL** (Uniform Resource Locator)—a URL is an address for a Web site. A URL example is `http://www.bearhome.com`.

◆ **Web server**—a computer connected to the Web that contains Web pages.

The Internet Publisher

The Internet Publisher will help you create new documents using the appropriate HTML codes. It will also convert an existing document into Web-ready HTML format. You should know, however, that if you do convert an existing document, there are several features not supported in HTML. Some of these include columns, drop caps, footnotes, page numbering, tabs and indents, and macros. For a complete list of unsupported features, turn to page 281 in the *WordPerfect User's Guide* that ships with the Personal Edition.

To create a new Web document:

1. Choose Internet Publisher from the File menu (**Figure 1**). The Internet Publisher window will open (**Figure 2**).

2. Click New Web Document. The Web Editor will appear with a blank document open in the editor window, ready for you to create your Web pages (**Figure 3**).

✔ Tip

■ The Web Editor is actually a special version of the normal document window setup to create Web pages.

Figure 1. Choose Internet Publisher from the File menu.

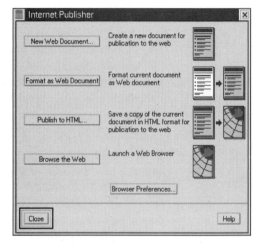

Figure 2. The Internet Publisher window helps you create Web-ready documents.

Figure 3. The new Web document opens in the Web Editor, ready for you to create your Web pages.

Figure 4. Open the document you want to convert.

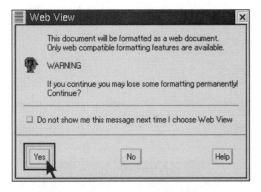

Figure 5. Before the actual conversion, WordPerfect warns you that some formatting may be lost.

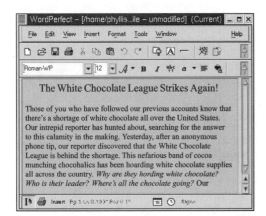

Figure 6. After the document is converted, it appears in the Web Editor window.

To convert an existing document to a Web document:

1. Open the document you want to convert (**Figure 4**).

2. Choose Internet Publisher from the File menu (**Figure 1**). The Internet Publisher window will open (**Figure 2**).

3. Click Format as Web Document. The Web View dialog box will open, telling you that some of the formatting will be lost (**Figure 5**).

4. Click Yes to continue with the conversion. The document is converted to a Web document and appears in the Web Editor window (**Figure 6**).

✔ Tips

- WordPerfect tries to save as much of the formatting of your document as possible when it performs the conversion. However, since a regular document and a Web document are two entirely different critters, they will look a bit different.

- If you decide that you didn't want to convert a document to Web format after all, you can revert it back to its previous form. Immediately after the conversion, click the Close button at the upper-right corner of the Web Editor window to close the document. When you open it again, you will see that it is in its original form.

Adding a Title

Now that you've created a new Web document and converted a regular document to Web format, it's time to add the text, graphics, and formatting that will make your Web pages distinctive.

The first thing you should do is add a title to your Web page. The title is displayed in the title bar of the Web browser. If you do not specify a title, WordPerfect automatically uses the first heading.

To add a title:

1. Choose Title from the Format menu (**Figure 7**). The Title dialog box will appear (**Figure 8**).

2. Select the Custom Title radio button, then type your title in the text box. The title shouldn't be too long, just something descriptive about the page or your Web site.

3. Click OK. The Title dialog box will close. You will see the title when you view the Web page with a browser (**Figure 9**).

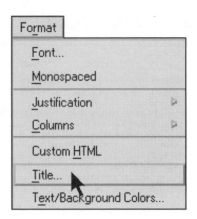

Figure 7. Choose Title from the Format menu.

Figure 8. In the Title area, select the Custom Title radio button, and then type the title in the text box.

Title bar

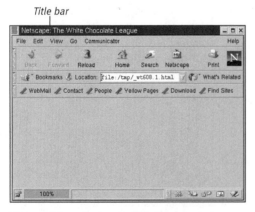

Figure 9. When you view the Web document in a browser, the title appears in the browser's title bar.

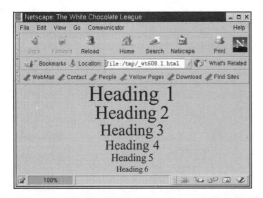

Figure 10. The six different heading sizes shown in a browser.

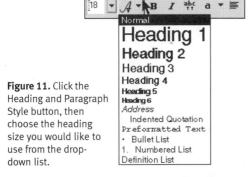

Figure 11. Click the Heading and Paragraph Style button, then choose the heading size you would like to use from the drop-down list.

Headings

Web pages use special heading styles. There are six levels—Heading 1 is the largest and Heading 6 the smallest. **Figure 10** shows the relative heading sizes.

To add a heading:

1. Click the Heading and Paragraph Style button on the Property Bar (**Figure 11**).

2. Choose the heading size you would like to use from the drop-down list.

3. Type the heading.

4. Press Enter on the keyboard to end the heading. Headings can really get folks' attention (**Figure 12**).

✔ Tip

■ You can also select text that you would like to format as a heading, then follow steps 2–3.

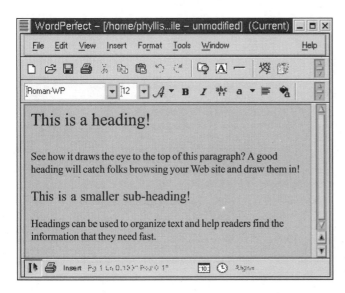

Figure 12. Headings can help organize your Web documents and draw attention where it's needed.

ADD HEADINGS

Entering and Formatting Text

Entering and formatting text in a Web document is the same as a normal WordPerfect document. All the skills you have learned previously in this book can be applied here. Text formatting can be divided into two categories, character level formatting and paragraph level formatting.

To add text:

Position the insertion point where you want to add the text, then type your text (**Figure 13**).

✔ Tips

■ When you press Enter to start a new paragraph, a double-spaced line will be inserted between the paragraphs.

■ If you want to start a new line without starting a new paragraph, choose Line Break from the Insert menu (**Figure 14**).

To edit text:

Select the text you would like to change, then type the replacement text (**Figure 15**). The selected text is deleted and the replacement text takes its place.

To delete text:

Select the text you want to delete, then press the Backspace or Delete keys on the keyboard.

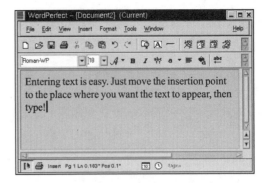

Figure 13. Typing text in a Web document is exactly the same as typing text in the regular WordPerfect document window.

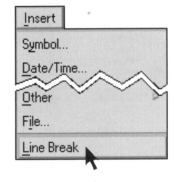

Figure 14. Choose Line Break from the Insert menu.

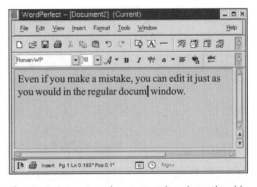

Figure 15. As you type the new text, it replaces the old, selected text.

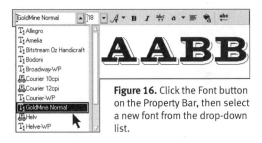

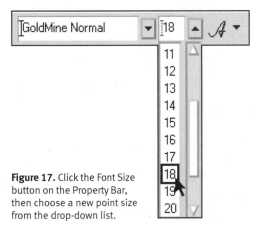

Figure 17. Click the Font Size button on the Property Bar, then choose a new point size from the drop-down list.

Figure 16. Click the Font button on the Property Bar, then select a new font from the drop-down list.

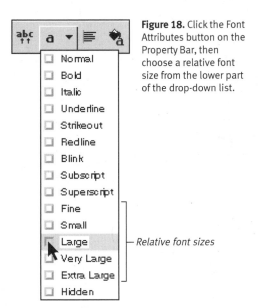

Figure 18. Click the Font Attributes button on the Property Bar, then choose a relative font size from the lower part of the drop-down list.

— Relative font sizes

To change fonts:

1. Select the text you want to change.

   or

   Position the insertion point where you would like the new font to start.

2. Click the Font button on the Property Bar and choose a new font from the drop-down list (**Figure 16**).

✔ Tip

■ If you use a special font, the folks browsing your Web pages must have that font loaded on their computers. Otherwise, the text will appear in the browser's default font which, most likely, would be some form of Times (also called Roman or Times Roman).

To make text larger or smaller:

1. Select the text you want to change.

2. Click the Font Size button on the Property Bar and choose a new font point size from the drop-down list (**Figure 17**).

   or

   Click the Font Attributes button on the Property Bar and choose a relative font size from the drop-down list (**Figure 18**). These sizes include Fine, Small, Large, Very Large, and Extra Large.

✔ Tip

■ For a discussion of font point sizing, turn to page 80. For details about relative font sizing, take a look at page 81.

CHANGE FONTS; MAKE TEXT LARGER OR SMALLER

To make text bold or italic:

1. Select the text you want to change.

2. Click the Bold or Italic button on the Property Bar.

   or

   Click the Font Attributes button on the Property Bar and choose Bold or Italic from the drop-down list (**Figure 19**).

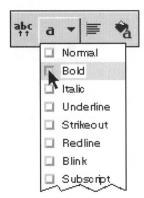

Figure 19. Click the Font Attributes button on the Property Bar and choose Bold from the drop-down list.

To make text underlined:

1. Select the text you want to change.

2. Click the Font Attributes button on the Property Bar and choose Underline from the drop-down list (**Figure 20**).

✔ Tip

■ You can activate more than one font attribute at a time, for instance, bold and italic.

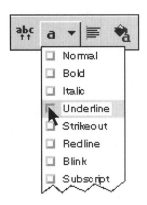

Figure 20. Click the Font Attributes button on the Property Bar and choose Underline from the drop-down list.

To make text blink:

1. Select the text you want to make blink.

2. Click the Font Attributes button on the Property Bar and choose Blink from the drop-down list (**Figure 21**).

✔ Tip

■ Use blinking text sparingly. It can get quite annoying if everything on a Web page is blinking!

To change the text's color:

1. Select the text you want to change.

2. Click the Font Color button on the Property Bar and choose a new color from the palette that appears (**Figure 22**).

Figure 21. Click the Font Attributes button on the Property Bar and choose Blink from the drop-down list.

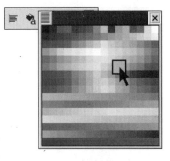

Figure 22. Click the Font Color button on the Property Bar and choose a new color from the palette.

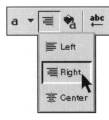

Figure 23. Click the Align button on the Property Bar and choose a justification from the drop-down list.

Figure 24. Choose Bullets & Numbering from the Insert menu.

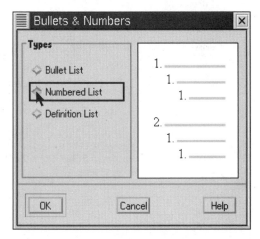

Figure 25. Select the radio button next to Bullet List or Numbered List, then click OK.

Paragraph Formatting

Just like a regular WordPerfect document, paragraph formatting in a Web document affects an entire paragraph of text. Some paragraph formatting includes justification, bulleted and numbered lists, and double indentation.

To justify paragraph text:

1. Select the text you want to justify.

2. Click the Align button on the Property Bar and choose a justification from the drop-down list (**Figure 23**).

To create a bulleted or numbered list:

1. Position the insertion point where you would like the list to start.

2. There are two ways to select a list style:

   A. Choose Bullets & Numbering from the Insert menu (**Figure 24**). The Bullets & Numbers dialog box will open (**Figure 25**).

   B. Select either the Bullet List or Numbered List radio button.

   C. Click OK. The Bullets & Numbers dialog box will close, returning you to the editor window.

   or

   Click the Heading and Paragraph Style button on the Property Bar and choose Bullet List or Numbered List from the drop-down list (**Figure 26**).

(continued)

CREATE A BULLETED OR NUMBERED LIST

3. Type the list, pressing the Enter key each time you want to add another list item.

4. To turn off the list style:

    A. Press Enter on the keyboard after your last list entry.

    B. Click the Heading and Paragraph Style button on the Property Bar and choose Normal from the drop-down list (**Figure 27**).

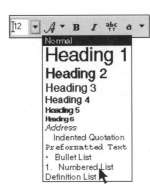

Figure 26. Click the Heading and Paragraph Style button on the Property Bar and choose Bullet List or Numbered List from the drop-down list.

✔ Tip

■ To move to a second or third level under a list item, press the Tab key on the keyboard.

To double indent a paragraph:

1. Select the text that you would like to indent on both the left and right sides.

2. Click the Heading and Paragraph Style button on the Property Bar and choose Indented Quotation from the drop-down list (**Figure 28**). The text will indent on both sides.

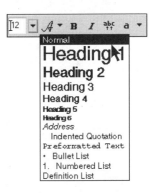

Figure 27. When you are finished with the list, press Enter on the keyboard, then choose Normal from the Heading and Paragraph Style drop-down list.

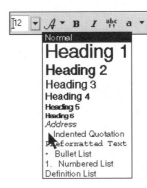

Figure 28. Click the Heading and Paragraph Style button on the Property Bar, then choose Indented Quotation from the drop-down list.

Figure 30. Use the Background Color/Wallpaper area to set your Web page's background.

Figure 29. Choose Text/Background Colors from the Format menu.

Figure 31. Click the tiny button to the right of Background Color, then choose a new color from the palette.

Figure 32. Use the Select File dialog box to find the image file. The dialog box will only let you select .gif files.

Figure 33. If you choose an image for your background, you will only be able to see it when the Web page is viewed in a browser. In this example, an image has been tiled across and down the Web page.

Background Colors and Images

Gray is the default background color in the Web Editor, but it doesn't have to be your choice. It's easy to set a new background color or choose an image that is *tiled* on the Web page. A tiled image is repeated, across and down the Web page to create a complete background.

To set a background color or image:

1. Choose Text/Background Colors from the Format menu (**Figure 29**). The Text/Background Colors dialog box will open (**Figure 30**).

2. **To set a background color:**

   A. Click the tiny button to the right of Background Color in the Background Color/Wallpaper area. A color palette will appear (**Figure 31**).

   B. Click the color you want to use. The color palette will close.

   To set an image as the background:

   A. Click the list button next to the Background Wallpaper text box. The Select File dialog box will appear (**Figure 32**).

   B. Use the Directory List and File List boxes to move to the directory where the image file is stored and then select it.

   C. Click OK. The full path of the image fill will appear in the Background Wallpaper text box.

3. Click OK. The Text/Background Colors dialog box will close. If you chose a color it will appear as the background of your Web document. If you chose an image, you will only be able to see it when you view your Web page with a browser (**Figure 33**).

SET A BACKGROUND COLOR OR IMAGE

Creating Links

Hyperlinks are one thing that makes the Web great. The cross-referencing power of links—the ability to jump from one Web page or site to another—is immense. Creating hypertext links is easy. All you need to do is associate selected text with the Web page or site you want to jump to.

To create a hypertext link:

1. Select the text that you want the user to click to jump to another Web page or site.

2. Choose Hyperlink from the Tools menu (**Figure 34**). The Create Hypertext Link dialog box will open (**Figure 35**).

3. Select the radio button next to Go To Other Document (**Figure 36**).

4. In the Go To Other Document text box, type the full URL of the Web page or site. For instance, `http://www.bearhome.com`.

5. Click OK. The Create Hypertext Link dialog box will close and the selected text will be underlined and change color, indicating that it is now a hypertext link.

✔ Tip

■ The default color of a hypertext link is blue. If you want to change it, take a look at the next page.

Figure 34. Choose Hyperlink from the Tools menu.

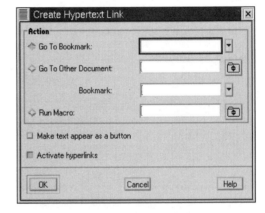

Figure 35. The Create Hypertext link dialog box is used to link URLs to selected text.

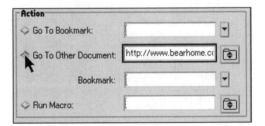

Figure 36. Select the Go To Other Document radio button, then type the URL of the Web site or page to which you want to link.

Figure 37. Choose Text/Background Colors from the Format menu.

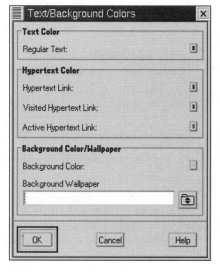

Figure 38. Use the Hypertext Color area to set your Web page's hypertext link colors.

To change hypertext link color:

1. Choose Text/Background Colors from the Format menu (**Figure 37**). The Text/Background Colors dialog box will open (**Figure 38**).

2. In the Hypertext Color area, click the tiny button to the right of Hypertext Link and select a new color from the palette that appears (**Figure 39**).

3. Click OK. The Text/Background Colors dialog box will close and your hyperlink text will change to the new color.

✔ Tip

■ If you wish to change the colors for Visited Hypertext Link and Active Hypertext Link, click the appropriate buttons in the Hypertext Color area and choose new colors from the palettes that appear.

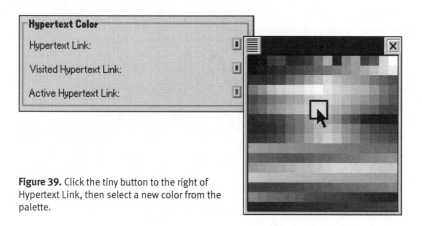

Figure 39. Click the tiny button to the right of Hypertext Link, then select a new color from the palette.

CHANGE HYPERTEXT LINK COLOR

Inserting Images

Pictures are worth a thousand words and Web images are no different! You can insert any of the clipart images that come with the Personal Edition of WordPerfect. The Web Editor will automatically convert them to the proper Web format.

Along with images go two things that need to be set:

◆ Alternate text—this is text that appears on the Web page while the image loads in the browser.

◆ Spacing around the graphic to set text flow.

Also, just like the graphics discussed in Chapter 6, *Clipart, Lines, & Charts*, you can add borders, fills, and captions. For details on how to add these items, turn to pages 101–106.

To insert an image:

1. Position the insertion point where you would like the image to appear.

2. Choose From File from the Graphics fly-out on the Insert menu (**Figure 40**). The Insert Image dialog box will appear (**Figure 41**).

3. Use the Directory List and File List boxes to move to where the image is stored and select it.

4. Click Insert. The image will appear on your Web page (**Figure 42**).

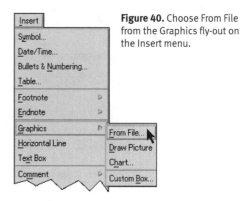

Figure 40. Choose From File from the Graphics fly-out on the Insert menu.

Figure 41. Use the Insert Image dialog box to locate the image file and select it.

Figure 42. The image appears where the insertion point is located. Any text near the image moves over to make room for the picture.

Figure 43.
Right click on the image and choose HTML Properties from the QuickMenu.

To set alternate text:

1. Right click on the image for which you want to set alternate text.

2. Choose HTML Properties from the QuickMenu (**Figure 43**). The HTML Properties dialog box will open (**Figure 44**).

3. Enter the text that you would like to appear while the image is loading into the Alternate Text box (**Figure 45**).

4. Click OK. The HTML Properties dialog box will close and the alternate text will appear when the Web page is loading into a browser.

Figure 44.
The HTML Properties dialog box is used to set alternate text and image links.

To set spacing around an image:

1. Right click on the image for which you want to set spacing.

2. Choose HTML Properties from the QuickMenu (**Figure 43**). The HTML Properties dialog box will open (**Figure 44**).

3. In the Display Options area, use the Horizontal Spacing, Vertical Spacing, and Border Width text boxes to set the space between the graphic and text. The number you enter is in pixels. (This is the unit of measure for Web pages.)

4. Click OK. The image will adjust its spacing and the text will appear the specified distance from the image (**Figure 46**).

Figure 45.
Type the text in the Alternate Text box.

Figure 46. The spacing around the image changes and the text moves to accommodate the new spacing.

SET ALTERNATE TEXT; SET IMAGE SPACING

To create an image link:

1. Right click on the image you want to set as a link.

2. Choose HTML Properties from the QuickMenu (**Figure 43**). The HTML Properties dialog box will open (**Figure 44**).

3. In the Define Mouse Click Action area, select the radio button next to Link (**Figure 47**).

4. Click the Link Properties button. The Edit Hypertext dialog box will open (**Figure 48**).

5. Select the radio button next to Go To Other Document, then type the full URL of the Web page or site. For instance, http://www.bearhome.com.

6. Click OK. The Edit Hypertext dialog box will close, returning you to the HTML Properties dialog box.

7. Click OK. The HTML Properties dialog box will close, returning you to the Web Editor. When you view your Web page in a browser, click the image, and the link will jump you to the specified Web page or site.

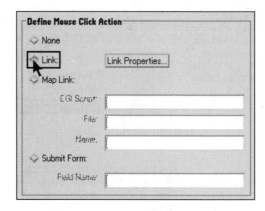

Figure 47. In the Define Mouse Click Action area, select the Link radio button, then click the Link Properties button.

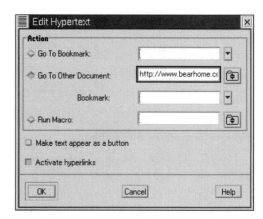

Figure 48. Click the Go To Other Document radio button, then type the Web page or site URL in the text box.

Help with Web Design

The best source for advice on the Web is the Web itself. There are many sites on the Web that offer advice on Web page design and style. Page design isn't just about pretty pictures, it includes creating user-friendly sites that make it easy for visitors to find the information they need. A few sites that offer interesting advice and tools for Web design are:

◆ Sun Microsystems Inc.'s Guide to Web Style: http://www.sun.com/styleguide

◆ Web Designer's Paradise: http://desktoppublishing.com/webparadise.html

◆ Web design links available at Yahoo: http://www.yahoo.com/Computers_and_Internet/ Internet/World_Wide_Web/Page_Creation

CREATE AN IMAGE LINK

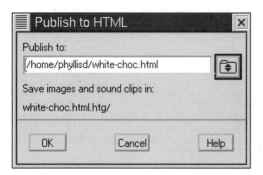

Figure 49. Type the location and name for the Web document in the Publish to text box, or click the list button and use the Select File dialog box to set the location and file name.

Figure 50. Use the Directory List box to move to the location where you want to store your Web document, then type the name in the Filename/Current Selection text box. It may seem confusing to use a "Select File" dialog box to name a Web document that has yet to be published, but it works fine all the same.

Figure 51. Choose View in Web Browser from the View menu.

Saving and Viewing Your Web Pages

After all the work is done the fun begins! It's easy to save your Web document in HTML format and view it in a browser. When a Web document is saved, WordPerfect considers that it has been *published*, meaning that it is ready for upload to a Web server.

To save your Web pages in HTML format:

1. Choose Internet Publisher from the File menu (**Figure 1**). The Internet Publisher window will appear (**Figure 2**).

2. Click Publish to HTML. The Publish to HTML dialog box will open (**Figure 49**).

3. In the Publish to text box type in the location where you would like the Web document saved.

    or

    A. Click the list button. The Select File dialog box will appear (**Figure 50**).

    B. Use the Directory List box to move to the location where you would like to store the Web document.

    C. Type the name that you would like to save the Web document as in the Filename/Current Selection text box.

    D. Click OK. The full pathname that the Web document will be saved as will appear in the Publish to text box.

4. Click OK. The Web document will be saved in HTML format. You can open the document and edit it like any other WordPerfect document.

To view your Web pages:

Choose View in Web Browser from the View menu (**Figure 51**). The Web page will load in your browser (**Figure 52**).

✔ Tips

■ If WordPerfect can't find your browser, choose Internet Publisher from the File menu to open the Internet Publisher dialog box (**Figure 2**). Click the Browser Preferences button to open the Browser Preferences dialog box (**Figure 53**). Click the File button next to the Full path to your Web Browser text box and use the Select File dialog box to locate the browser.

■ Viewing Web pages in a browser is handy. You can check out hypertext and image links to make sure they work, and see exactly how the Web page appears in the browser.

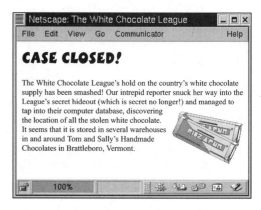

Figure 52. Your Web page appears in the browser.

Figure 53. In the Web Browser area, enter the full path of your browser in the text box.

Summary

In this chapter you learned how to:

- ◆ Create a new Web document
- ◆ Convert an existing document to a Web document
- ◆ Add a title to your Web page
- ◆ Add headings
- ◆ Add, edit, and delete text
- ◆ Change font and font size
- ◆ Make text bold, italic, or underlined
- ◆ Make text blink

- ◆ Change text color
- ◆ Create bulleted and numbered lists
- ◆ Double indent paragraphs
- ◆ Create hypertext links
- ◆ Set background colors and images
- ◆ Create an image link
- ◆ Save your Web document
- ◆ View your Web document in a browser

14

PRINTING

Figure 1. Choose Print from the File menu.

Printing can be used in many ways. Besides printing a document when it is completed, you can print draft documents to see how they look on paper. You can try a special effect and then print it to see how it looks (many times the printed page appears quite different from what you see on the monitor). Or you can even print a document for good old red pencil editing.

To print a document:

1. Choose Print from the File menu (**Figure 1**) or click the Print button on the WordPerfect 8 Toolbar. The Print dialog box will open with Full Document selected in the Print Selection area (**Figure 2**).

2. Click OK. The document will print.

✔ Tip

■ It's a good idea to always save your document before you print.

Figure 2. Click OK to print the document.

To print more than one copy of a document:

1. Choose Print from the File menu (**Figure 1**) or click the Print button on the WordPerfect 8 Toolbar. The Print dialog box will open (**Figure 2**).

2. In the Copies area on the right side of the dialog box, type a number in the Number of Copies text box or click the little up arrow to increase the number (**Figure 3**).

3. Click OK.

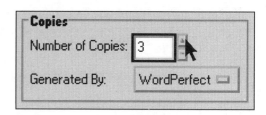

Figure 3. Use the Number of Copies text box to set how many copies of a document will print.

To print the current page:

1. Position the insertion point on the page you would like to print.

2. Choose Print from the File menu (**Figure 1**) or click the Print button on the WordPerfect 8 Toolbar. The Print dialog box will open (**Figure 2**).

3. Select the radio button next to Current Page in the Print Selection area (**Figure 4**).

4. Click OK. The page will print.

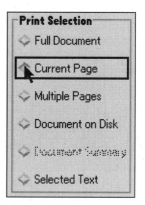

Figure 4. In the Print Selection area, select the radio button next to Current Page.

To print specific text:

1. Select the text you would like to print.

2. Choose Print from the File menu (**Figure 1**) or click the Print button on the WordPerfect 8 Toolbar. The Print dialog box will open (**Figure 2**).

3. Select the radio button next to Selected Text in the Print Selection area (**Figure 5**).

4. Click OK. The text will print.

Figure 5. In the Print Selection area, select the radio button next to Selected Text.

Figure 6. In the Print Selection area, select the radio button next to Multiple Pages.

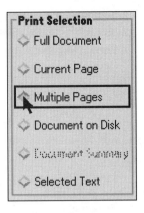

To print specific pages:

1. Choose Print from the File menu (**Figure 1**) or click the Print button on the WordPerfect 8 Toolbar. The Print dialog box will open (**Figure 2**).

2. Select the Multiple Pages radio button in the Print Selection area (**Figure 6**).

3. Click OK. The Multiple Pages dialog box will open (**Figure 7**).

4. In the Page(s) text box, enter the page numbers you want to print.

5. Click OK. Both the Multiple Pages and Print dialog boxes will close and the pages you specified will print.

✔ Tip

■ If you are printing specific pages, you can specify page numbers, such as 2, 6, or 9, or a *page range*. For instance, if you enter 2–9, pages 2 through 9 would print. If you enter –4, pages 1 through 4 would print. If you enter 6–, page 6 through the end of the document would print.

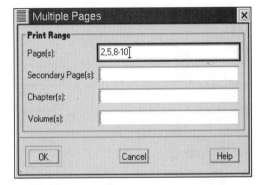

Figure 7. Use the Page(s) text box to set the pages you want printed, then click OK. In this example, pages 2, 5, 8, 9, and 10 will print.

To print a draft of a document without graphics:

1. Choose Print from the File menu (**Figure 1**) or click the Print button on the WordPerfect 8 Toolbar. The Print dialog box will open (**Figure 2**).

2. In the Document Settings area, use the Print Quality drop-down list to select Draft (**Figure 8**).

3. Select the box next to Do Not Print Graphics.

4. Click OK to print the document.

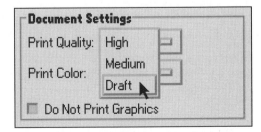

Figure 8. Use the Print Quality drop-down list to select Draft, then select the box next to Do Not Print Graphics.

To print a document back to front:

1. Choose Print from the File menu (**Figure 1**) or click the Print button on the WordPerfect 8 Toolbar. The Print dialog box will open (**Figure 2**).

2. Click the Output Options button. The Output Options dialog box will open (**Figure 9**).

3. In the Formatting Options area, select the check box next to Print in Reverse Order (Back to Front) (**Figure 10**).

4. Click OK. The Formatting Options dialog box will close, returning you to the Print dialog box.

5. In the Print Selection area, select how much of the document you want to print, either the Full Document or Multiple Pages.

6. Click OK. If you selected Full Document in step 5, the document will print. If you selected Multiple Pages in step 5, the Multiple Pages dialog box will open (**Figure 11**). Type the page numbers you would like to print in the Pages text box, then click OK. Both the Multiple Pages and Print dialog boxes will close and the pages will print.

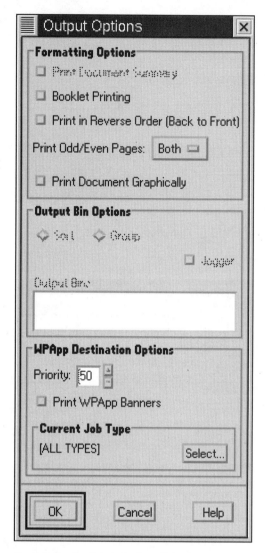

Figure 9. Use the Output Options dialog box to set whether a document will print from back to front, print odd or even pages (or both), or print a banner.

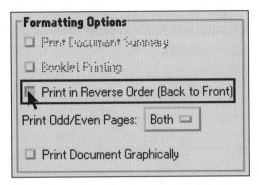

Figure 10. In the Formatting Options area, select the check box next to Print in Reverse Order (Back to Front).

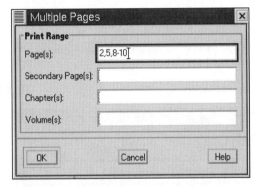

Figure 11. Use the Page(s) text box to set the pages you want printed, then click OK. In this example, pages 2, 5, 8, 9, and 10 will print.

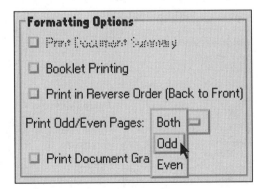

Figure 12. Use the Print Odd/Even Pages drop-down list to set whether odd or even pages (or both) are printed.

To print odd or even pages:

1. Choose Print from the File menu (**Figure 1**) or click the Print button on the WordPerfect 8 Toolbar. The Print dialog box will open (**Figure 2**).

2. Click the Output Options button. The Output Options dialog box will open (**Figure 9**).

3. Use the Print Odd/Even Pages drop-down list to select either odd or even (**Figure 12**).

4. Click OK. The Formatting Options dialog box will close, returning you to the Print dialog box.

5. In the Print Selection area, select how much of the document you want to print, either the Full Document or Multiple Pages.

6. Click OK. If you selected Full Document in step 5, the document will print. If you selected Multiple Pages in step 5, the Multiple Pages dialog box will open (**Figure 11**). Type the page numbers you would like to print in the Pages text box, then click OK. Both the Multiple Pages and Print dialog boxes will close and the pages will print.

Banners

Banners are used to separate print jobs. If you are printing many documents or work in an office where one printer is used by many people, it can be handy to print a banner that separates one document from another. A banner consists of 2 pages, one printed before the document and one printed after. The page that is printed before a document usually includes the name of the person who printed the document, as well as the document's filename, and the date and time it was sent.

To print banners:

1. Choose Print from the File menu (**Figure 1**) or click the Print button on the WordPerfect 8 Toolbar. The Print dialog box will open (**Figure 2**).

2. Click the Output Options button. The Output Options dialog box will open (**Figure 13**).

3. In the WPApp Destination Options area, select the check box next to Print WPApp Banners (**Figure 14**).

4. Click OK. The Output Options dialog box will close, returning you to the Print dialog box.

5. In the Print Selection area, select how much of the document you want to print.

6. Click OK to print the document.

✔ Tip

- If you are not using a shared printer, the WPApp Destination Options area will be grayed out and unavailable.

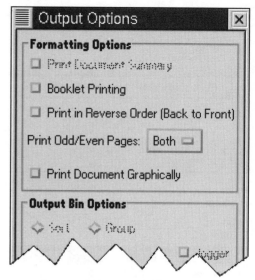

Figure 13. Use the Output Options dialog box to set whether a banner is printed.

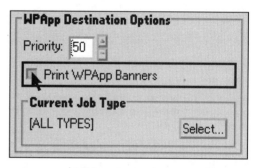

Figure 14. In the WPApp Destination Options area, select the check box next to Print WPApp Banners. This option will only be available if a shared printer is selected.

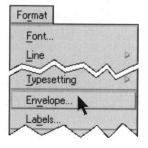

Figure 15. Choose Envelope from the Format menu.

PRINT BANNERS

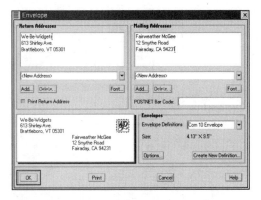

Figure 16. Use the Envelope dialog box to enter the return address, mailing address, and envelope size.

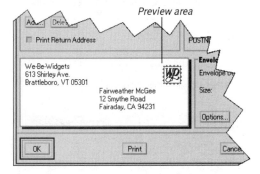

Figure 17. As you create the envelope a preview appears in the preview area.

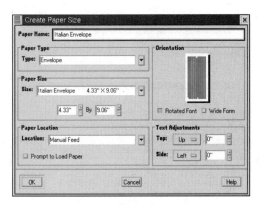

Figure 18. Use the Create Paper Size dialog box to set the paper name, type of paper, and its size.

Printing Envelopes

Printing envelopes is easy. WordPerfect sets up the spacing automatically for you, so all you have to do is enter a return address and the addressee's information.

To print an envelope:

1. Choose Envelope from the Format menu (**Figure 15**). The Envelope dialog box will appear (**Figure 16**).

2. If you want to print a return address:

   A. In the Return Addresses area, type the return address in the text box.

   B. Select the box next to Print Return Address in the Return Addresses area.

3. In the Mailing Addresses area, type the name and address of the person to whom you are sending the envelope.

4. In the Envelopes area, use the Envelope Definitions drop-down list to select the envelope size you are using.

5. Load the envelope in your printer.

6. Click Print. The Envelope dialog box will close and the envelope will be printed.

✔ Tips

- As you enter the information for your envelope, a preview of the envelope appears in the preview area (**Figure 17**).

- For details on how to set up an envelope mail merge to quickly print a list full of addresses, turn to pages 197–199.

- If there are no envelope sizes available in the Envelope Definitions drop-down list, take a look at page 238 for directions on how to add envelopes.

To create an envelope definition:

1. Choose Envelope from the Format menu (**Figure 15**). The Envelope dialog box will open (**Figure 16**).

2. Click Create New Definition. The Create Paper Size dialog box will appear (**Figure 18**).

3. Type a name for your new envelope in the Paper Name text box.

4. In the Paper Type area, use the Type drop-down list to select Envelope (**Figure 19**).

5. In the Paper Size area, use the Size drop-down list to select the size of envelope you are using (**Figure 20**).

6. In the Paper Location area use the Location drop-down list to select the location where your envelopes will be loaded on your printer. By default, this is Manual Feed.

7. Click OK. The Create New Definition dialog box will close, returning you to the Envelope dialog box. The envelope definition you created will now be selected and available in the Envelope Definitions drop-down list (**Figure 21**).

8. Click OK to close the Envelope dialog box without printing an envelope or fill in the Return Addresses and Mailing Addresses text boxes and click Print to print an envelope.

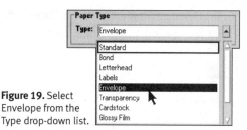

Figure 19. Select Envelope from the Type drop-down list.

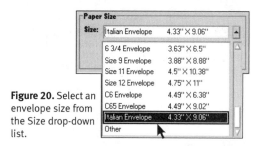

Figure 20. Select an envelope size from the Size drop-down list.

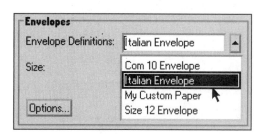

Figure 21. The envelope you created appears in the Envelope Definitions drop-down list.

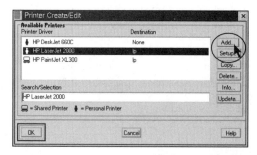

Figure 23. In the Printer Create/Edit dialog box, click Add.

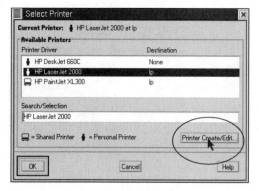

Figure 22. In the Select Printer dialog box, click Printer Create/Edit.

CREATE AN ENVELOPE DEIFINITION

Figure 24. Use the Available Printer Drivers list box to select the printer you want to add.

Figure 25. Click OK to close the Create Printer dialog box.

Figure 26. The printer you added appears in the list box.

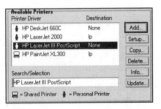

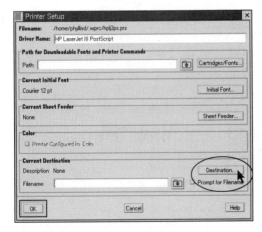

Figure 27. In the Printer Setup dialog box, click the Destination button.

Adding More Printers

Some folks have access to more than one printer. You can add and delete printers, and set printer properties using the Select Printer dialog box.

To add a printer:

1. Choose Print from the File menu (**Figure 1**) or click the Print button on the WordPerfect 8 Toolbar. The Print dialog box will open (**Figure 2**).

2. In the Current Printer area, click Select. The Select Printer dialog box will appear (**Figure 22**).

3. Click the Printer Create/Edit button. The Printer Create/Edit dialog box will open (**Figure 23**).

4. Click Add. The Add Printer Driver dialog box will appear (**Figure 24**).

5. Use the Available Printer Drivers list box to select the printer you want to use.

6. Click OK. The Create Printer dialog box will open with a suggested name for that printer in the text box (**Figure 25**).

7. Click OK. The Create Printer and Add Printer Driver dialog boxes will close, returning you to the Printer Create/Edit dialog box. The new printer you selected will appear in the Printer Driver list box (**Figure 26**).

8. If "None" is displayed in the Destination Column of your new printer:

    A. Click Setup. The Printer Setup dialog box will open (**Figure 27**).

    B. Click Destination. The Select Destination dialog box will appear (**Figure 28**).

    C. Click lp to select the local printer.

    (continued)

ADD A PRINTER

D. Click OK to close the Select Destination dialog box, then click OK again to close the Printer Setup dialog box and return to the Printer Create/Edit dialog box.

9. Click OK. The Printer Create/Edit dialog box will close, returning you to the Select Printer dialog box.

10. Click OK again to close the Select Printer dialog box and return to the Print dialog box. The printer that you added will be listed in the Current Printer area (**Figure 29**).

11. If you want to print a document select the other print options you would like, then click OK to print. Otherwise, click Cancel to close the Print dialog box. Even though you click Cancel, the new printer will be available and selected the next time you print.

✔ Tip

■ You can only add a network printer if you are logged on as root (or su to root) and have launched WordPerfect as an administrator. For details on how to launch WordPerfect as an administrator, see page 84, steps 4–7.

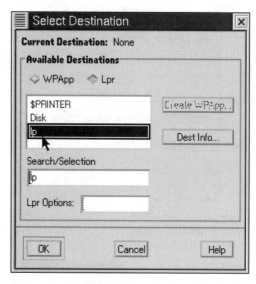

Figure 28. In the Available Destinations area, select lp to link the new printer driver you just installed to the actual printer itself. "lp" stands for local printer.

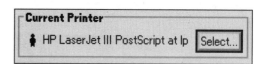

Figure 29. The new printer you installed appears in the Current Printer area at the top of the Print dialog box.

ADD A PRINTER

Summary

In this chapter you learned how to:

◆ Print a document

◆ Print more than one copy of a document

◆ Print the current page

◆ Print selected text

◆ Print specified pages

◆ Print a draft without graphics

◆ Print a document back to front

◆ Print odd or even pages

◆ Print banners

◆ Print envelopes

◆ Add envelope definitions

◆ Add a printer

INDEX

INDEX

What else would you like to see?

If I write a sequel to this book, what topics and features would you like me to cover? Send an e-mail with your suggestions to: phyllis@bearhome.com

---